My Cat is Such a Weirdo

1

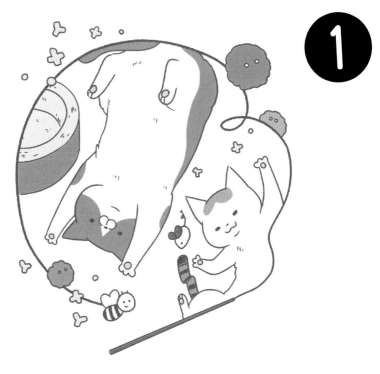

Story and Art by
Tamako Tamagoyama

Prologue

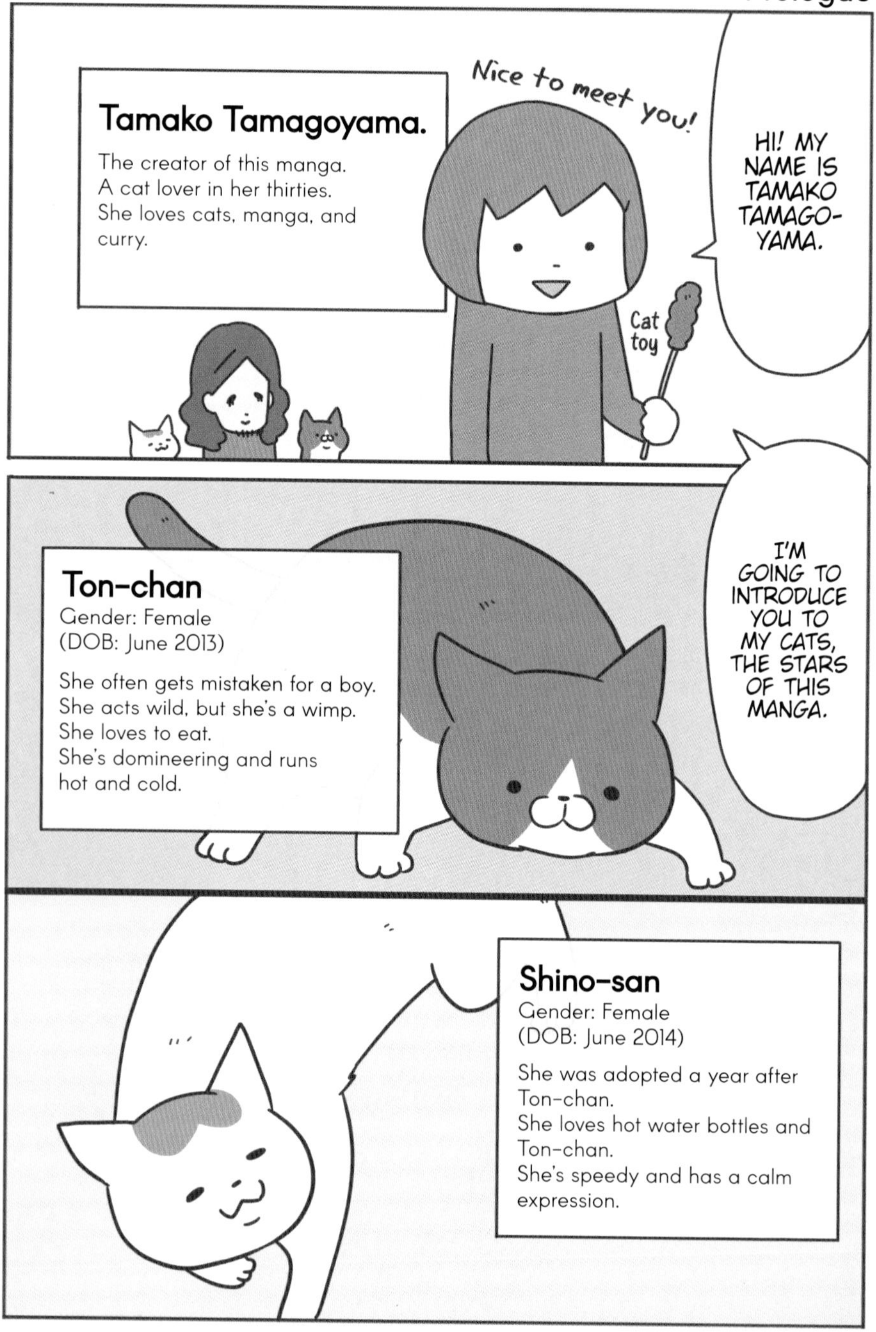
HI! MY NAME IS TAMAKO TAMAGO-YAMA.
Nice to meet you!
Cat toy
Tamako Tamagoyama.
The creator of this manga. A cat lover in her thirties. She loves cats, manga, and curry.
I'M GOING TO INTRODUCE YOU TO MY CATS, THE STARS OF THIS MANGA.
Ton-chan
Gender: Female
(DOB: June 2013)
She often gets mistaken for a boy. She acts wild, but she's a wimp. She loves to eat. She's domineering and runs hot and cold.
Shino-san
Gender: Female
(DOB: June 2014)
She was adopted a year after Ton-chan. She loves hot water bottles and Ton-chan. She's speedy and has a calm expression.

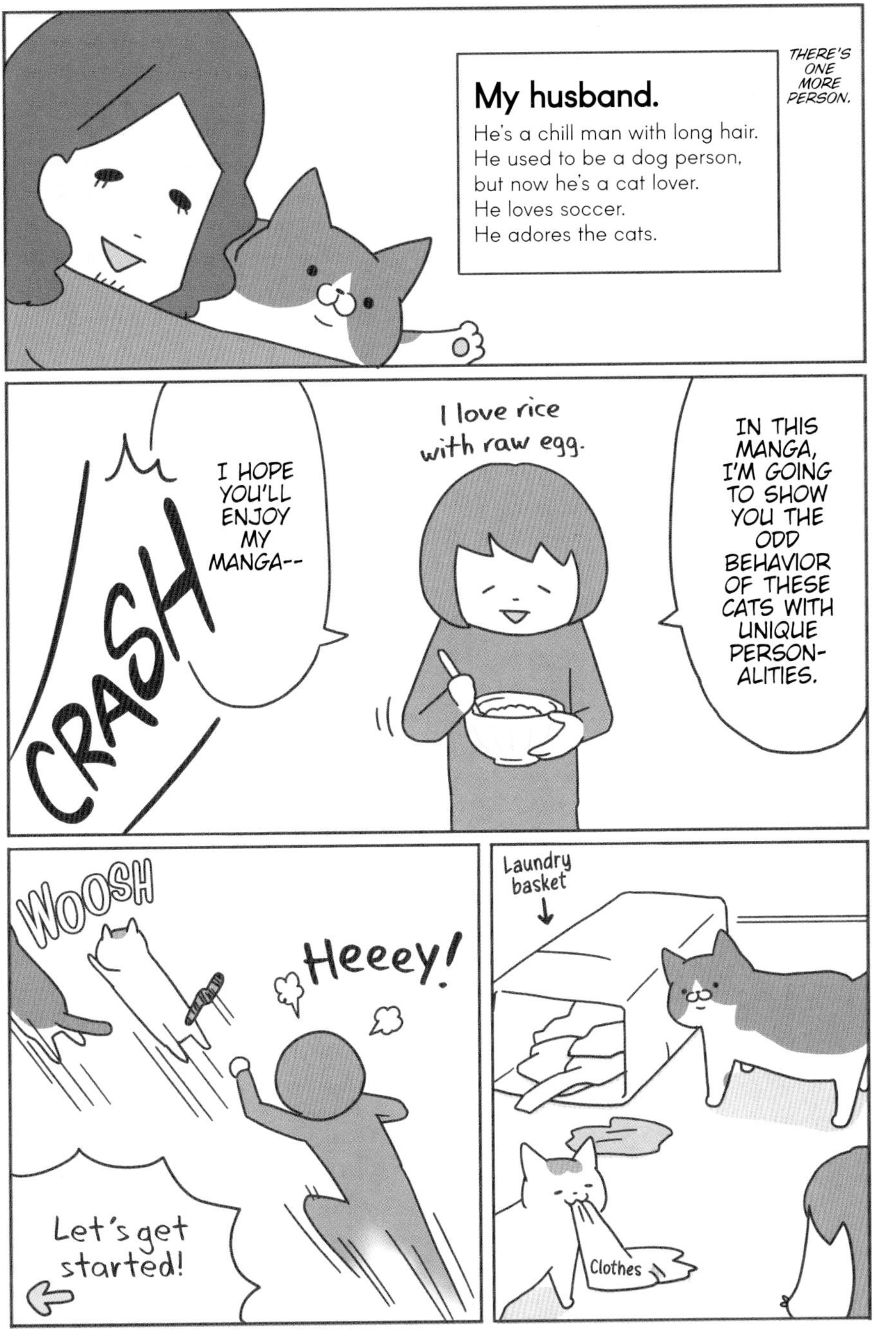
THERE'S ONE MORE PERSON.
My husband.
He's a chill man with long hair.
He used to be a dog person,
but now he's a cat lover.
He loves soccer.
He adores the cats.
IN THIS MANGA, I'M GOING TO SHOW YOU THE ODD BEHAVIOR OF THESE CATS WITH UNIQUE PERSON-ALITIES.
I love rice with raw egg.
I HOPE YOU'LL ENJOY MY MANGA--
CRASH
Laundry basket
Clothes
WOOSH
Heeey!
Let's get started!

contents

Prologue 002

Chapter 1 My Cats Are Such Weirdos 007
Column **The Anatomy of My Cats** 017
Column **The Care Routine for My Cats** 025

Chapter 2 My Cats and Objects 035
Column **Nail Trim Penalty** 043
Column **Breaking Their Toys Again** 051

Chapter 3 My Cats and Food 061
Column **Cat Food** 071

Chapter 4 The Dilemma of Being a Cat Owner 081
Column **My Cats' Favorite Things** 089
Signature Collection! Cat Photo Album 096

Chapter 5 A Peaceful Life with My Cats   107
    Column **Cleaning**   116
    Column **Interior Decorating**   117
    Bonus Manga **Personifying My Cats**   126

Chapter 6 My Parents' Cats   137

Chapter 7 Meeting My Cats   149
    Column **Meeting at the Adoption Event**   157
    Column **Meeting through an Online**
            Adoption Ad   161
    Memories of Ton and Shino   168

    Afterword   172

Chapter 1

My Cats Are Such Weirdos

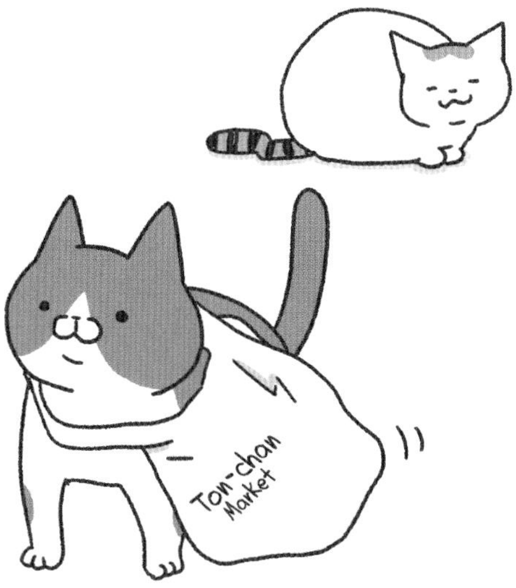
Ton-chan Market

Difficult to Understand

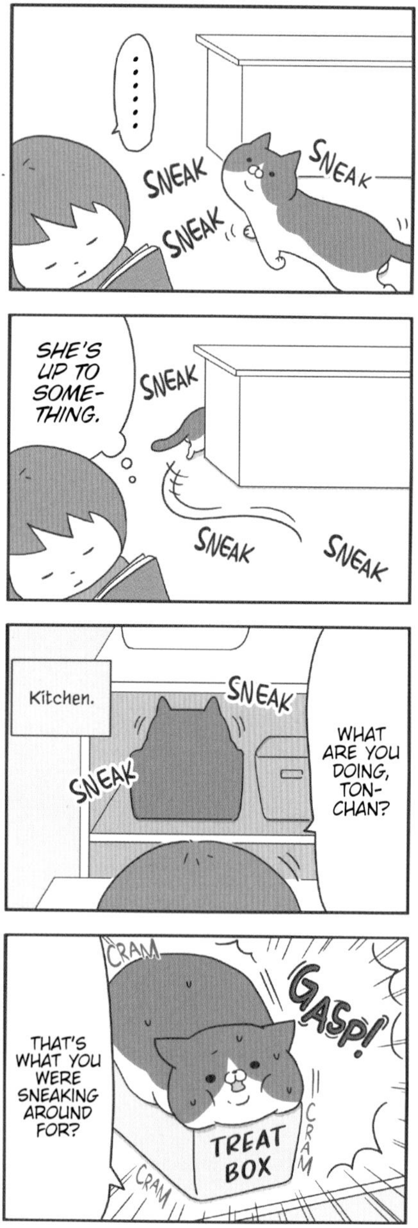
SNEAK
……
SNEAK
SNEAK
SNEAK
SHE'S UP TO SOME-THING.
SNEAK
SNEAK
SNEAK
WHAT ARE YOU DOING, TON-CHAN?
Kitchen.
SNEAK
GASP!
CRAM
CRAM
THAT'S WHAT YOU WERE SNEAKING AROUND FOR?
TREAT BOX
CRAM

Getting into a box of treats must have been a big mission for Ton-chan.

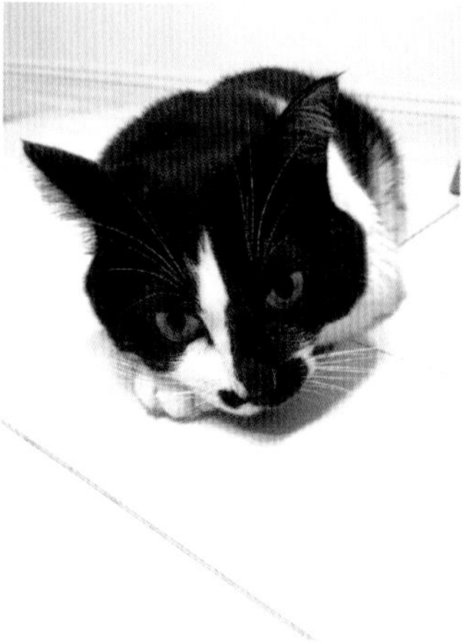

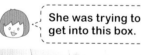

She was trying to get into this box.

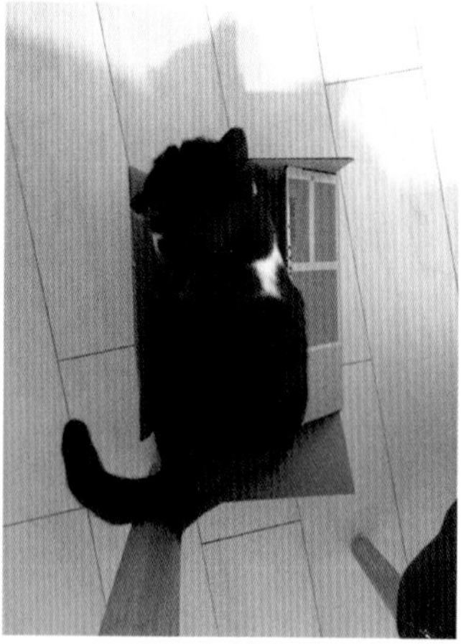

Don't Do It

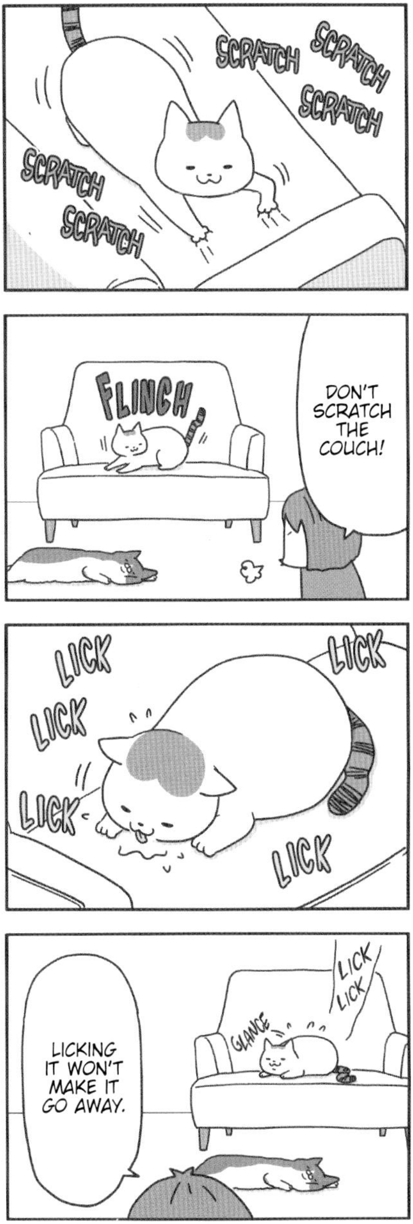
SCRATCH SCRATCH
SCRATCH
SCRATCH
SCRATCH
FLINCH
DON'T SCRATCH THE COUCH!
LICK
LICK
LICK
LICK
LICK
LICK LICK
GLANCE
LICKING IT WON'T MAKE IT GO AWAY.

There's no fixing it.

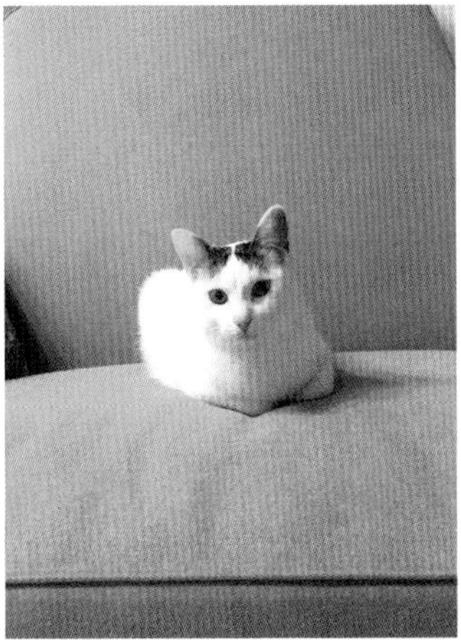

"I'm sorry."

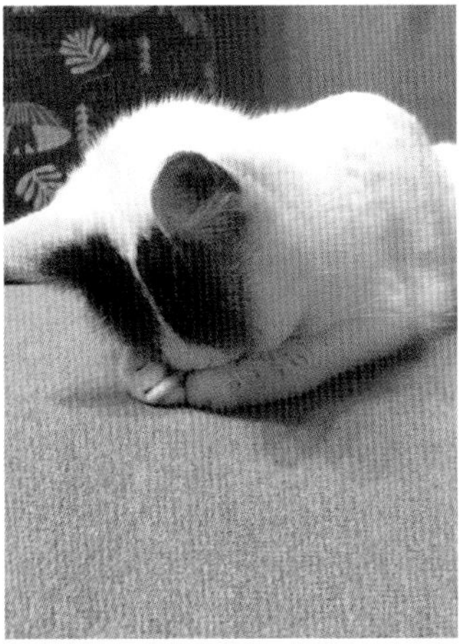

Meowing

I CAUGHT HER RED-HANDED.
AH!
HEEEY!!
Countertop
Off-Limits to Cats
WSH WSH WSH
WHACK
Mysterious feint movement.
CLATTER
THUD
MEOW!!
DON'T "MEOW" ME!

You think you can play dumb? Not a chance!

The cute act won't work on me.

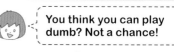

Dead Set on Rubbing Her Cheeks

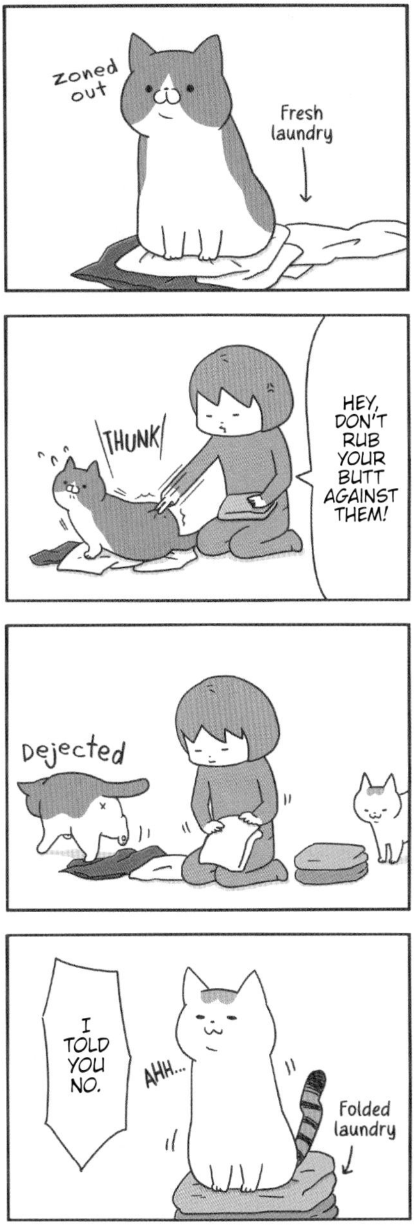
zoned out
Fresh laundry
HEY, DON'T RUB YOUR BUTT AGAINST THEM!
THUNK
Dejected
I TOLD YOU NO.
AHH...
Folded laundry

They eagerly rubbed their butts against my fresh laundry.

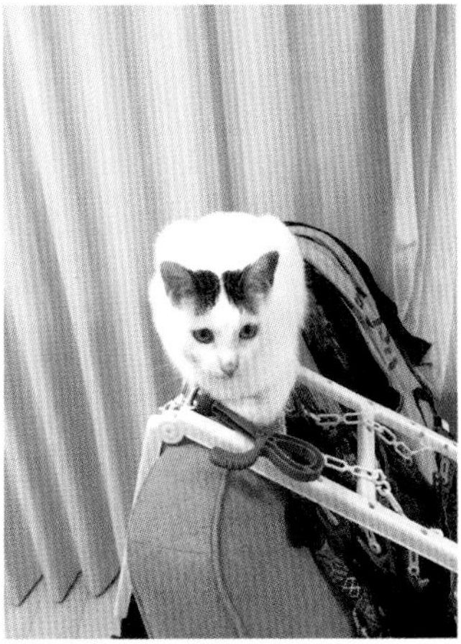

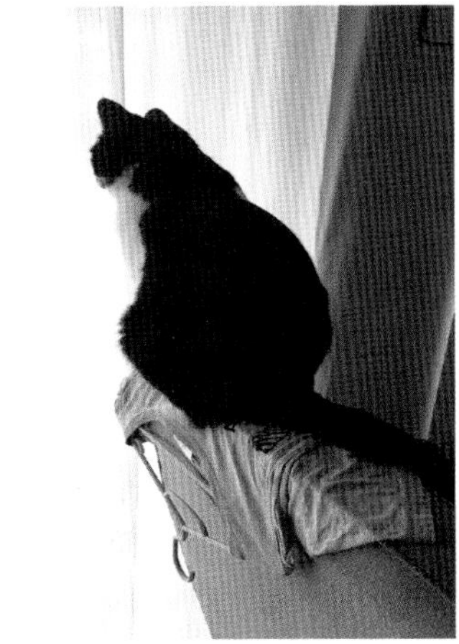

Scratch Away

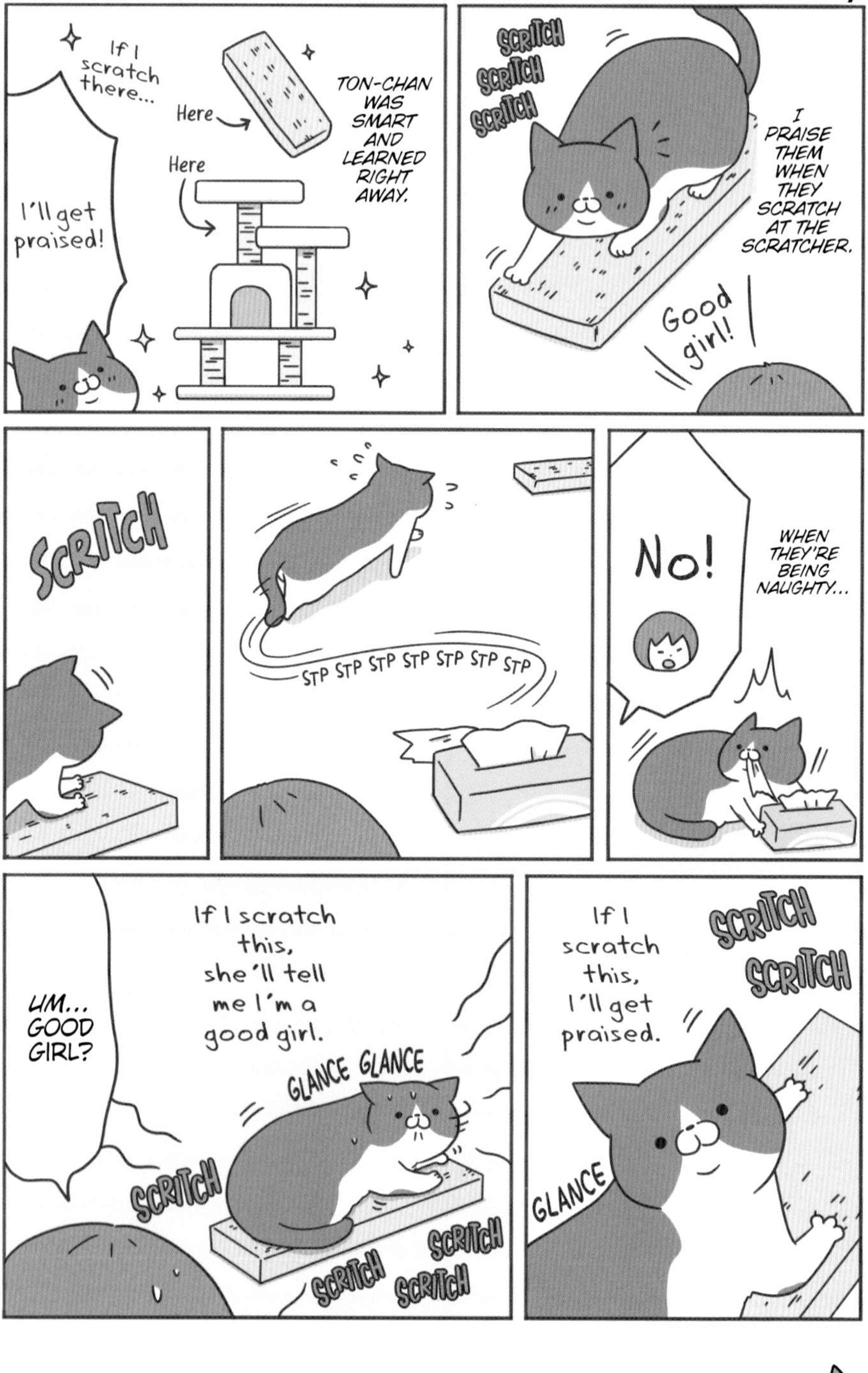

SCRITCH SCRITCH SCRITCH
I PRAISE THEM WHEN THEY SCRATCH AT THE SCRATCHER.
Good girl!
If I scratch there...
Here
Here
TON-CHAN WAS SMART AND LEARNED RIGHT AWAY.
I'll get praised!
WHEN THEY'RE BEING NAUGHTY...
No!
STP STP STP STP STP STP STP
SCRITCH
If I scratch this, I'll get praised.
SCRITCH
SCRITCH
GLANCE
If I scratch this, she'll tell me I'm a good girl.
GLANCE GLANCE
UM... GOOD GIRL?
SCRITCH
SCRITCH
SCRITCH
SCRITCH

Trying Hard to Pretend to Sleep

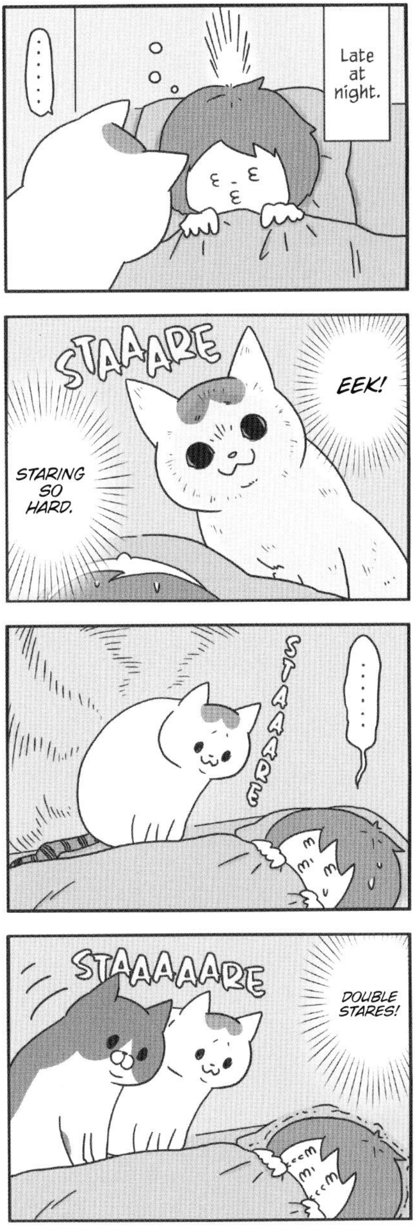
Late at night.
……
EEK!
STAAARE
STARING SO HARD.
……
STAAARE
DOUBLE STARES!
STAAAAARE

When I refused to wake up, they finally gave up.

This was Shino-san with her pupils dilated. So scary!

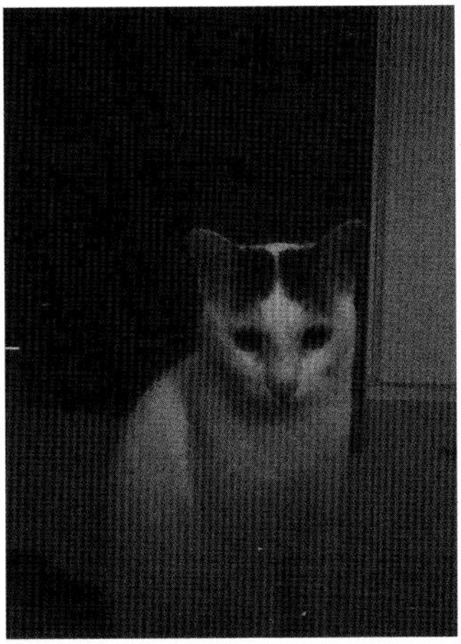

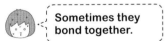

Sometimes they bond together.

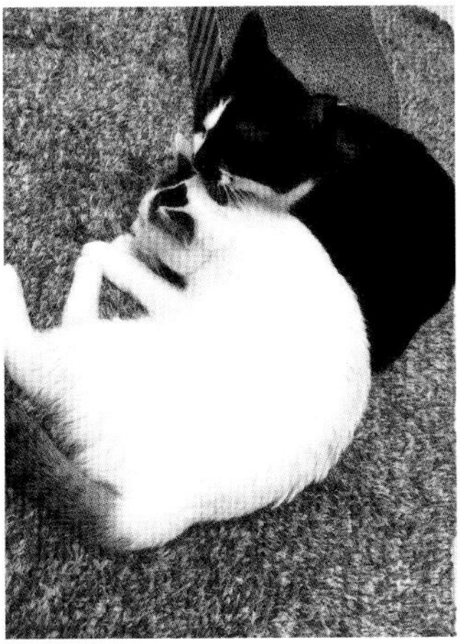

Why Stick Your Paw In?

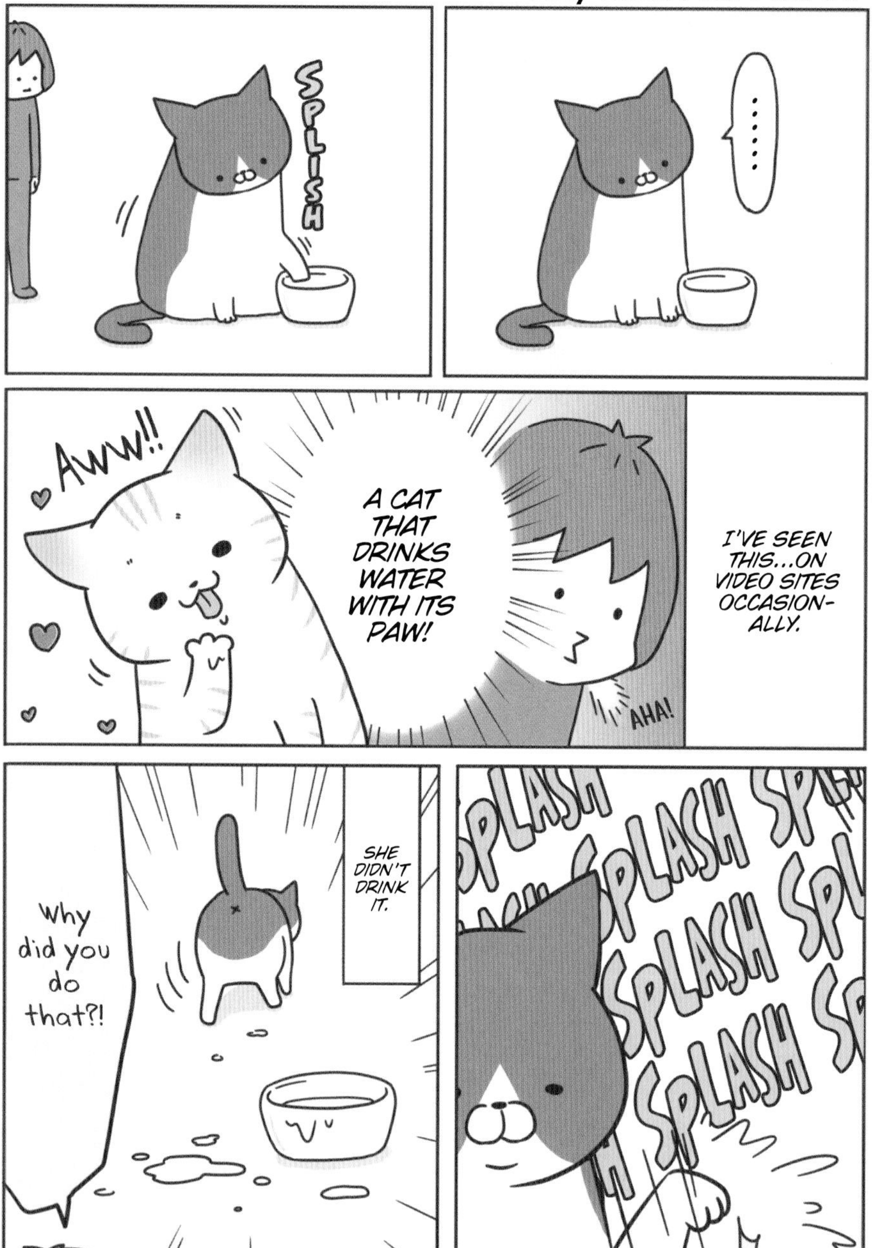
......
SPLISH
I'VE SEEN THIS...ON VIDEO SITES OCCASION-ALLY.
A CAT THAT DRINKS WATER WITH ITS PAW!
AHA!
Aww!!
SPLASH SPLASH SPLASH SPLASH SPLASH
SHE DIDN'T DRINK IT.
Why did you do that?!

Deep Anxiety

WHY DOES MY CAT...
STARE
WHAT'S UP? YOU'RE ADORABLE!
SOMETIMES...
WHAT? WHAT'S THE MATTER?
STARE DEEPLY...
SAY SOMETHING!
INTO MY EYES?
Stop staring at me!

Ton-chan is photogenic but doesn't normally make eye contact.

There's probably no deep meaning to it...but please stop!

As Immovable as a Mountain

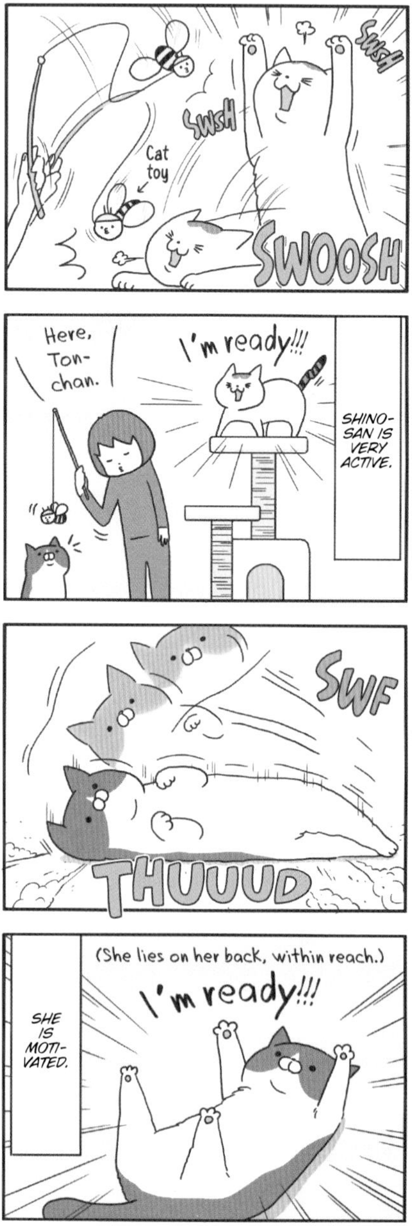
SWSH
SWSH
Cat toy
SWOOSH
SHINO-SAN IS VERY ACTIVE.
I'm ready!!!
Here, Ton-chan.
SWF
THUUUD
(She lies on her back, within reach.)
I'm ready!!!
SHE IS MOTIVATED.

She's really up for it. She just doesn't like to move around.

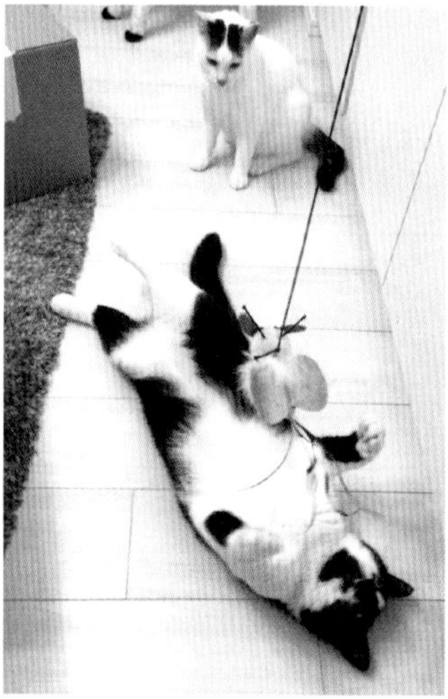

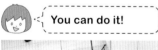

You can do it!

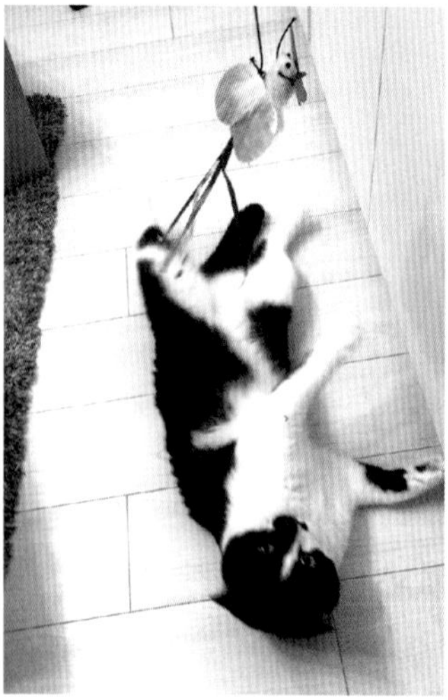

The Anatomy of My Cats

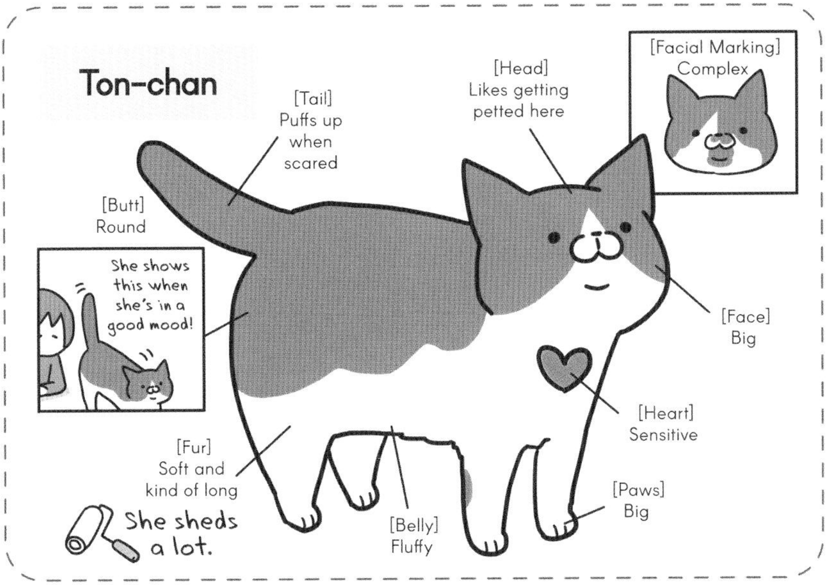

Ton-chan
[Facial Marking]
Complex
[Head]
Likes getting petted here
[Tail]
Puffs up when scared
[Butt]
Round
She shows this when she's in a good mood!
[Face]
Big
[Heart]
Sensitive
[Fur]
Soft and kind of long
[Paws]
Big
[Belly]
Fluffy
She sheds a lot.

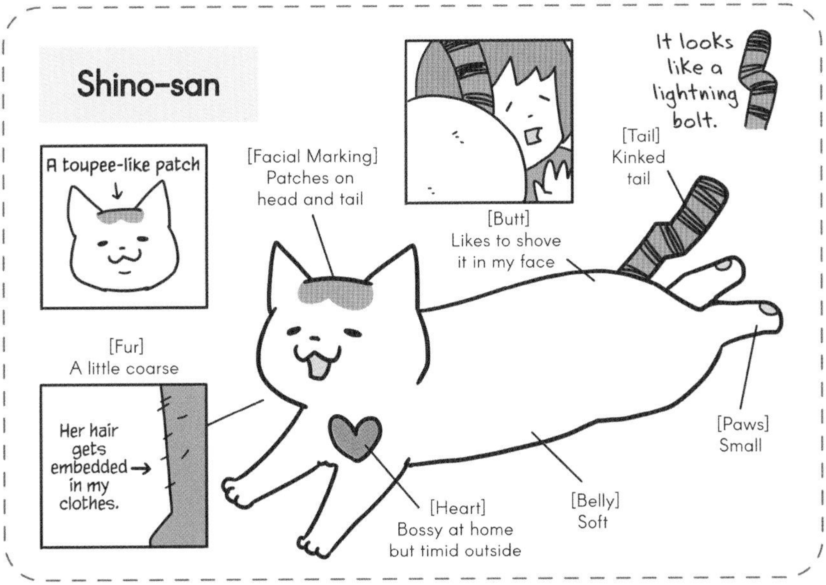

Shino-san
It looks like a lightning bolt.
[Tail]
Kinked tail
A toupee-like patch
[Facial Marking]
Patches on head and tail
[Butt]
Likes to shove it in my face
[Fur]
A little coarse
Her hair gets embedded in my clothes.
[Paws]
Small
[Belly]
Soft
[Heart]
Bossy at home but timid outside

Speaker

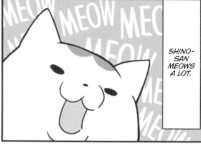

MEOW MEOW MEOW MEOW MEOW
SHINO-SAN MEOWS A LOT.
SHE MAKES THIS SOUND WHEN SHE'S HUNGRY.
MEOWW MEOWW
MEW MEW
MEW MEW
THIS MEANS SHE WANTS TO PLAY.
WHAT'S THIS?
Meooow
Meooow
Meooow
SHE'S MEOWING JUST FOR THE HECK OF IT.

I want to know why she's meowing, but she's probably just saying, "Hey, hey, hey!" most of the time.

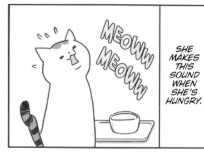

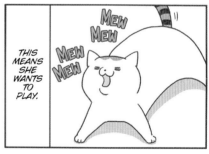

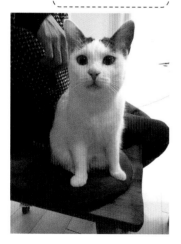

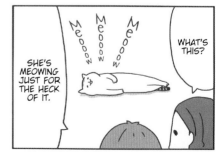

Doing Her Best

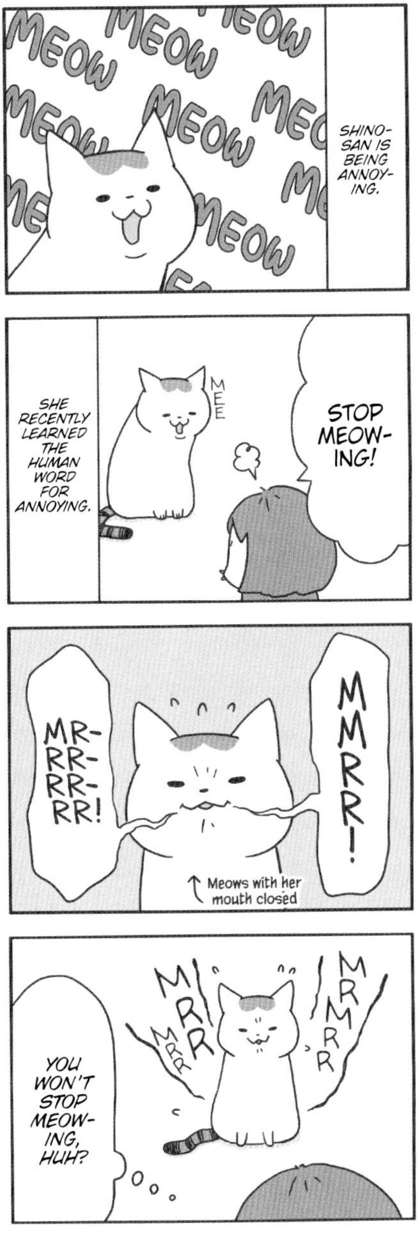
SHINO-SAN IS BEING ANNOY-ING.
MEOW
MEOW
MEOW
MEOW
MEOW
MEOW
MEOW
STOP MEOW-ING!
MEE
SHE RECENTLY LEARNED THE HUMAN WORD FOR ANNOYING.
MMRRR!
MR-RR-RR-RR!
Meows with her mouth closed
MRMRR
MRR
MRR
YOU WON'T STOP MEOW-ING, HUH?

Being Sensitive

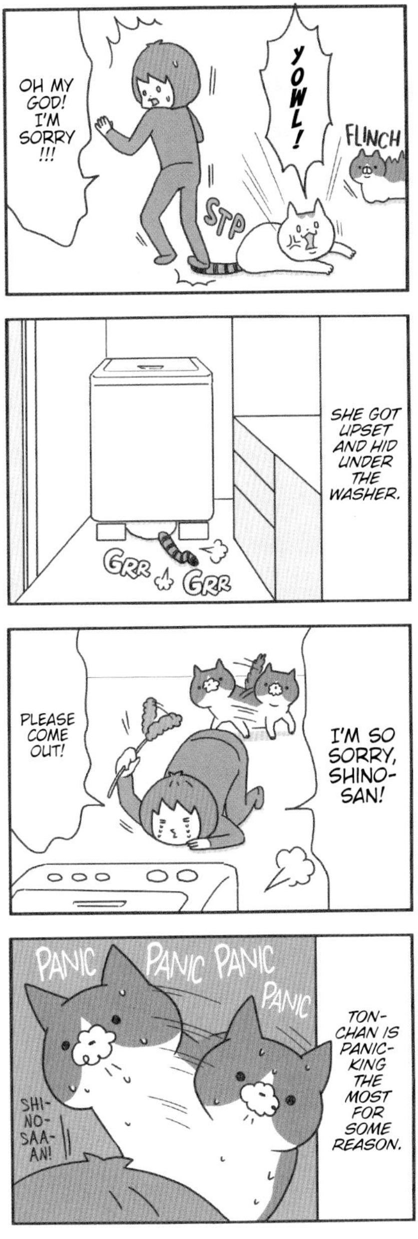
FLINCH
YOWL!
OH MY GOD! I'M SORRY!!!
STP
SHE GOT UPSET AND HID UNDER THE WASHER.
GRR GRR
I'M SO SORRY, SHINO-SAN!
PLEASE COME OUT!
TON-CHAN IS PANIC-KING THE MOST FOR SOME REASON.
PANIC PANIC PANIC PANIC
SHI-NO-SAA-AN!

Realization

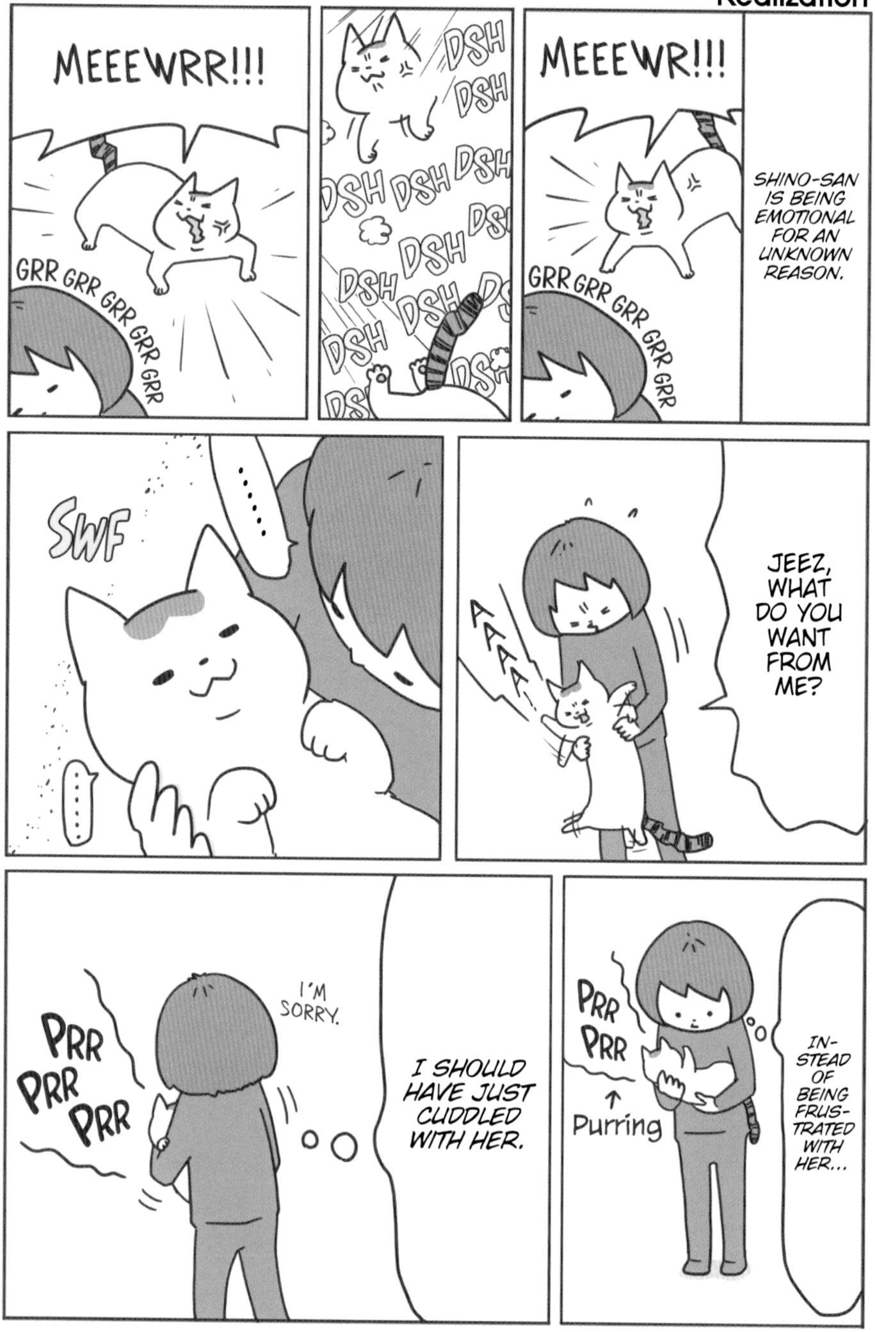
SHINO-SAN IS BEING EMOTIONAL FOR AN UNKNOWN REASON.
MEEEWR!!!
GRR GRR GRR GRR GRR
DSH DSH DSH DSH DSH DSH DSH DSH DSH DSH DSH DSH DSH DSH
MEEEWRR!!!
GRR GRR GRR GRR GRR
JEEZ, WHAT DO YOU WANT FROM ME?
AAAA
SWF
......
......
IN-STEAD OF BEING FRUS-TRATED WITH HER...
PRR PRR
Purring
I SHOULD HAVE JUST CUDDLED WITH HER.
I'M SORRY.
PRR PRR PRR

Not Cool

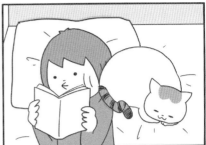

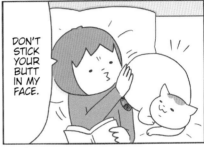

DON'T STICK YOUR BUTT IN MY FACE.
TWIRL TWIRL TWIRL
TWIRL TWIRL
NO, IT'S NOT!
COOL!!

This isn't cool at all.

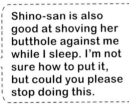

Shino-san is also good at shoving her butthole against me while I sleep. I'm not sure how to put it, but could you please stop doing this.

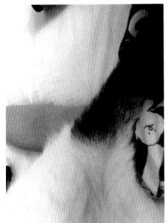

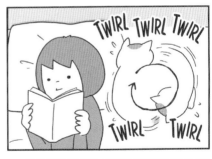

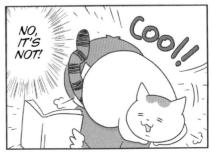

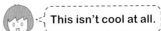

The Best Position at the Moment

SHINO-SAN HAS RECENTLY BEEN SLEEPING LIKE THIS.
BRISTLE BRISTLE
LICK LICK
LICK LICK
BRISTLE BRISTLE
My arm: It gets licked and scraped
My face: It holds her butt
CUT IT OUT WITH YOUR BUTT.
Mew!
SHOVE SHOVE
I GET CHEWED OUT INSTEAD.

A CAT SHOVING ITS BUTT AGAINST ITS OWNER INDICATES TRUST OR INTENTION TO PROTECT THEM.
I appreciate the thought, but no thanks.

Shino-san's New Skill

Late at night.
Let's play!
MEOW!
I'M NOT PLAYING!!
......
SMACK
...
SMACK
SMACK
SMAC
SMA
!...
URRRGGHH.

Shino-san has a kinked tail. That kink looks painful to me.

First Winter with the Heated Floor

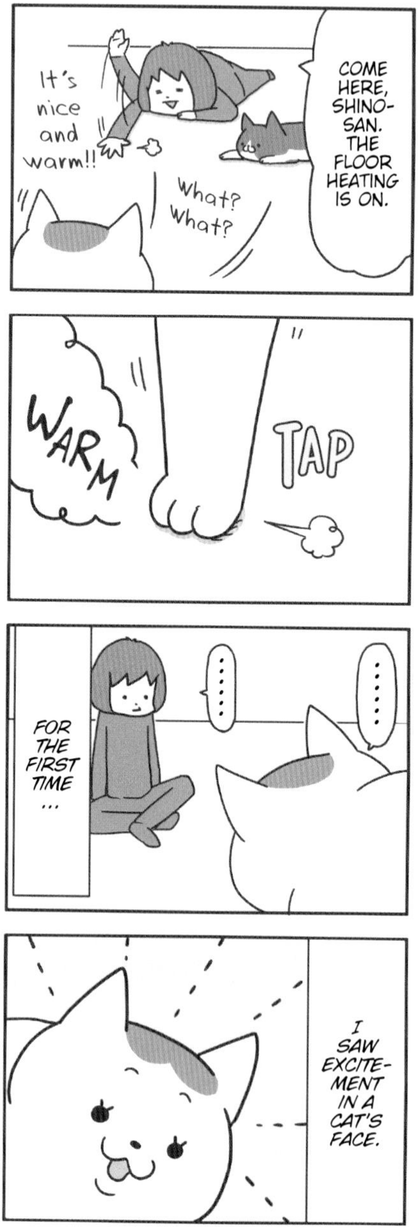
COME HERE, SHINO-SAN. THE FLOOR HEATING IS ON.
It's nice and warm!!
What? What?
TAP
WARM
......
......
FOR THE FIRST TIME ...
I SAW EXCITE-MENT IN A CAT'S FACE.

She really looked excited.

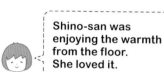

Shino-san was enjoying the warmth from the floor. She loved it.

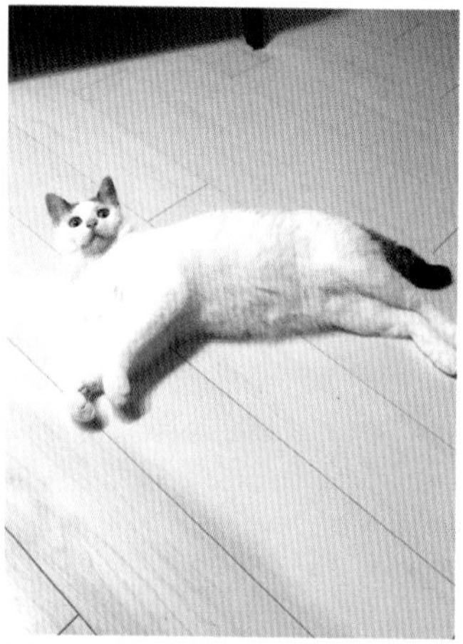

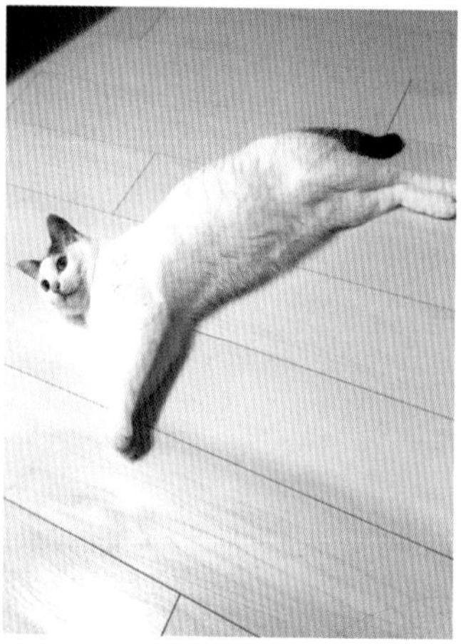

The Care Routine for My Cats

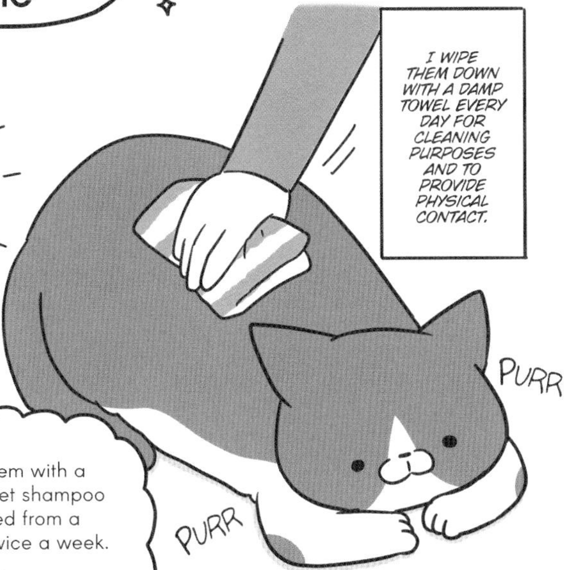
I WIPE THEM DOWN WITH A DAMP TOWEL EVERY DAY FOR CLEANING PURPOSES AND TO PROVIDE PHYSICAL CONTACT.
PURR
PURR

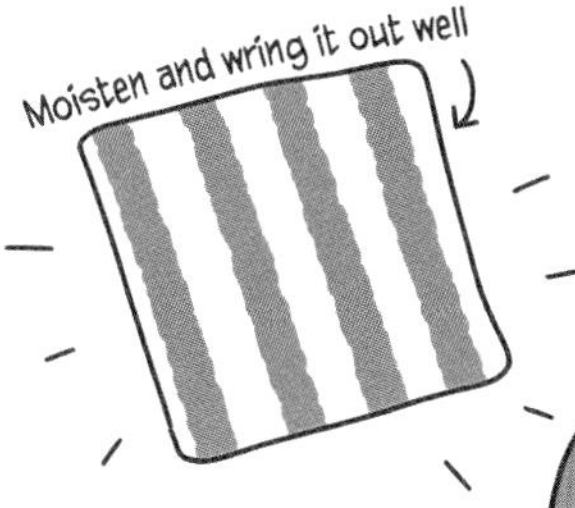
Moisten and wring it out well

I use a microfiber cloth from a 100 yen shop.

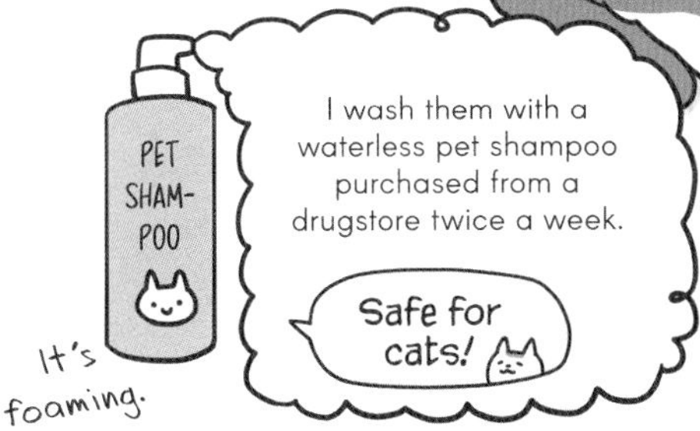
PET SHAM-POO
It's foaming.
I wash them with a waterless pet shampoo purchased from a drugstore twice a week.
Safe for cats!

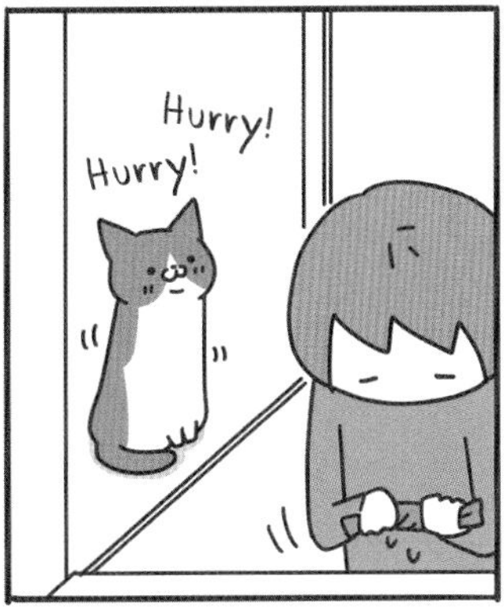
Hurry!
Hurry!

Ton-chan loves to get wiped down. She comes over when I get a towel ready.

I brush them almost daily to reduce shedding.

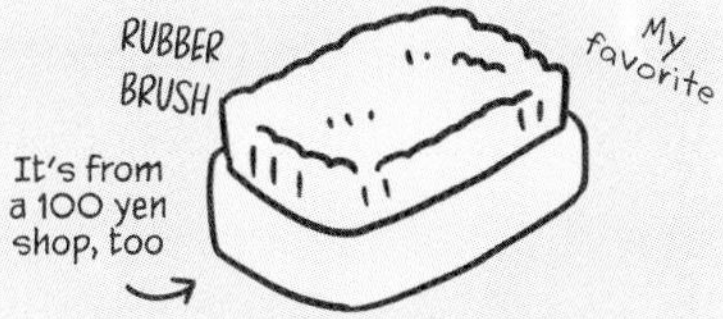
RUBBER BRUSH
My favorite
It's from a 100 yen shop, too

They seem to like this better than being petted since it creates less static charge.

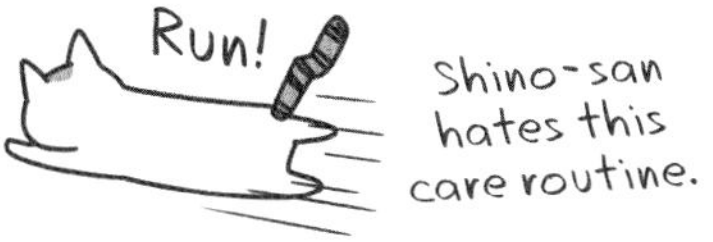
Run!
Shino-san hates this care routine.

Brushing

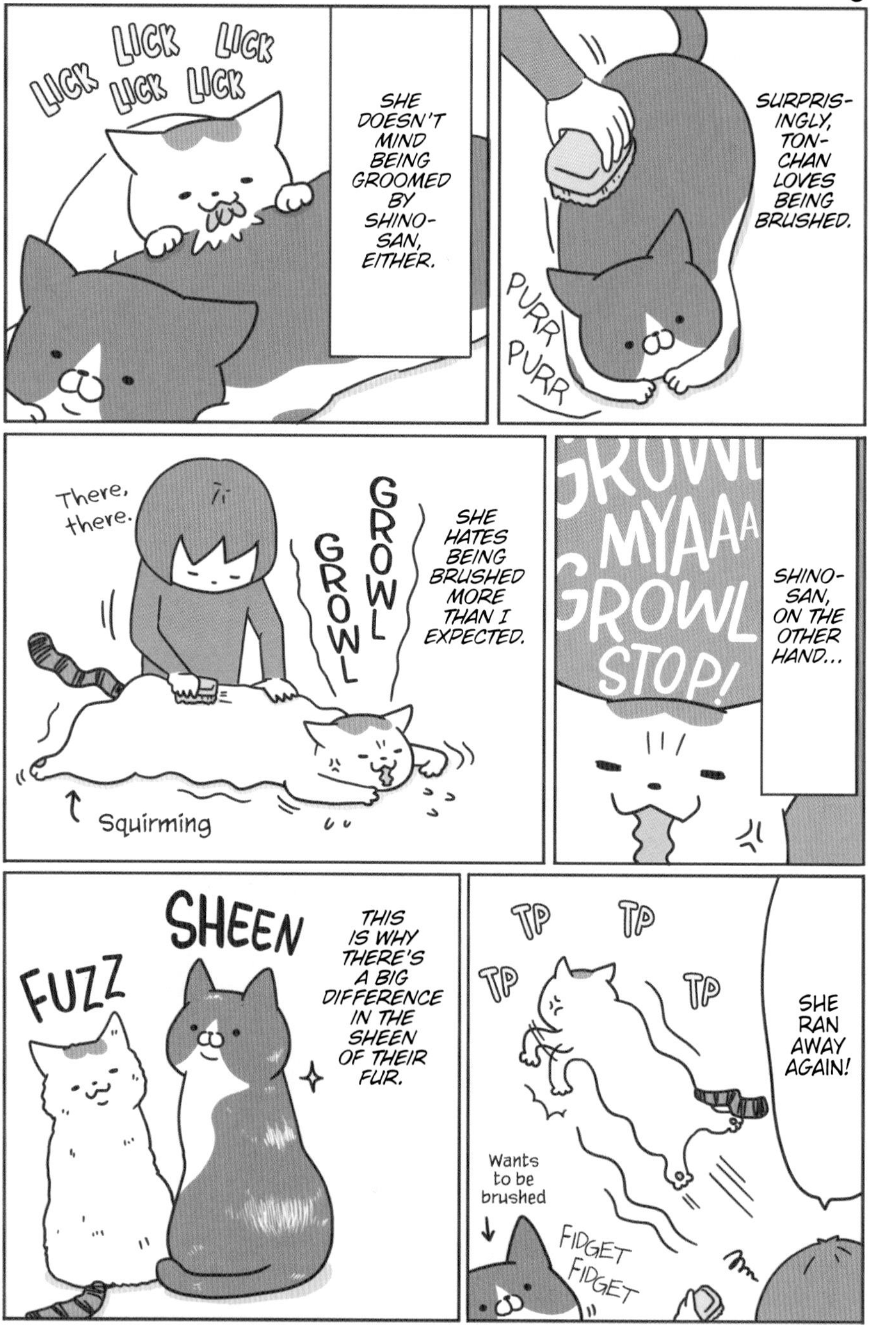
SURPRISINGLY, TON-CHAN LOVES BEING BRUSHED.
PURR PURR
SHE DOESN'T MIND BEING GROOMED BY SHINO-SAN, EITHER.
LICK LICK LICK LICK LICK
SHINO-SAN, ON THE OTHER HAND...
GROWL MYAAA GROWL STOP!
SHE HATES BEING BRUSHED MORE THAN I EXPECTED.
GROWL GROWL
There, there.
Squirming
SHE RAN AWAY AGAIN!
TP TP TP TP
Wants to be brushed
FIDGET FIDGET
THIS IS WHY THERE'S A BIG DIFFERENCE IN THE SHEEN OF THEIR FUR.
SHEEN
FUZZ

Out of It

SPACED OUT
……
SPACED OUT
Are you alive?
SPACED OUT
ZZZ
ZZZ
IS SHE ASLEEP?!
Her eyes are open

She spaced out even while I took pictures of her.

Sometimes she's so spaced out, it worries me.

Ton-chan's Secret Technique

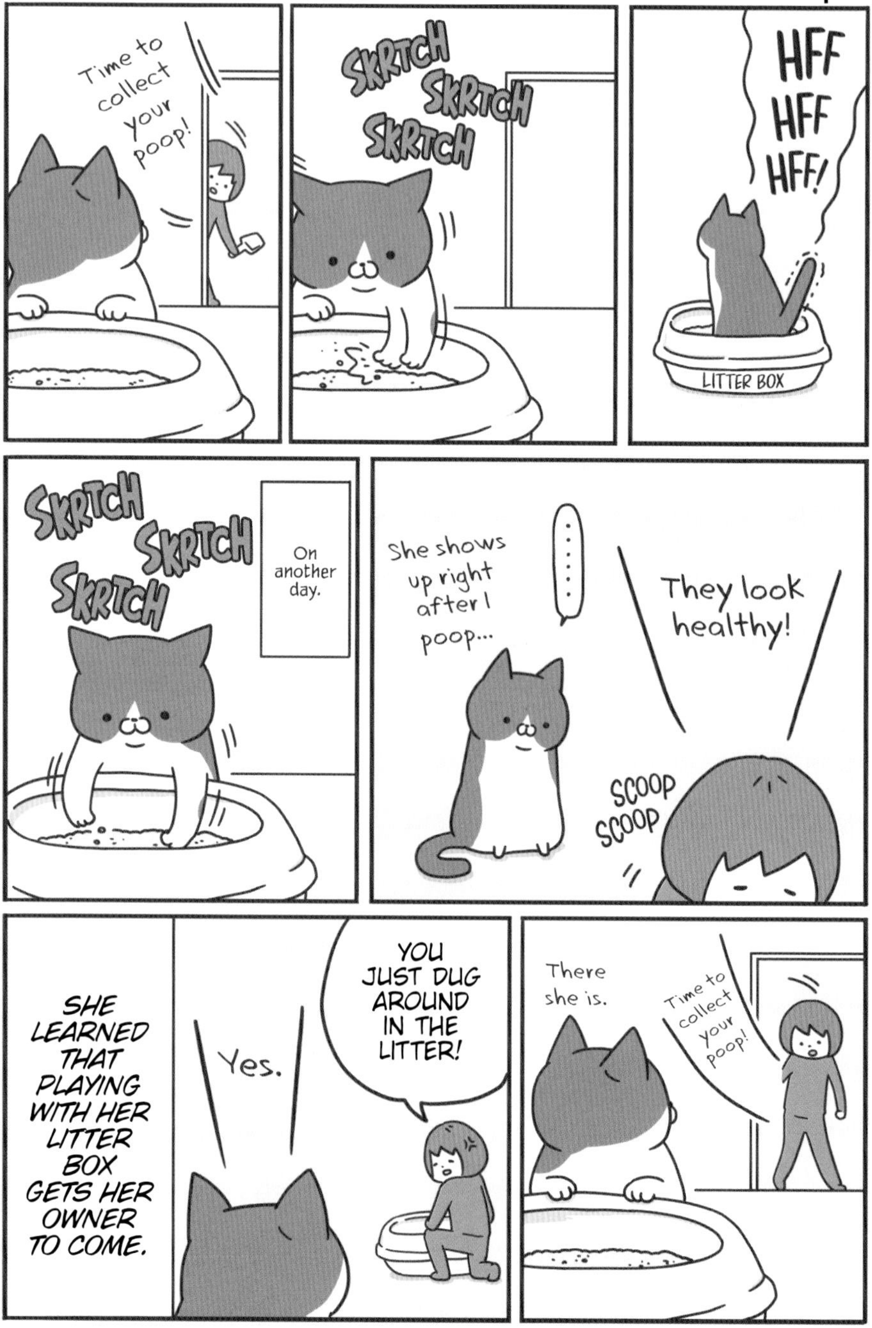
HFF
HFF
HFF!
LITTER BOX
SKRTCH
SKRTCH
SKRTCH
Time to collect your poop!
They look healthy!
......
She shows up right after I poop...
SCOOP
SCOOP
On another day.
SKRTCH
SKRTCH
SKRTCH
Time to collect your poop!
There she is.
YOU JUST DUG AROUND IN THE LITTER!
Yes.
SHE LEARNED THAT PLAYING WITH HER LITTER BOX GETS HER OWNER TO COME.

Did You Call Me?

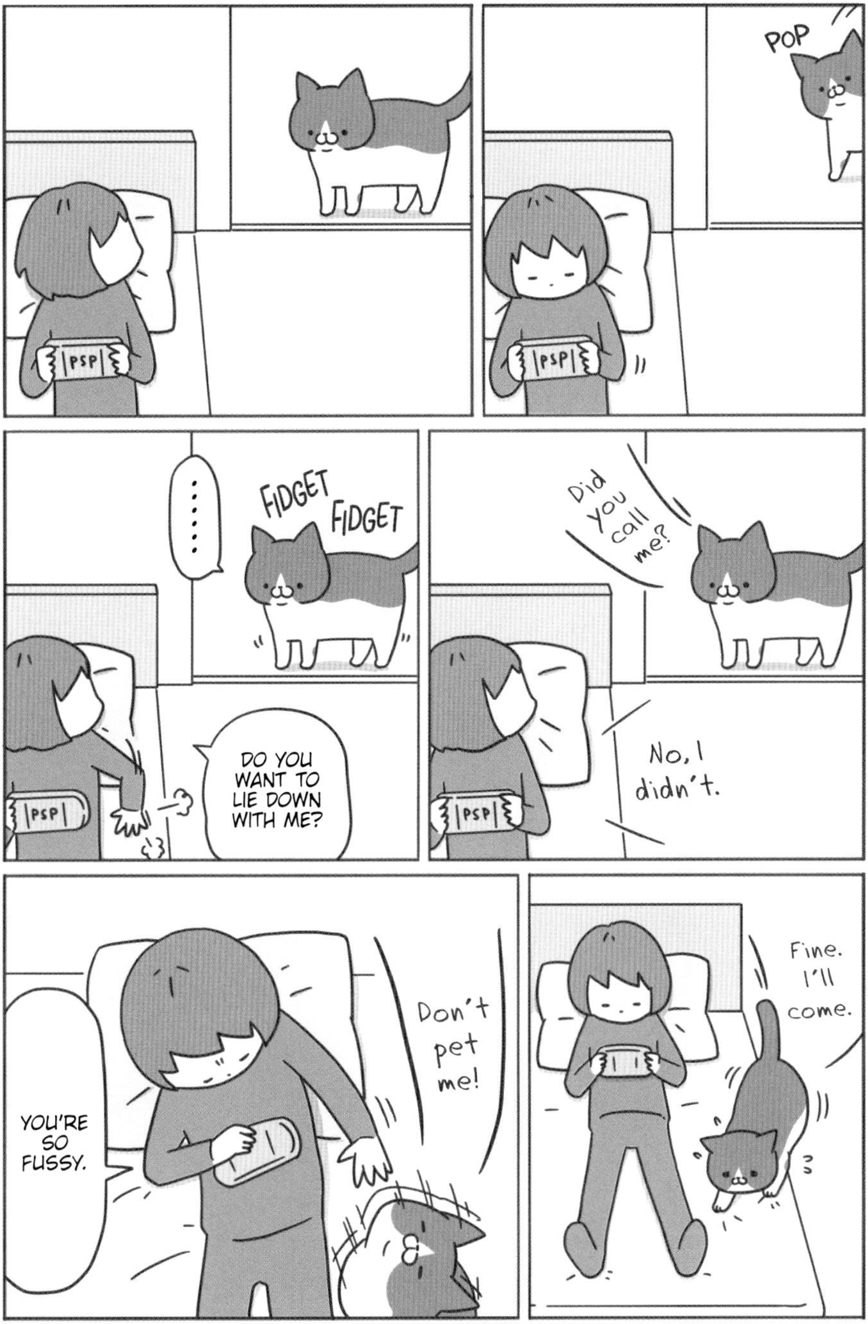
POP
FIDGET FIDGET
......
DO YOU WANT TO LIE DOWN WITH ME?
Did you call me?
No, I didn't.
Fine. I'll come.
Don't pet me!
YOU'RE SO FUSSY.

Ton-chan Is a Big Pain

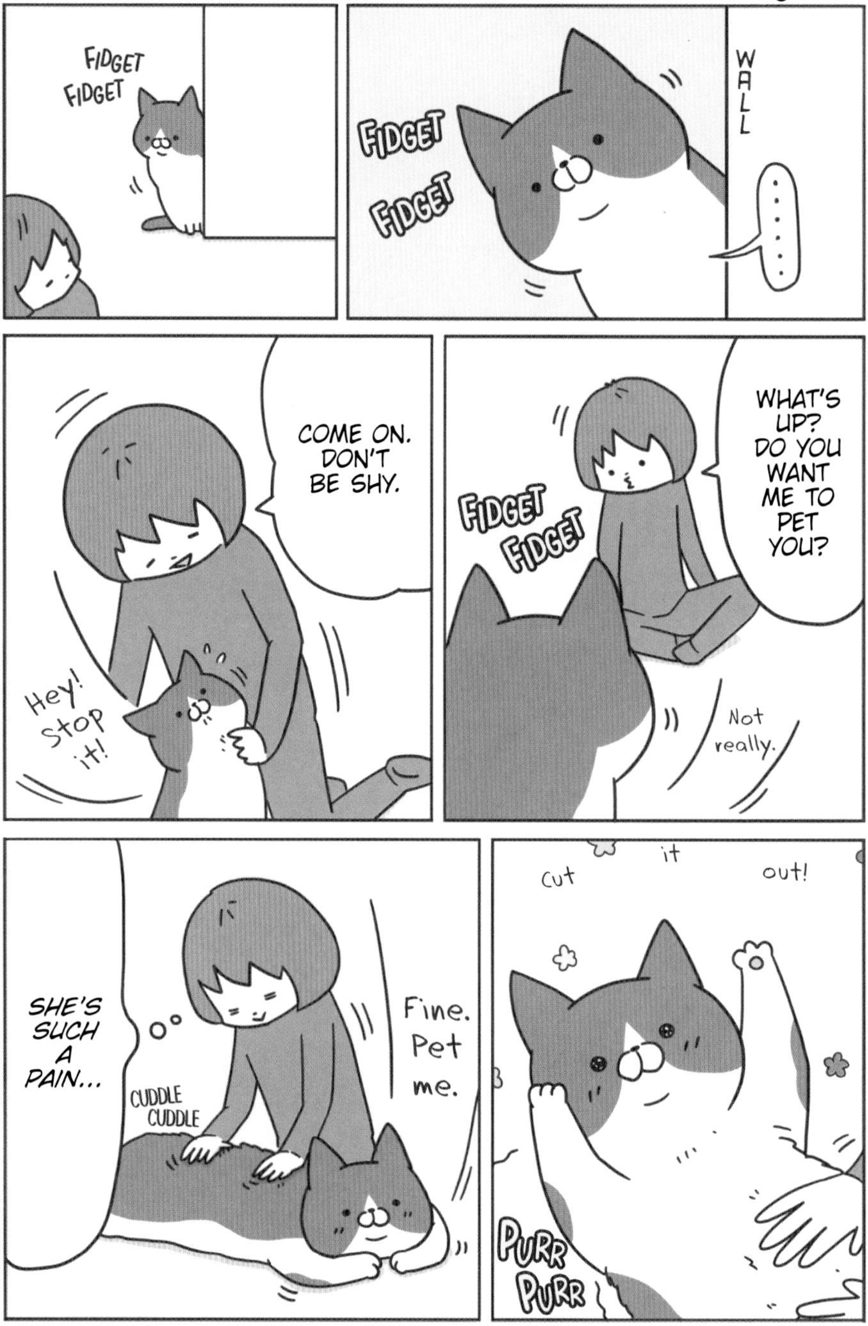

FIDGET
FIDGET
WALL
......
FIDGET
FIDGET
WHAT'S UP? DO YOU WANT ME TO PET YOU?
FIDGET
FIDGET
Not really.
COME ON. DON'T BE SHY.
Hey! Stop it!
Cut it out!
PURR
PURR
SHE'S SUCH A PAIN...
Fine. Pet me.
CUDDLE
CUDDLE

She's Not That Much of a Pain

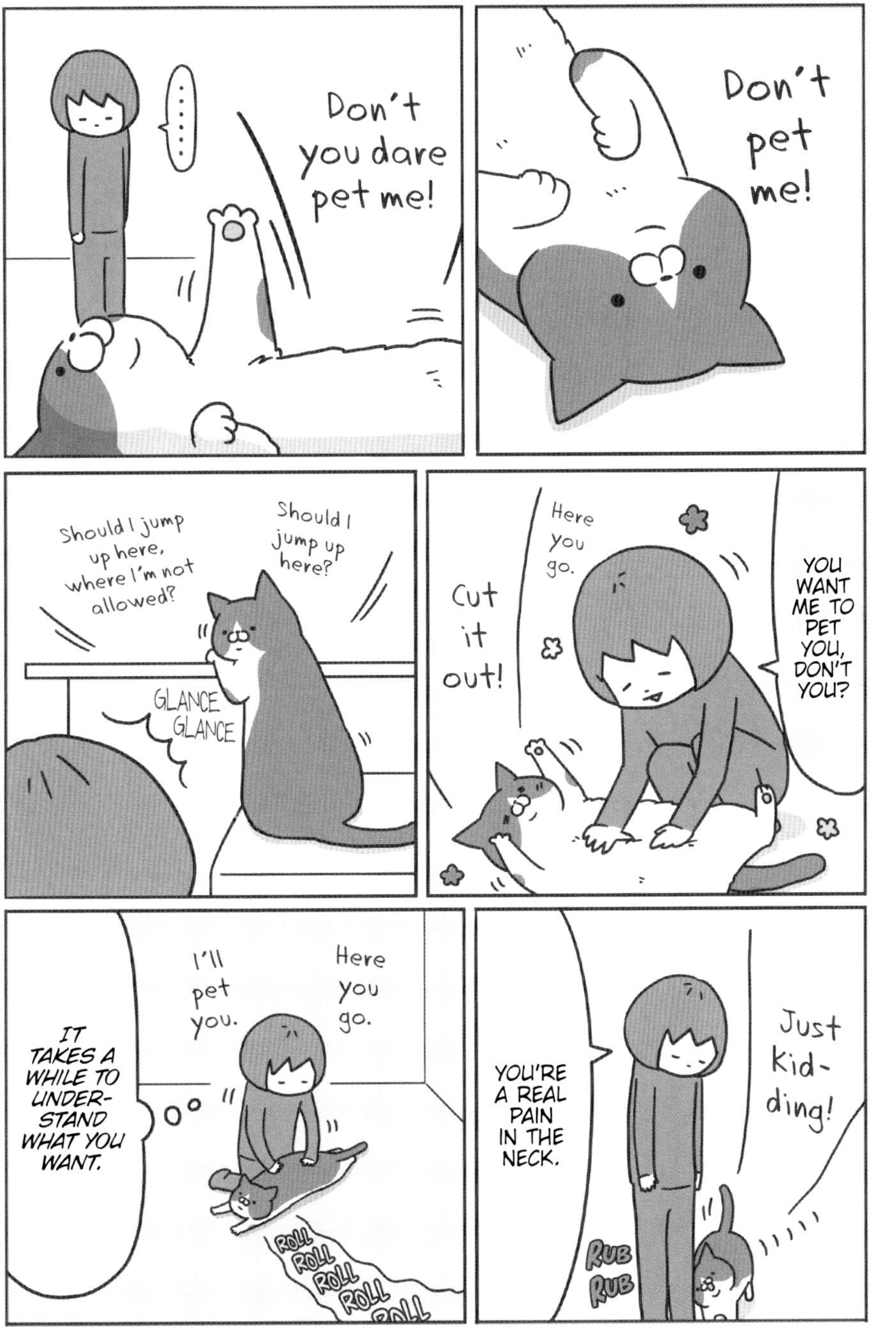
Don't pet me!
...
Don't you dare pet me!
Here you go.
YOU WANT ME TO PET YOU, DON'T YOU?
Cut it out!
Should I jump up here?
Should I jump up here, where I'm not allowed?
GLANCE GLANCE
Just kid-ding!
YOU'RE A REAL PAIN IN THE NECK.
RUB RUB
Here you go.
I'll pet you.
IT TAKES A WHILE TO UNDER-STAND WHAT YOU WANT.
ROLL ROLL ROLL ROLL ROLL

A Grain of Rice

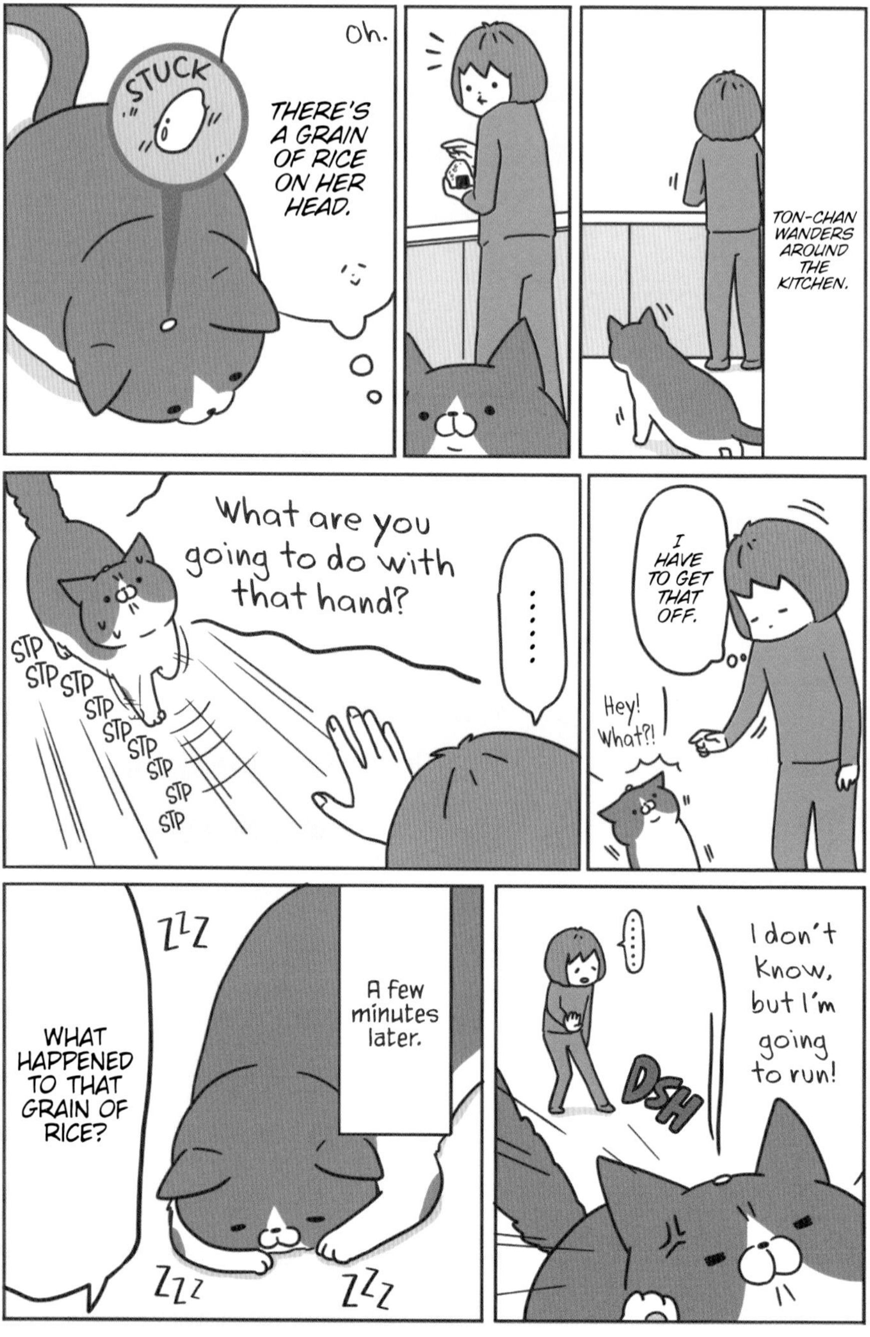
TON-CHAN WANDERS AROUND THE KITCHEN.
Oh.
THERE'S A GRAIN OF RICE ON HER HEAD.
STUCK
I HAVE TO GET THAT OFF.
Hey! What?!
What are you going to do with that hand?
......
STP STP STP STP STP STP STP STP STP
......
I don't know, but I'm going to run!
DSH
A few minutes later.
ZZZ
WHAT HAPPENED TO THAT GRAIN OF RICE?
ZZZ
ZZZ

Ton-chan Gets Mad

TON-CHAN IS MAD AT ME.
THAT'S BECAUSE I STEPPED ON HER TAIL YESTERDAY.
Oh! Sorry!
SCRUNCH
. . . . . .
She doesn't cry
SMACK
SMACK
Sorry...
I'm so sorry.
SHE WAS STILL UPSET THE NEXT MORNING.
SHE PROBABLY FORGOT WHY SHE WAS MAD.
Presses against me

She was mad at me.

It's off-topic, but her paws looked like pork buns.

My Cat
is Such a
Weirdo

Chapter 2

My Cats and Objects

← remote control

A Failed Negotiation

HEY!
I WAS GOING TO WEAR THAT TODAY!
Don't care!
HERE, SLEEP ON THIS MAT.
Problem solved.
FOR CATS
WSH
IT DIDN'T SOLVE ANY-THING.
GRAB

A final measure.
STRIPPING
My shirt
DRAG
Go sit on that.
DRAG

Maintenance Duty

THESE ARE MY FLUFFY SLIPPERS.
WARM
Oh...
FLUFFY
FLUFFY
These fluffy things...
must be groomed.
LICK
LICK
LICK
LICK
EW!
THEY FELT WARM AND DAMP.

I guess she wanted to take care of me.

Give it back.

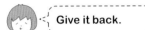

She services Ton-chan too.

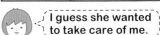

Their Main Object

Amazun
Amazun
CAT HOUSE
Whee!
Whee!

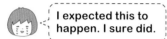

I expected this to happen. I sure did.

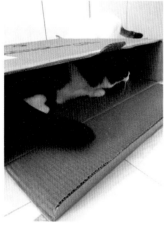

My Stuff Belongs to My Cats

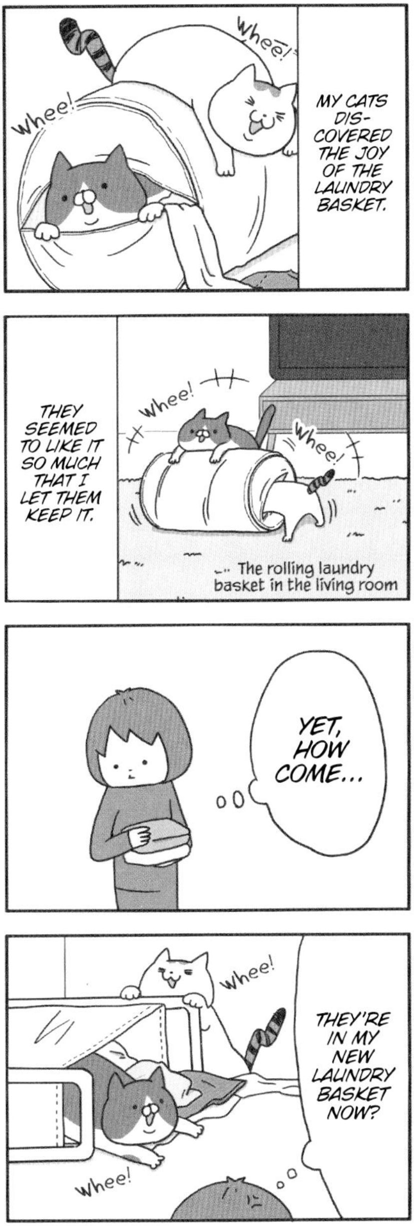
MY CATS DIS-COVERED THE JOY OF THE LAUNDRY BASKET.
Whee!
Whee!
Whee!
Whee!
THEY SEEMED TO LIKE IT SO MUCH THAT I LET THEM KEEP IT.
... The rolling laundry basket in the living room
YET, HOW COME...
THEY'RE IN MY NEW LAUNDRY BASKET NOW?
Whee!
Whee!

I tried to buy one that wouldn't interest them, but it was futile.

They got into both my old and new laundry baskets.

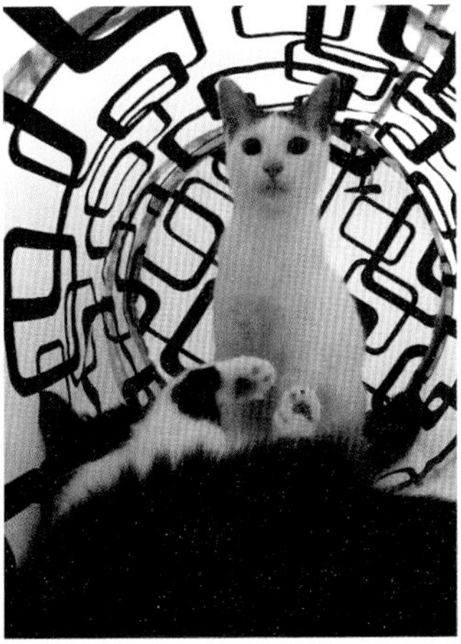

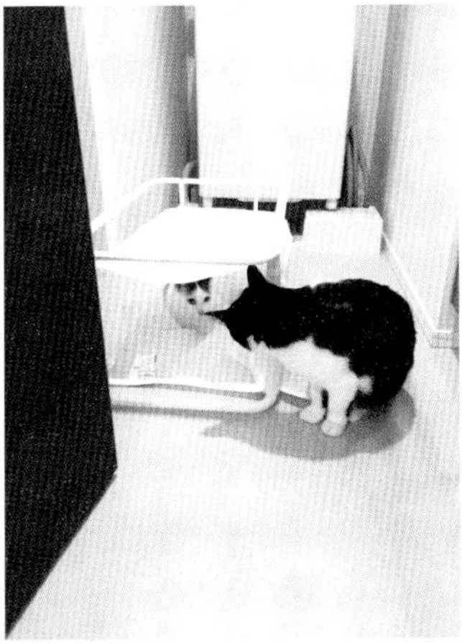

Another Way of Thinking

MY UPHOLSTERED OTTOMAN IN THE LIVING ROOM...
SCRATCH SCRATCH
SEEMS TO WORK PERFECTLY AS A SCRATCHER.
SCRATCH SCRATCH
AT FIRST I TRIED TO KEEP THEM AWAY FROM IT.
Stop it!
RIP RIP RIP
SCRATCH SCRATCH
AS IT GOT MORE SCRATCHED UP, I STOPPED CARING ABOUT IT.
SCRATCH SCRATCH SCRATCH SCRATCH
NOW I CONSIDER IT A SCRATCHING OTTOMAN AND LIVE IN PEACE.
Ha ha ha!
SCRATCH SCRATCH SCRATCH
SCRATCH SCRATCH SCRATCH

This is their big scratcher.

Resistance was futile the moment they set their eyes on it.

I didn't expect it to become this fuzzy mess when I bought it.

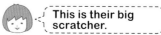

Even Though It Says It's Safe to Swallow

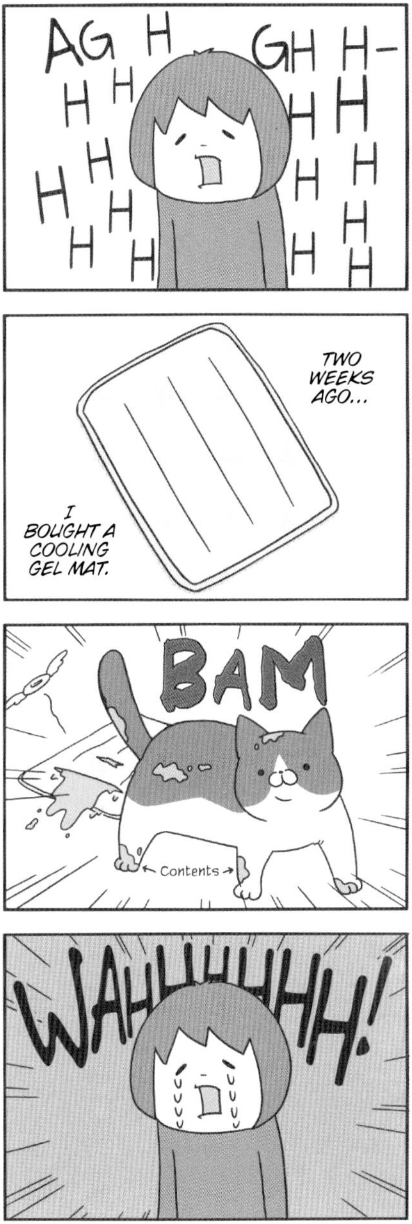
AGH GH H-HHHHHHHHHHHHHH
TWO WEEKS AGO...
I BOUGHT A COOLING GEL MAT.
BAM
Contents
Contents
WAHHHHHH!

Ton-chan and the Bath Part 1

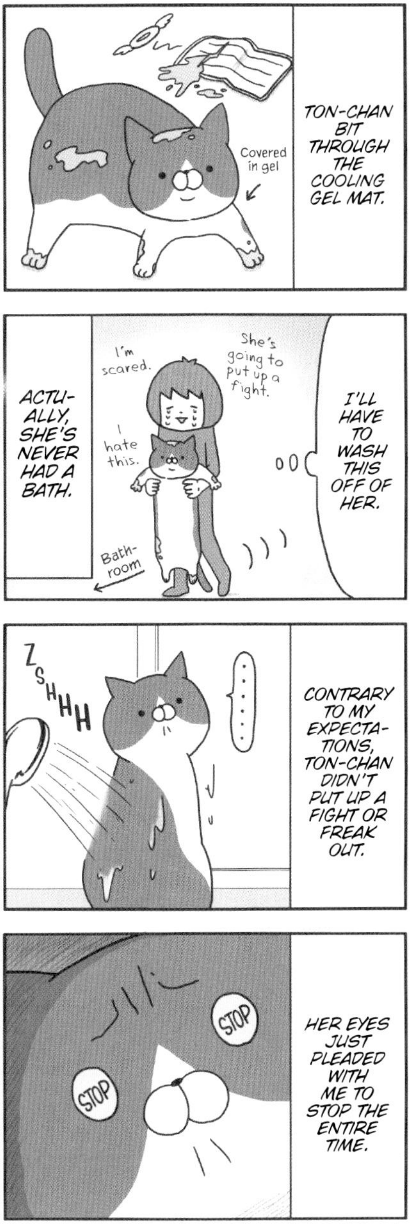
TON-CHAN BIT THROUGH THE COOLING GEL MAT.
Covered in gel
I'LL HAVE TO WASH THIS OFF OF HER.
She's going to put up a fight.
I'm scared.
I hate this.
Bathroom
ACTUALLY, SHE'S NEVER HAD A BATH.
CONTRARY TO MY EXPECTATIONS, TON-CHAN DIDN'T PUT UP A FIGHT OR FREAK OUT.
......
ZSHHH
HER EYES JUST PLEADED WITH ME TO STOP THE ENTIRE TIME.
STOP
STOP

Ton-chan and the Bath Part 2

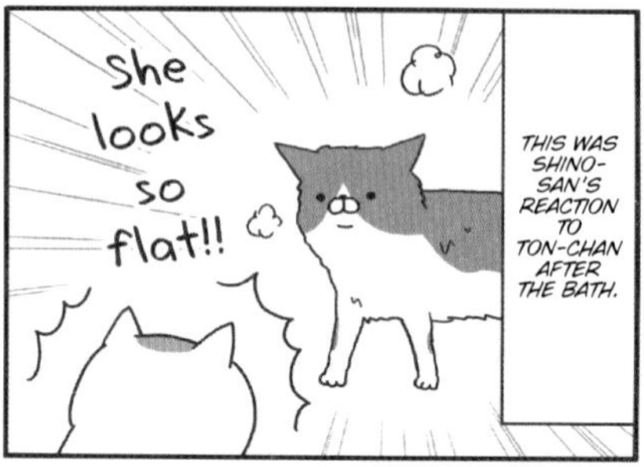
THIS WAS SHINO-SAN'S REACTION TO TON-CHAN AFTER THE BATH.
She looks so flat!!

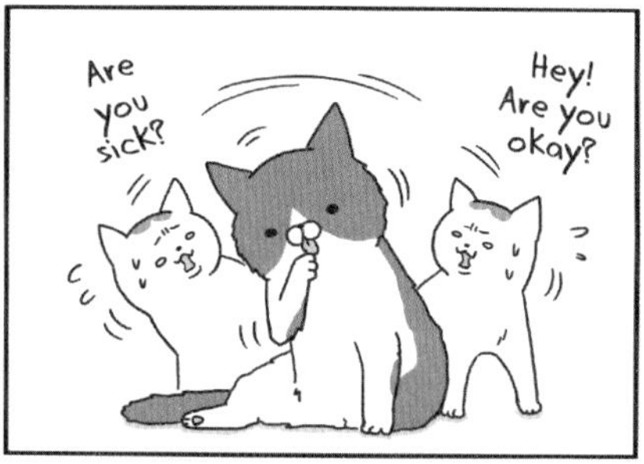
Hey! Are you okay?
Are you sick?

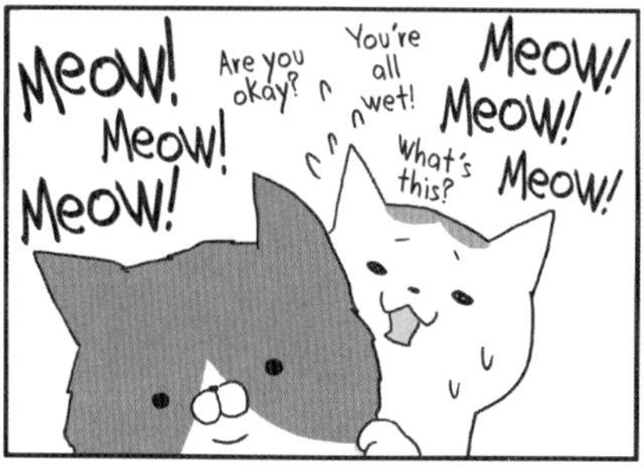
Meow!
Meow!
Meow!
What's this?
You're all wet!
Are you okay?
Meow!
Meow!
Meow!

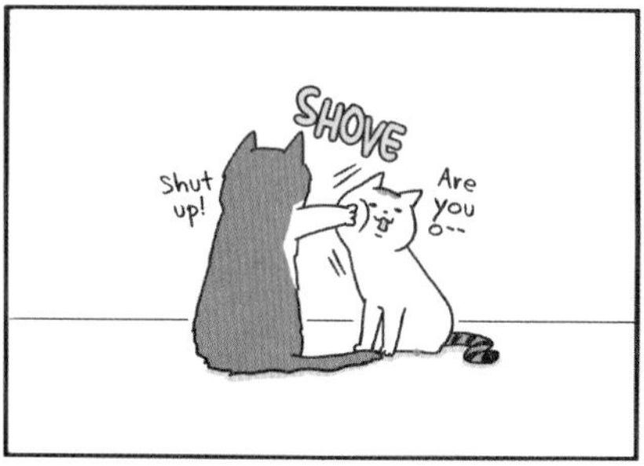
SHOVE
Are you o--
Shut up!

Ton-chan didn't look small at all when she was wet.

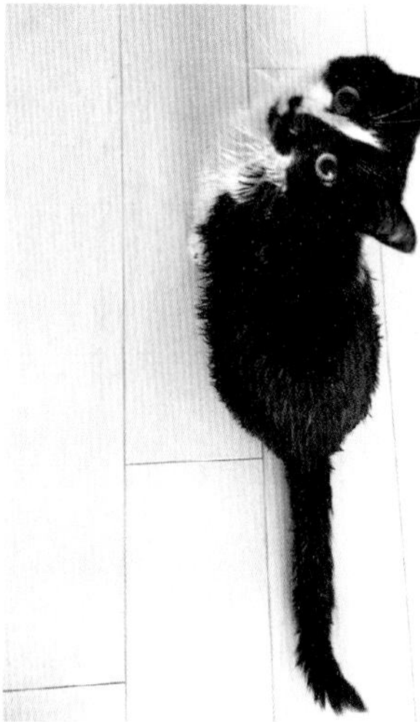

Shino-san, who was worried, kept meowing in front of the bathroom door.

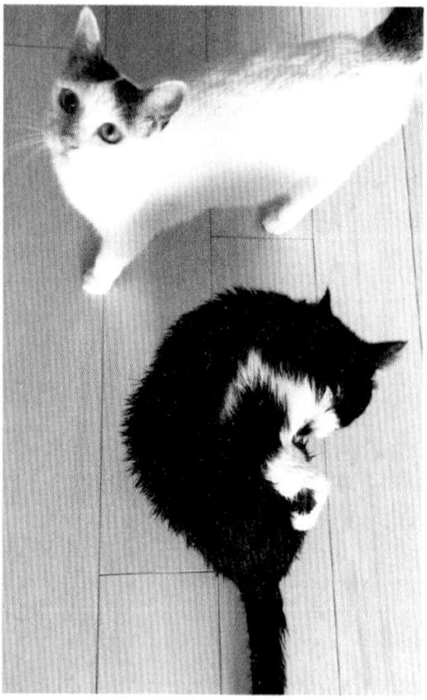

Nail Trim Penalty

Both of my cats hate getting their nails cut.
I wanted to avoid doing something they don't like,
so I made nail trimming a punishment.

① **No!**

When they do something bad...

CLOTHES

② They get their nails trimmed...

as punishment.

RESTRAINT

This method worked well enough
on my cats to lessen their
bad habits, but it also limited
my chances to cut their nails.
What do I do about this?

GOOD CATS HAVE LONG NAILS.

TON-CHAN'S NAILS.

❀ Thick and hard to clip
❀ Whitish in color

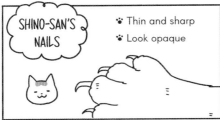

SHINO-SAN'S NAILS

❀ Thin and sharp
❀ Look opaque

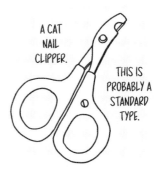

A CAT NAIL CLIPPER.

THIS IS PROBABLY A STANDARD TYPE.

Welcome Home

THMP THMP THMP THMP THMP
I'M HOME!
GOOD GIRL, TON-CHAN.
THANKS FOR COMING OUT.
RUB RUB
RUB
......
AH!
RUB RUB RUB RUB RUB RUB
HEY! SHE ONLY CAME OUT TO SCENT-MARK!!
Erase the other scents.
Put my scent on this.
RUB RUB RUB RUB RUB RUB

She's more diligent with marking my husband's running shoes.
RUB
RUB
RUB
RUB

Ton-chan looked satisfied. My shoes were covered in her hair.

Punch It for Now

REALLY?

I MIS-
PLACED
MY
PHONE.

Sign: Husband

I'LL CALL YOUR PHONE.

ZZ
ZZ

 Ton-chan got upset at Shino-san for interrupting her nap.

URZZ
RMB RMB
RMB RMB RMB
RMB RMB RMB
RMB RMB
RMB RMB

JOLT

STOP!!

Damn you!!

POW

Toothpaste

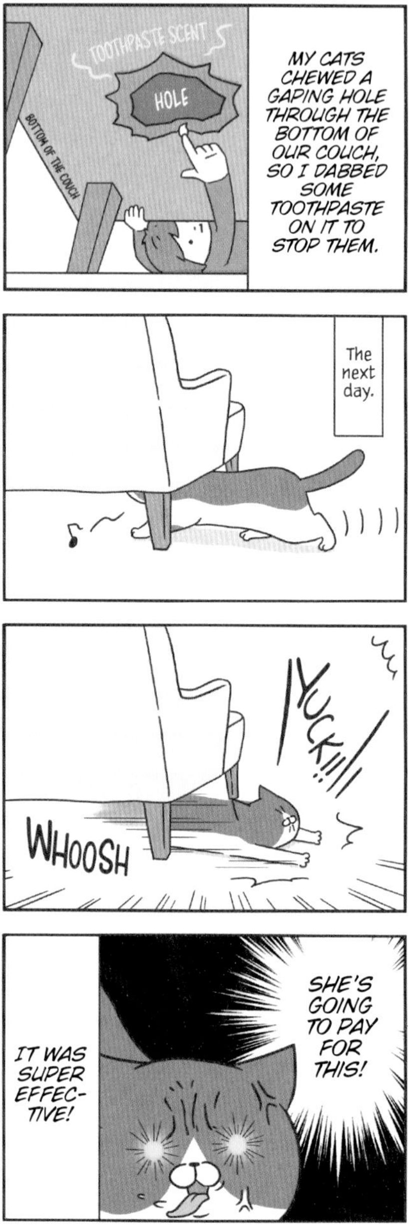

TOOTHPASTE SCENT
HOLE
BOTTOM OF THE COUCH
MY CATS CHEWED A GAPING HOLE THROUGH THE BOTTOM OF OUR COUCH, SO I DABBED SOME TOOTHPASTE ON IT TO STOP THEM.
The next day.
YUCK!!!
WHOOSH
SHE'S GOING TO PAY FOR THIS!
IT WAS SUPER EFFECTIVE!

She seems to hate the scent of toothpaste.

We closed up the hole on the couch, but it was full of hair.

A Cat Can Tell the Difference

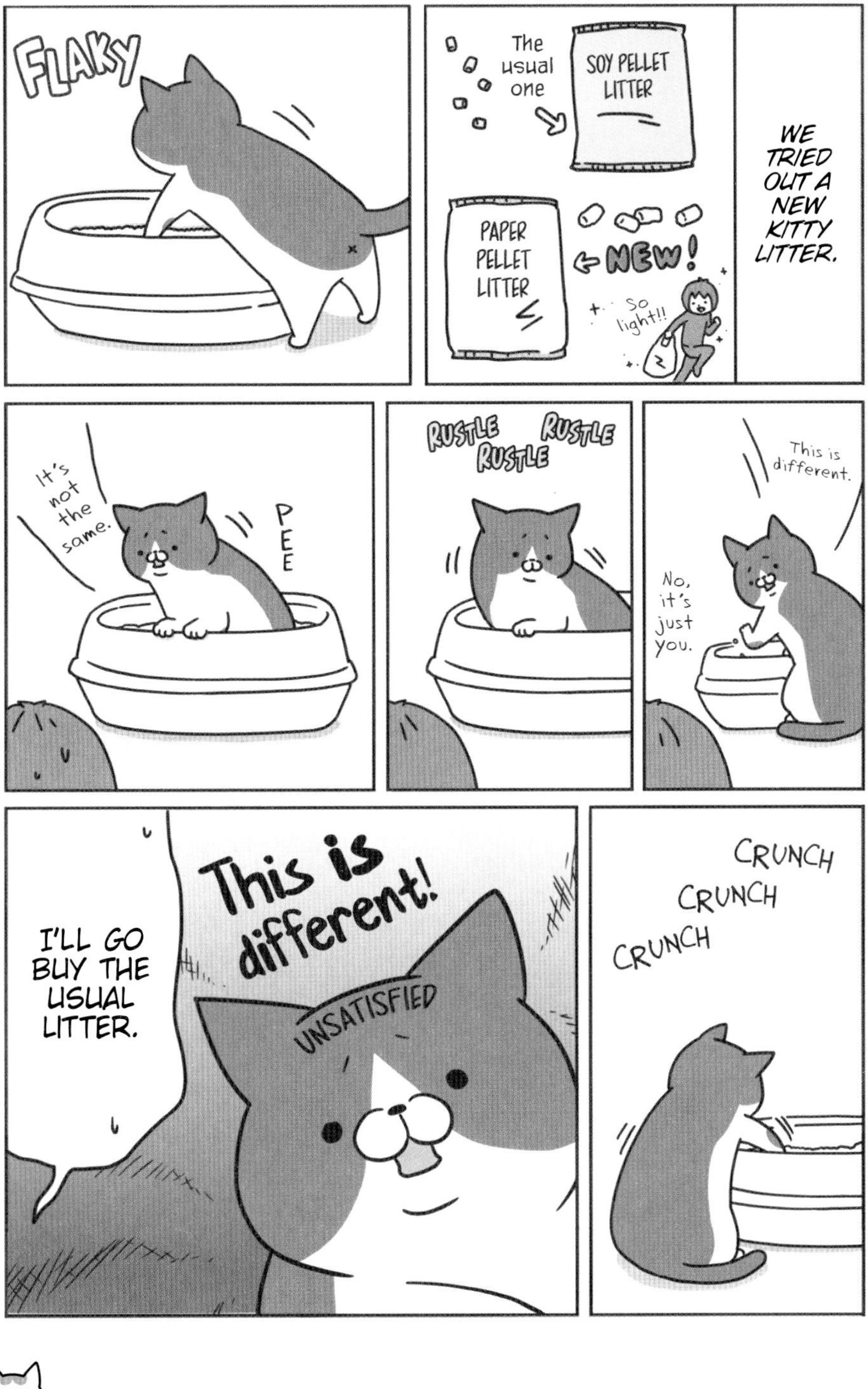

WE TRIED OUT A NEW KITTY LITTER.
The usual one
SOY PELLET LITTER
PAPER PELLET LITTER
NEW!
So light!!
FLAKY
This is different.
No, it's just you.
RUSTLE RUSTLE RUSTLE
It's not the same.
PEE
CRUNCH
CRUNCH
CRUNCH
This is different!
UNSATISFIED
I'LL GO BUY THE USUAL LITTER.

Pom-Pom Mystery

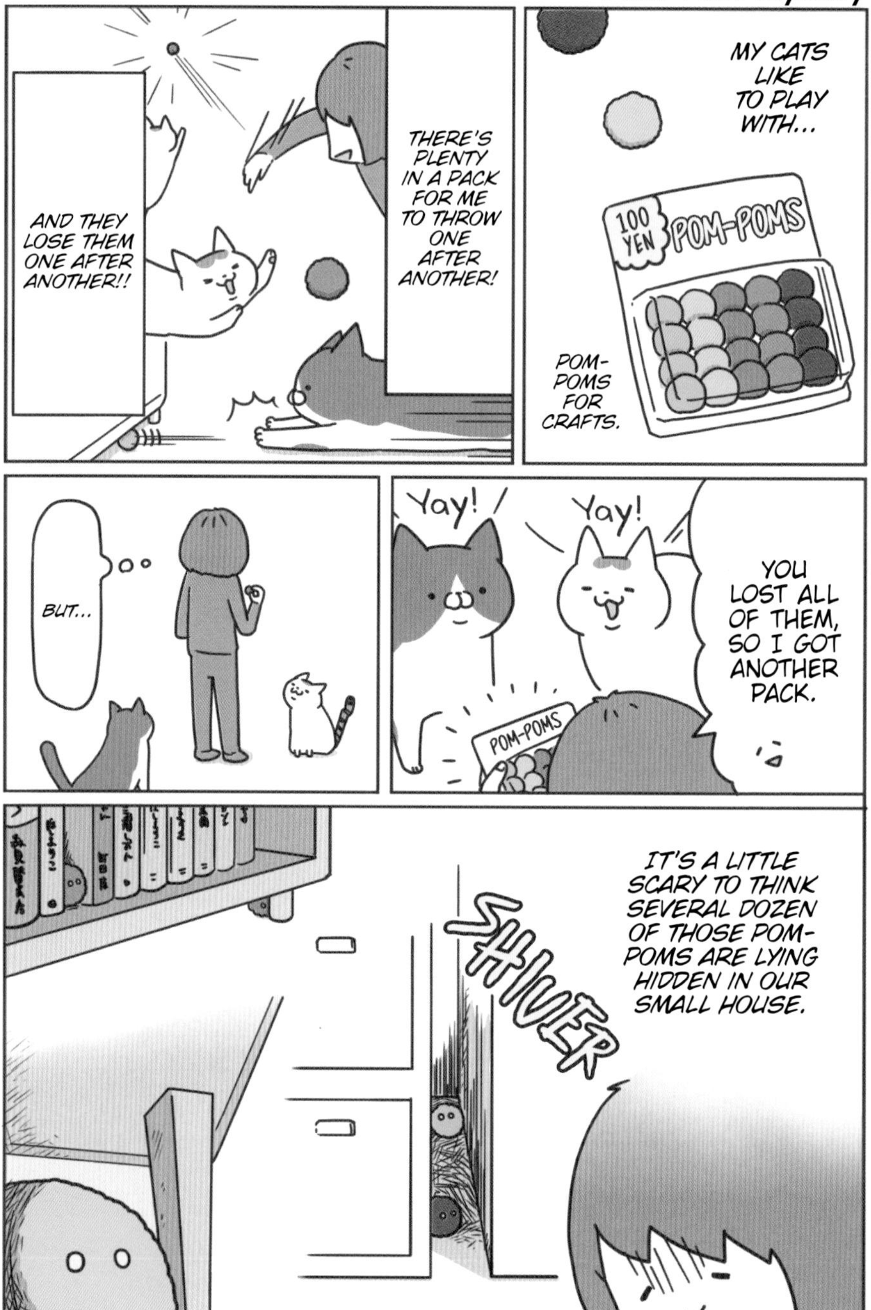

MY CATS LIKE TO PLAY WITH...
100 YEN
POM-POMS
POM-POMS FOR CRAFTS.
THERE'S PLENTY IN A PACK FOR ME TO THROW ONE AFTER ANOTHER!
AND THEY LOSE THEM ONE AFTER ANOTHER!!
Yay!
Yay!
YOU LOST ALL OF THEM, SO I GOT ANOTHER PACK.
POM-POMS
BUT...
IT'S A LITTLE SCARY TO THINK SEVERAL DOZEN OF THOSE POM-POMS ARE LYING HIDDEN IN OUR SMALL HOUSE.
SHIVER

Dipping in the Water

THEY HAVE A FELT BALL.
WHEEEEEE
HFF! HFF!
HFF! HFF!
WATER
......
SPLISH
THEY DIP IT IN THE WATER BEFORE THEY PLAY WITH IT FOR SOME REA-SON.
WOOHOO!

I'm glad they're having fun.

They don't get bored with these pom-poms. I stock up on a lot of them.

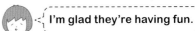

Locally Made

THIS TOY DIDN'T LAST.
Ton-chan usually chews them up.
I'LL BUY IT!
DURABLE, MADE IN JAPAN
CAT TOY
BUY
THIS ONE SHOULDN'T BREAK THAT EASILY.
Ha ha!
Don't under-estimate products made in Japan!
SNAP
WHERE IT WAS MADE DIDN'T MATTER.

Shino-san rarely breaks her toys since she knows that means she won't be able to play with them anymore. Ton-chan tries to destroy them right away.

When Ton-chan breaks a toy, she does a good job.

Breaking Their Toys Again

Even though cat owners are destined to have their cats ruin their toys...

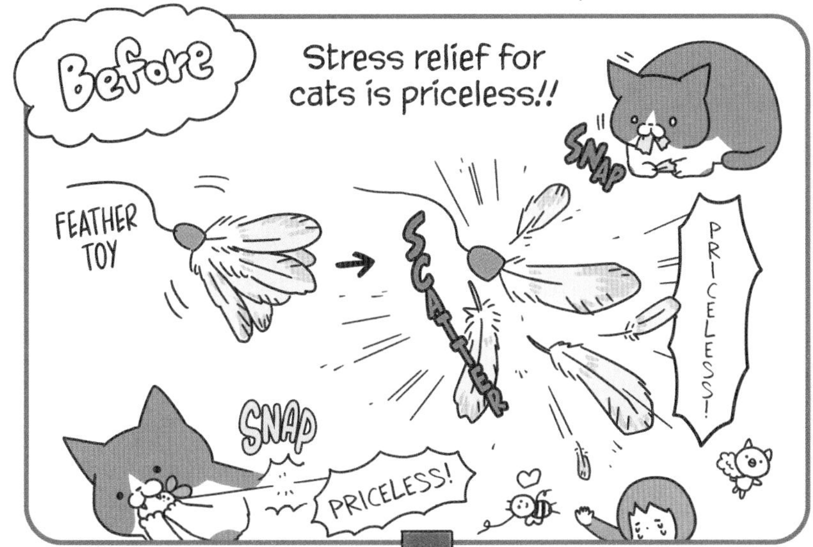
Before
Stress relief for cats is priceless!!
SNAP
PRICELESS!
SCATTER
FEATHER TOY
SNAP
PRICELESS!

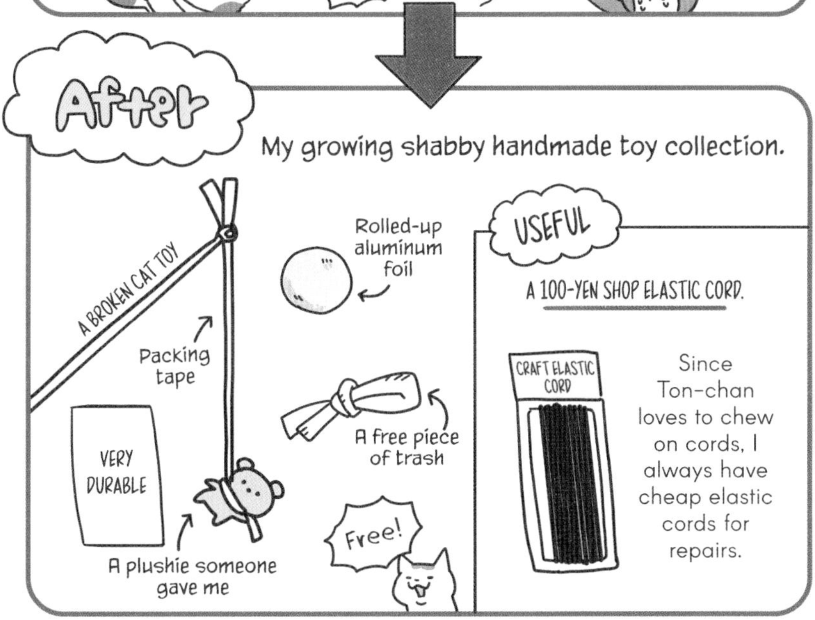
After
My growing shabby handmade toy collection.
USEFUL
A 100-YEN SHOP ELASTIC CORD.
Since Ton-chan loves to chew on cords, I always have cheap elastic cords for repairs.
CRAFT ELASTIC CORD
Rolled-up aluminum foil
A free piece of trash
Free!
A BROKEN CAT TOY
Packing tape
VERY DURABLE
A plushie someone gave me

It's Not That They Wanted It

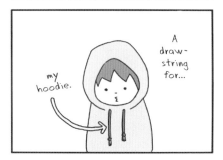

A drawstring for...
my hoodie.
MY CATS TRY TO GET TO IT ALL THE TIME.
WSH
......
PLOP
HERE, YOU CAN HAVE IT.
What's this?
I don't want it.
COME ON!

They're only interested in it when it's dangling.

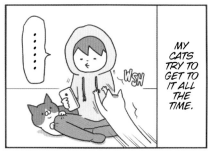

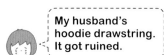

My husband's hoodie drawstring. It got ruined.

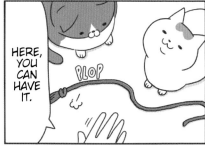

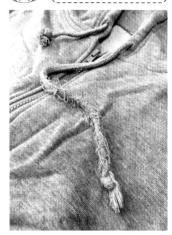

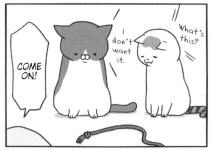

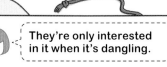

My Cats and Their Toys

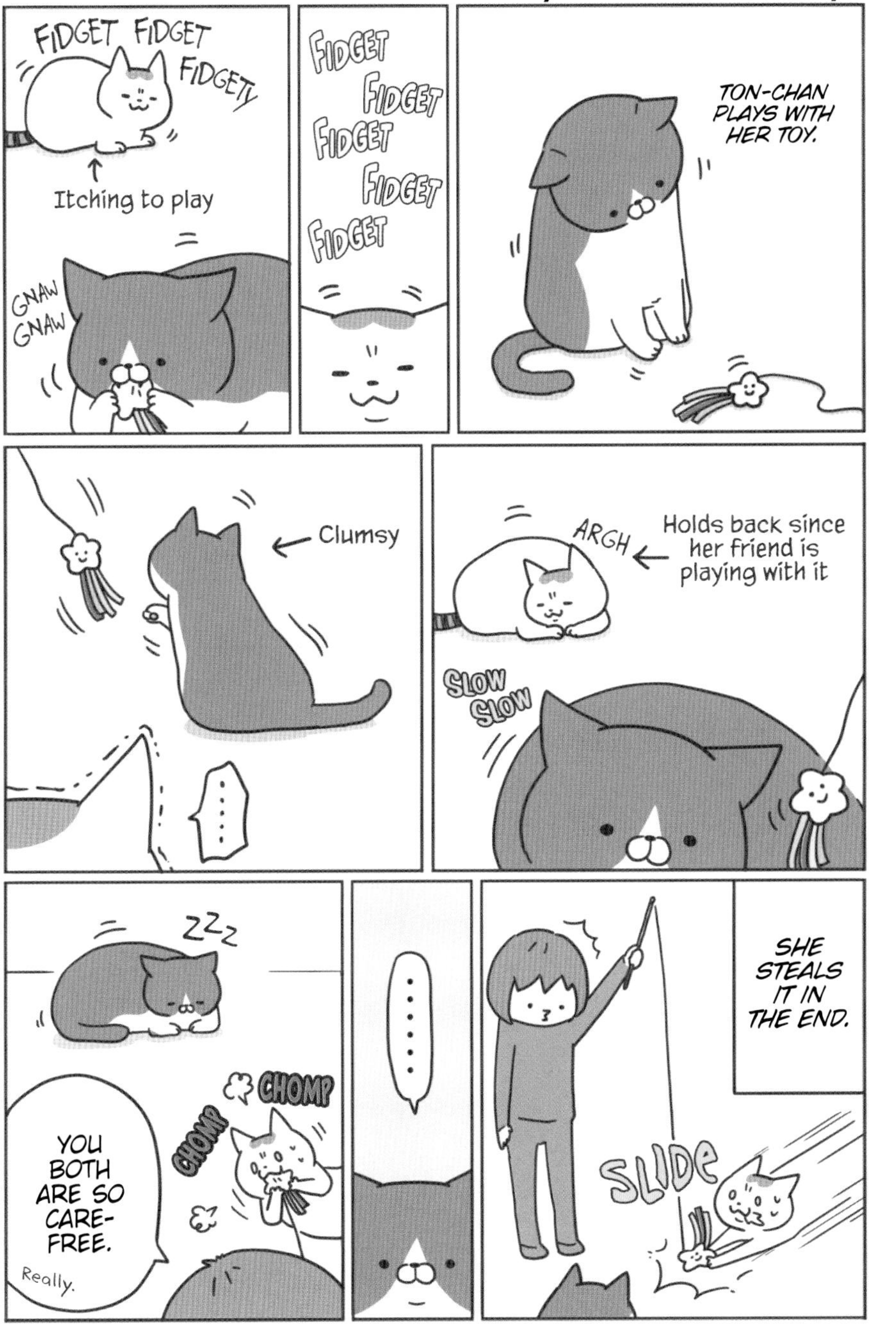
TON-CHAN PLAYS WITH HER TOY.
FIDGET FIDGET FIDGET FIDGET FIDGET
FIDGET FIDGET FIDGETY
Itching to play
GNAW GNAW
ARGH
Holds back since her friend is playing with it
SLOW SLOW
Clumsy
......
SHE STEALS IT IN THE END.
SLIDE
......
ZZZ
CHOMP
CHOMP
YOU BOTH ARE SO CARE-FREE.
Really.

Looking Cute from Behind

ONE DAY...
TON-CHAN WAS SITTING STILL IN MY BED-ROOM.
COMFORTER
FWIP
FLINCH
TON-CHAN, WHAT ARE YOU DOING?
WERE YOU ZONING OUT?
What's the matter?
What's the matter?
SHE WAS PEE-ING.
WAHHHHHHH!!
Had a distant look all along
PEE

She did it to me three times.

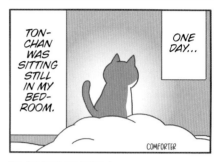

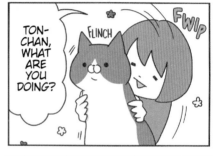

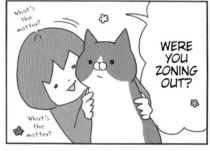

This was back when Ton-chan was a kitten. She doesn't have accidents anymore.

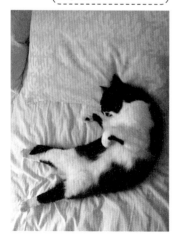

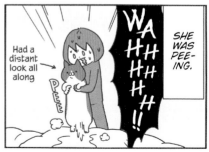

My Cats and a Box

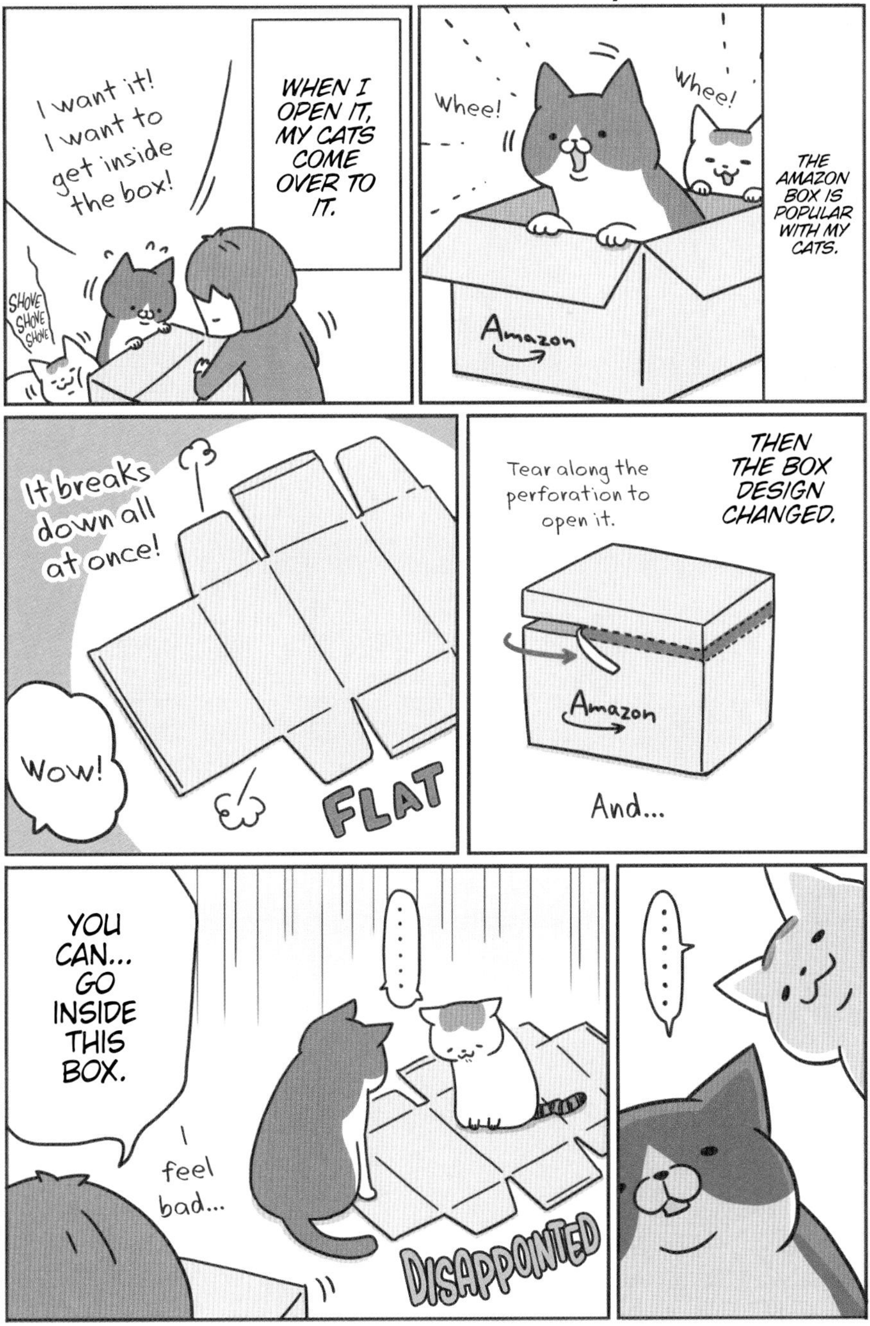
THE AMAZON BOX IS POPULAR WITH MY CATS.
Whee!
Whee!
Amazon
WHEN I OPEN IT, MY CATS COME OVER TO IT.
I want it! I want to get inside the box!
SHOVE SHOVE SHOVE
THEN THE BOX DESIGN CHANGED.
Tear along the perforation to open it.
Amazon
And...
It breaks down all at once!
FLAT
Wow!
......
......
YOU CAN... GO INSIDE THIS BOX.
I feel bad...
DISAPPOINTED

Enjoying It a Lot

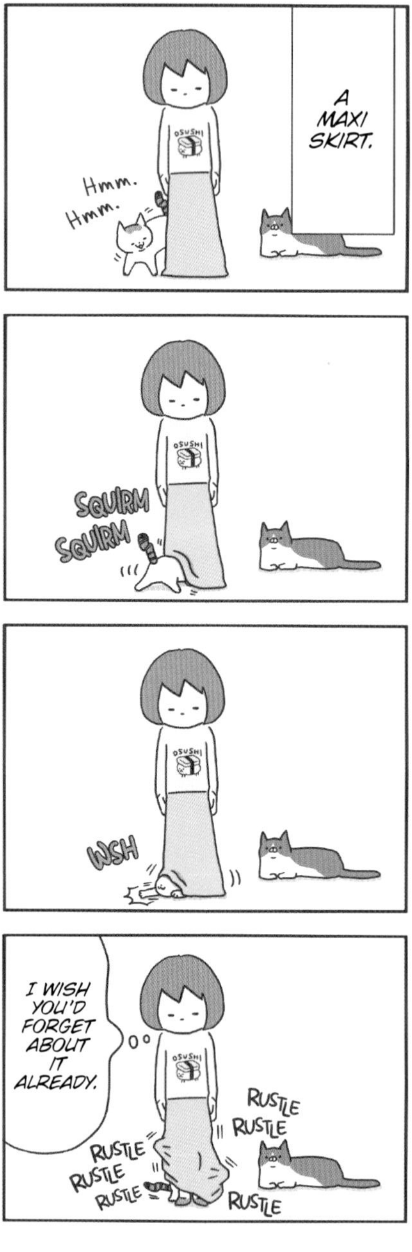
A MAXI SKIRT.
Hmm. Hmm.
SQUIRM SQUIRM
WSH
I WISH YOU'D FORGET ABOUT IT ALREADY.
RUSTLE RUSTLE
RUSTLE RUSTLE RUSTLE
RUSTLE

Shino-san likes to get in my clothes. She'll do that and go crazy with them.

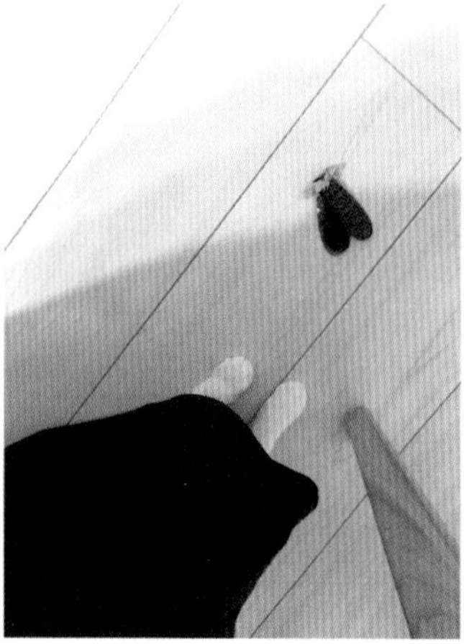

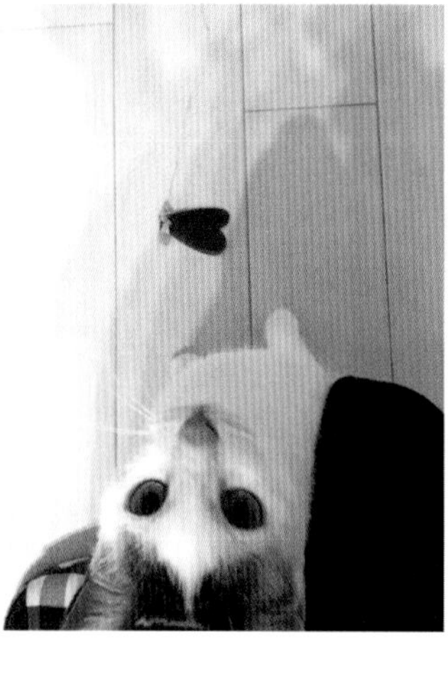

Still on Trend

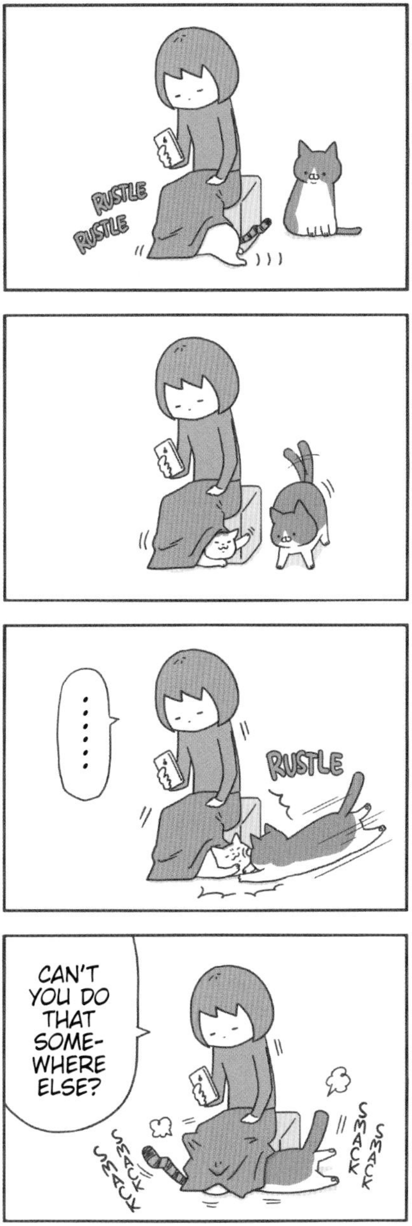
RUSTLE
RUSTLE
......
RUSTLE
CAN'T YOU DO THAT SOME-WHERE ELSE?
SMACK
SMACK
SMACK
SMACK

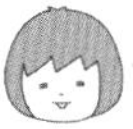

I keep wearing the maxi skirt while I tell them to stop. I have such a blast with it.

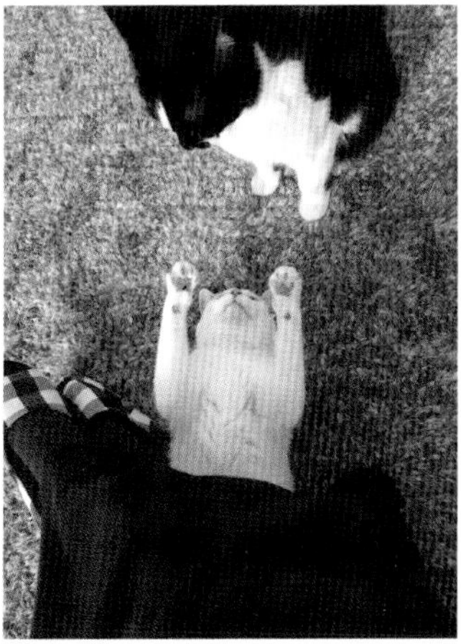

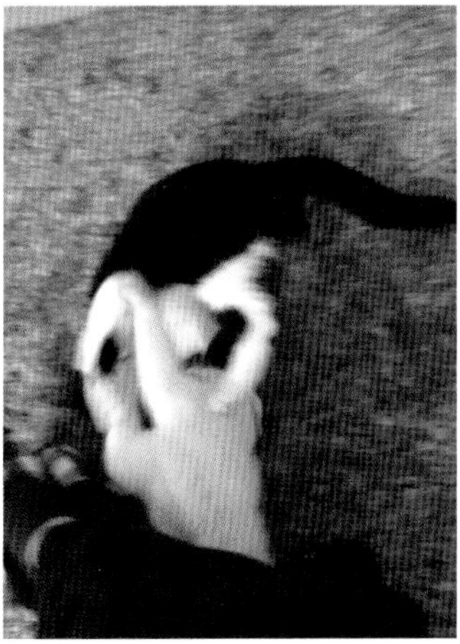

Escaping Out of a Skirt

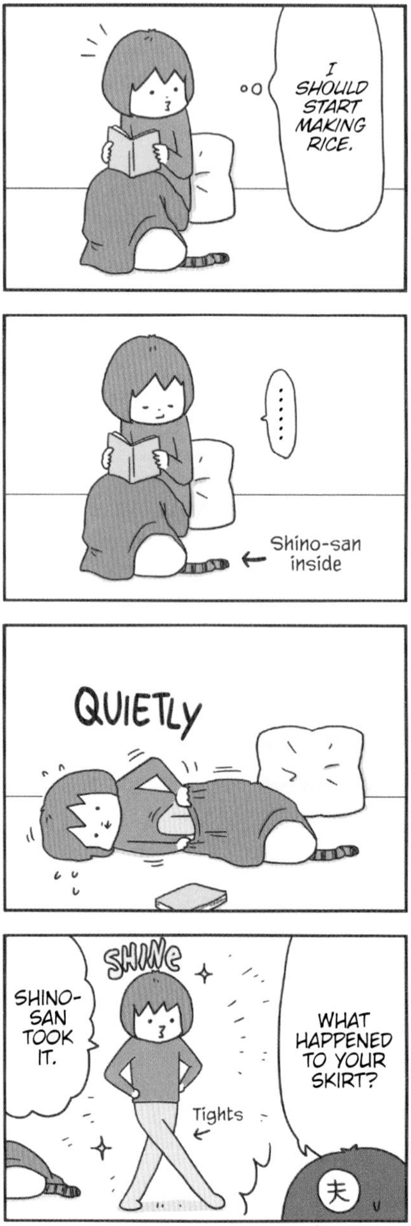
I SHOULD START MAKING RICE.
......
Shino-san inside
QUIETLY
WHAT HAPPENED TO YOUR SKIRT?
SHINE
SHINO-SAN TOOK IT.
Tights
夫

Sign: Husband

I had no other way.

Here's the skirt Shino-san took. It moved little by little and freaked Ton-chan out.

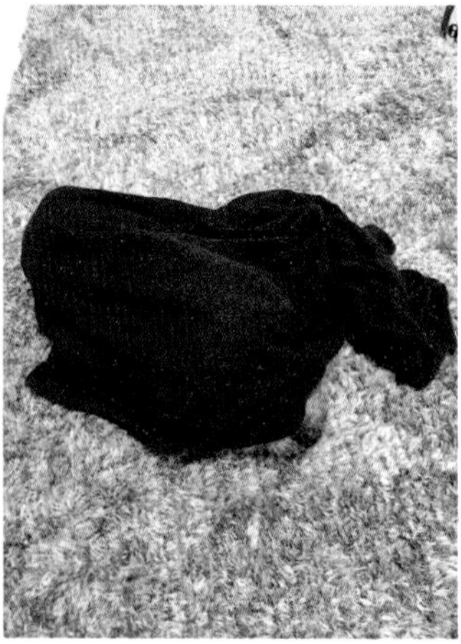

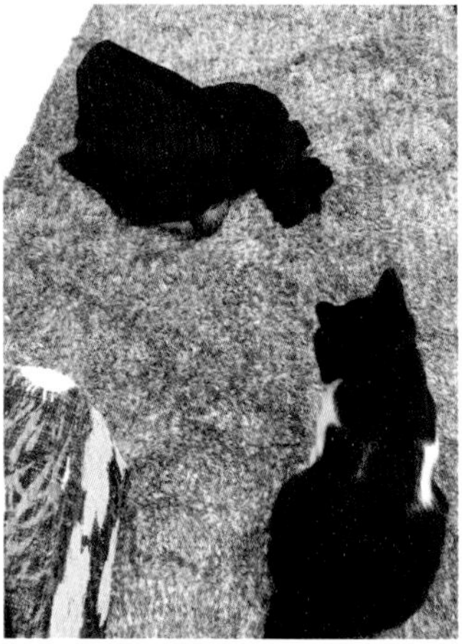

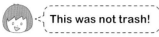

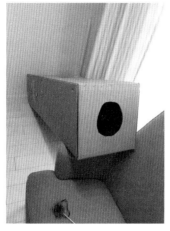

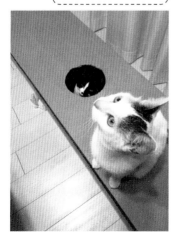

Eliminator

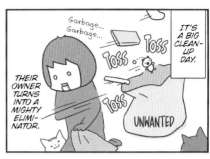

IT'S A BIG CLEAN-UP DAY.
Toss
Garbage... Garbage...
Toss
Toss
THEIR OWNER TURNS INTO A MIGHTY ELIMINATOR.
UNWANTED
The Eliminator's ☆ Eye
TARGET
A BIG CARDBOARD BOX
MEE MEOWW
!!!
WE'RE KEEPING THIS!
WE KEPT IT FOR THE NEW YEAR.

This was not trash!

A piece of knotted twine in the left corner of the photo wasn't trash, either!

※Because the cats liked it.

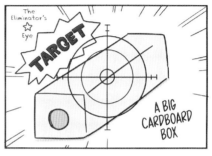

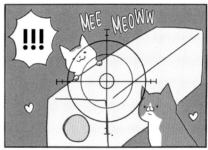

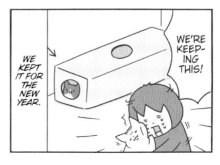

My Cat is Such a Weirdo

Chapter 3

My Cats and Food

New ☆ Food ☆ Texture

I GAVE A PIECE OF TUNA SASHIMI...
MUNCH
MUNCH
MUNCH
TO MY CAT THAT USUALLY ONLY EATS CAT FOOD.
Wh-wh-what the heck is this?
CHEWY CHEWY CHEWY
Wh-what the heck is this?!
GROSS!!!
BLERGH
But yum!!!
MUNCH
MUNCH
SHE FINISHED IT DESPITE BEING SUPER CON-FUSED BY IT.

When I gave her tuna a year later, she wouldn't eat it. The dry food is her favorite right now.

Individual Expressions

WHEN I WAS GRILLING...
SHO CHU
A DRIED FIREFLY SQUID...
VERY TASTY
MY CATS CAME OVER AND DEMANDED I GIVE THEM SOME.
Gimme!
Gimme!
You can't have it.
THIS IS WHEN SHINO-SAN WOULD MEOW VERY LOUDLY TO ANNOY ME.
GIMME!
Sometimes rolls her tongue
TON-CHAN MOSTLY STAYS QUIET...
BUT GIVES ME AN ANNOYING LOOK.
Mee...
Meow...
Mumbling

They each approach me in a different way.

This is her annoying look.

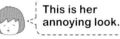

She Usually Ignores My Calling

A bowl of super-hot miso soup
Another bowl of super-hot miso soup
SLOWLY
Hot, hot!
SLOWLY
TABLE
Hff hff.
SLOWLY
Hot, hot!
TROT TROT
SLOWLY
Hey, what are you doing? What's that you're holding? Come on!
TROT TROT
Stop!
TUG TUG

Just before my husband left for a run, Ton-chan rushed out to protect his shoes.

Not for You

PLUNK
TOMATOES
WOOSH
SPLOSH
EXCITED
EXCITED
WHAT?
What?......

This is when she hangs around with a surprised look for a while.

Touch It for Now

TON-CHAN KNOWS THAT HER TREATS COME FROM THE FRIDGE.
What did you just take out of the fridge?
Chicken? Is it chicken?
IT'S TOFU.
I know you won't eat it.
SNIFF SNIFF SNIFF SNIFF SNIFF SNIFF SNIFF
......
TAP
HEY, DON'T TOUCH IT.

I made Szechuan bean curd with this tofu.

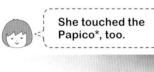

She touched the Papico*, too.

*Papico is a frozen treat in a plastic bottle.

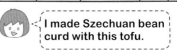

Crunchy Pickled Plum

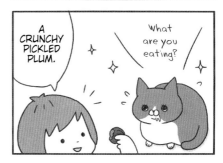

What are you eating?
A CRUNCHY PICKLED PLUM.
YOU WON'T LIKE THIS.
SNIFF SNIFF SNIFF SNIFF SNIFF
See? It smells sour.
Hell... no.
No way!
THIS TURNS YOU OFF THAT MUCH?!

She said no way. I didn't think she'd want it.

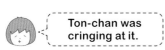

Ton-chan was cringing at it.

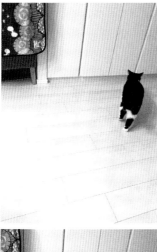

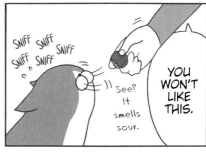

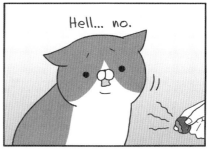

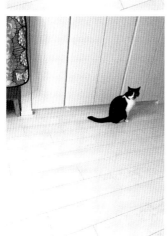

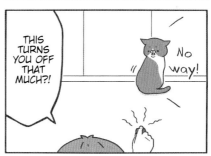

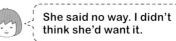

Broccoli

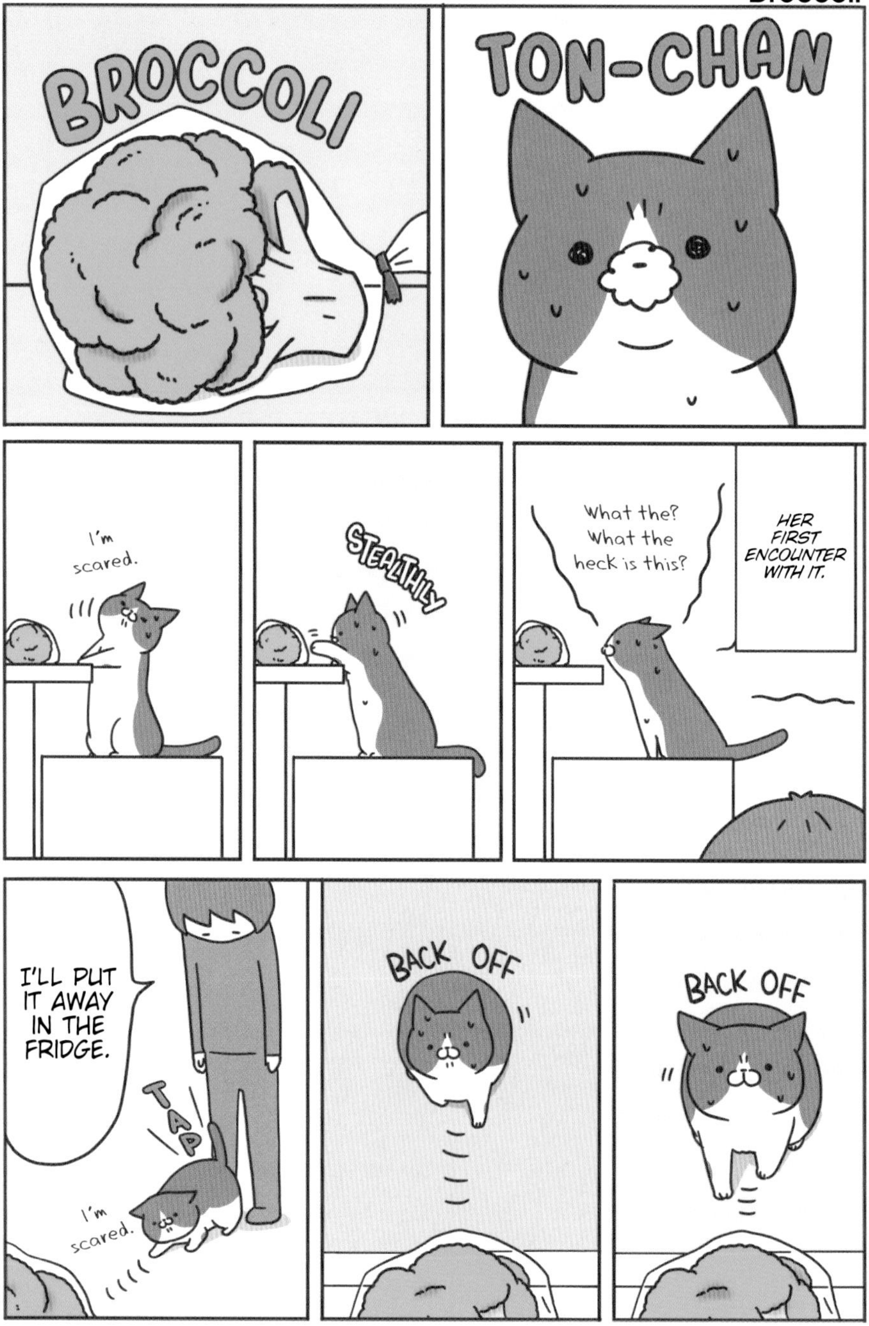
TON-CHAN
BROCCOLI
HER FIRST ENCOUNTER WITH IT.
What the? What the heck is this?
STEALTHILY
I'm scared.
BACK OFF
BACK OFF
I'LL PUT IT AWAY IN THE FRIDGE.
TAP
I'm scared.

A Matter of Feelings

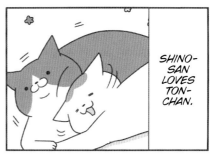

SHINO-SAN LOVES TON-CHAN.
SHINO-SAN, YOU SHOULD DRINK MORE WATER FOR YOUR HEALTH.
I'll add some to your wet food.
WHEN SHE'S COLD, SHE WON'T DRINK MUCH WATER.
BUT SHE LIKES DRINKING IT FROM A BOWL IN TON-CHAN'S CRATE.
GULP
GULP
GULP
YOU HAVE THE SAME BOWL IN YOUR CRATE...
SHE LOOKS CON-TENT.
LAP LAP LAP

She tries to eat Ton-chan's food too.

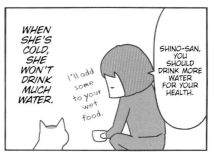

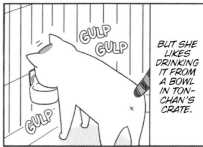

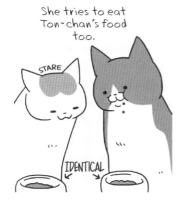

STARE
IDENTICAL

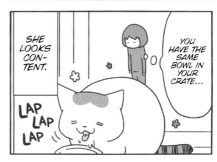

The Missing Treat

TREAT
TIME FOR YOUR TREATS!
WOO HOO!
NOM NOM NOM NOM NOM
It's gone. ......
Gone!! Our treats are gone!!
THAT'S BECAUSE YOU ATE ALL OF IT.
Oh, come on!

This happens every time.

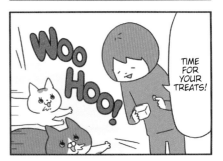

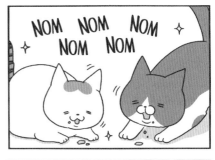

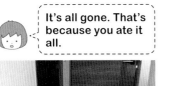

It's all gone. That's because you ate it all.

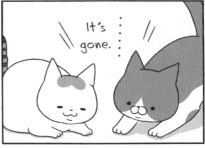

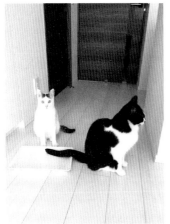

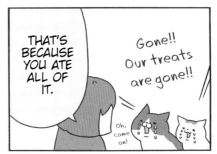

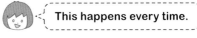

Cat Food

WET FOOD
EVENING
WET FOOD
Share
DRY FOOD
MORNING AND NIGHT

I basically give them some dry food in the morning and at night and have them share a can of wet food as a treat in the evening. I try to have them eat both the dry and wet food in case I'm limited in choice in an emergency.

Soft food!
Crunchy food!
Ton-chan likes the dry food. Shino-san likes the wet food.
They both love Kurokan brand.
KUROKAN
They tend to over-eat it, so they only have it once a month.
Yay!
Yay!

Treats

① I chop up and freeze a piece of chicken breast.

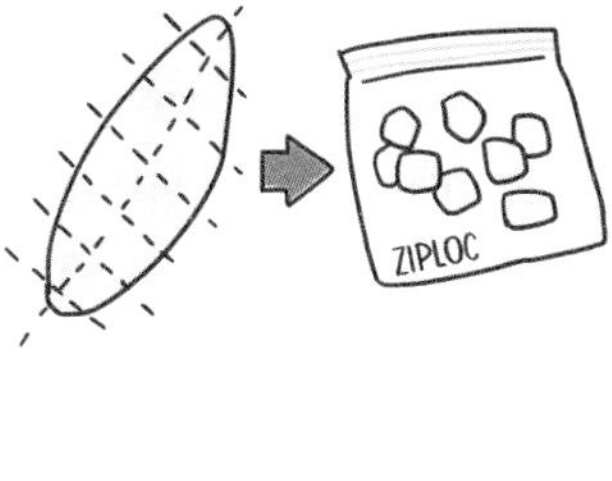

ZIPLOC

② I then boil, cool down, and shred the chicken before giving it to them.

SHREDDED CHICKEN

It's a quick and easy treat for them.

But...
I don't give it to them that often.
You could gain weight.
Oh, no!
Oh, no!

Least Favorite Food

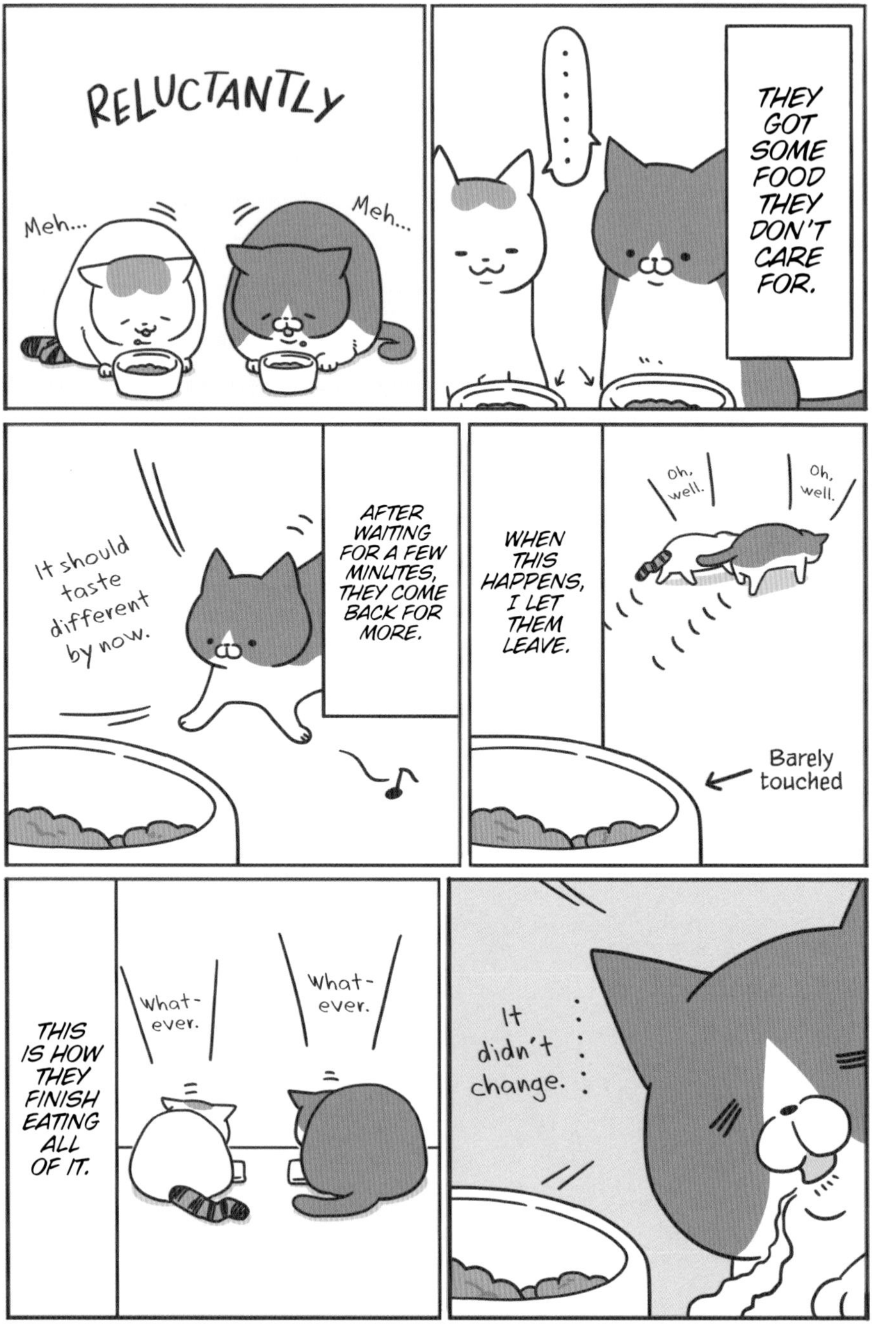
THEY GOT SOME FOOD THEY DON'T CARE FOR.
......
RELUCTANTLY
Meh...
Meh...
AFTER WAITING FOR A FEW MINUTES, THEY COME BACK FOR MORE.
It should taste different by now.
Oh, well.
Oh, well.
WHEN THIS HAPPENS, I LET THEM LEAVE.
Barely touched
It didn't change.
What-ever.
What-ever.
THIS IS HOW THEY FINISH EATING ALL OF IT.

Nuisance

FIDGET
FIDGET
FIDGET
FIDGET
CA FOOD
CLATTER
CLATTER
STEALTHILY
KLUNK
KLUNK
NOT YET.
PANT
PANT
CLATTER
CLATTER
CLATTER
SHOVE
HEY! YOU'RE IN THE WAY!
CLUNK
CLUNK
CLUNK
CLUNK

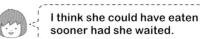

I think she could have eaten sooner had she waited.

My absent-minded husband opened this bag of cat food. So sloppy and careless.

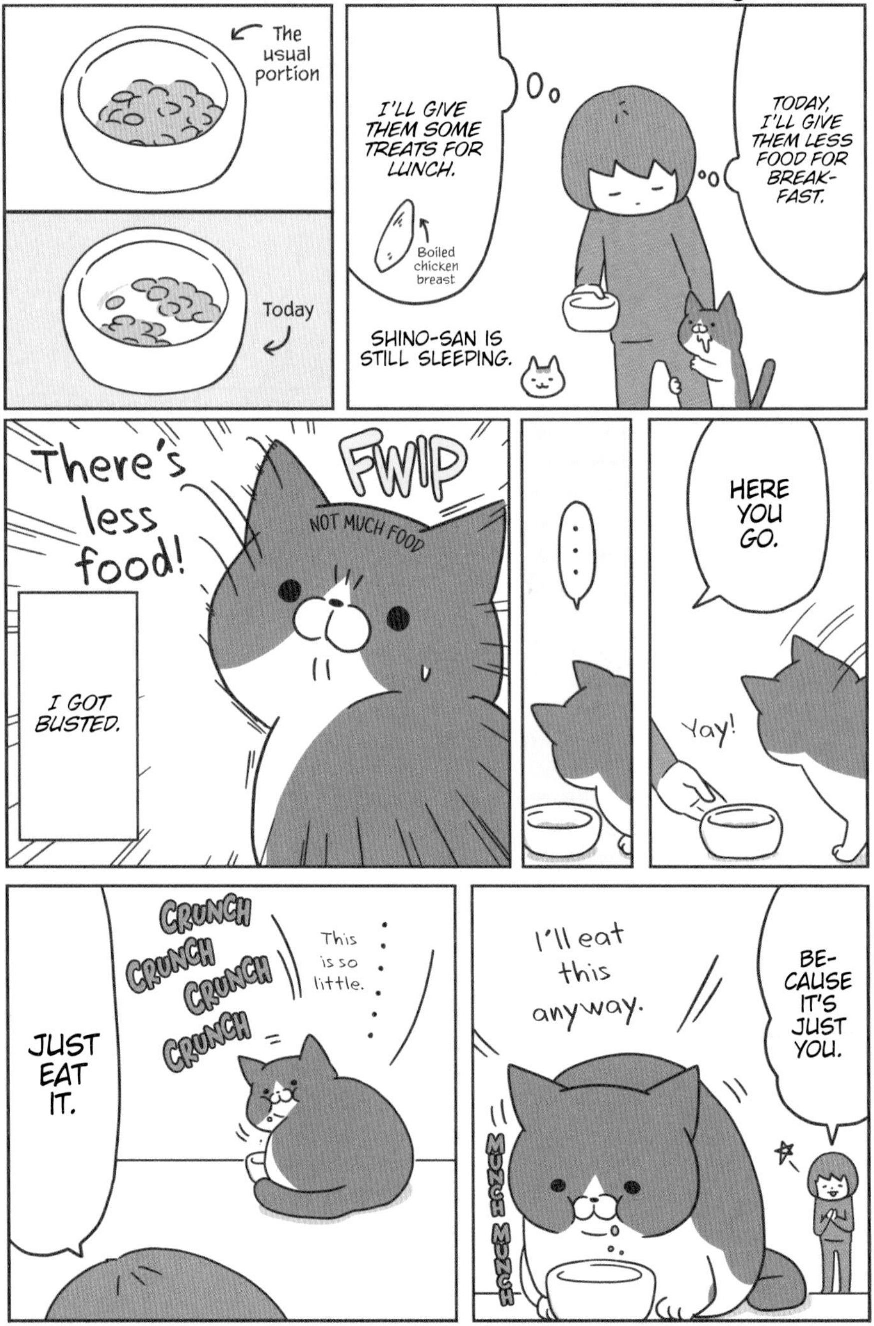
TODAY, I'LL GIVE THEM LESS FOOD FOR BREAK- FAST.
I'LL GIVE THEM SOME TREATS FOR LUNCH.
Boiled chicken breast
SHINO-SAN IS STILL SLEEPING.
The usual portion
Today
HERE YOU GO.
Yay!
...
FWIP
There's less food!
NOT MUCH FOOD
I GOT BUSTED.
BE- CAUSE IT'S JUST YOU.
I'll eat this anyway.
MUNCH MUNCH
This is so little.
CRUNCH
CRUNCH
CRUNCH
CRUNCH
JUST EAT IT.

I didn't think it was so bad since she doesn't get treats very often.

Ton-chan Is Strong

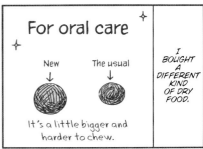

I BOUGHT A DIFFERENT KIND OF DRY FOOD.
For oral care
The usual
New
It's a little bigger and harder to chew.
CHOMP CRUNCH CRUNCH
Yum!
MUNCH MUNCH
Yum!
CRUNCH CRUNCH CRUNCH CRUNCH CRUNCH
Crunchy!
GRIND GRIND
So crunchy!!
I LEARNED THE DIFFERENCE BETWEEN TON-CHAN'S AND SHINO-SAN'S JAW STRENGTH.
I can't chew them!
I'M SORRY, SHINO-SAN. YOU CAN HAVE THE USUAL FOOD.
CRUNCH CRUNCH CRUNCH CRUNCH CRUNCH CRUNCH CRUNCH

Shino-san has a weaker jaw. The poor cat had a rough time: couldn't chew→couldn't chew→spat it out→couldn't chew→swallowed it whole→vomited. I deeply regretted it.

Super Early Riser

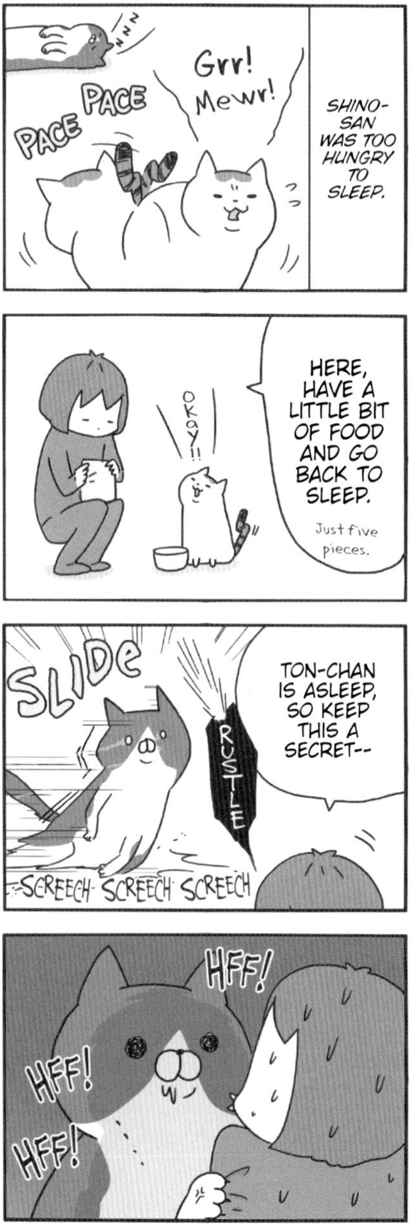

NNN
Grr! Mewr!
PACE PACE
SHINO-SAN WAS TOO HUNGRY TO SLEEP.
HERE, HAVE A LITTLE BIT OF FOOD AND GO BACK TO SLEEP.
Just five pieces.
Okay!!
TON-CHAN IS ASLEEP, SO KEEP THIS A SECRET--
SLIDE
RUSTLE
SCREECH SCREECH SCREECH
HFF!
HFF!
HFF!

You were sound asleep a second ago.

Ton-chan is rarely disturbed by sounds, but she reacts to the sound of food in a flash.

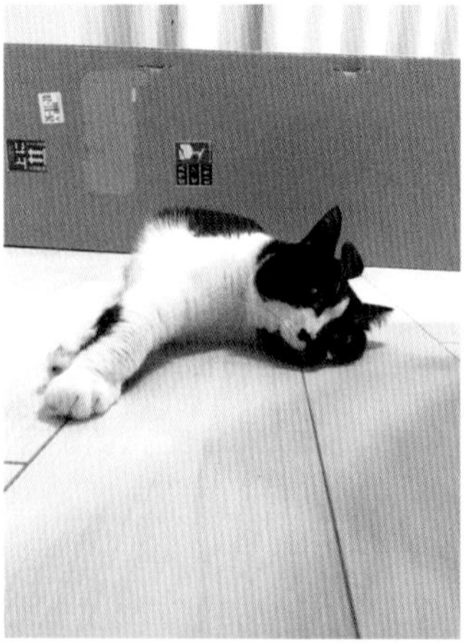

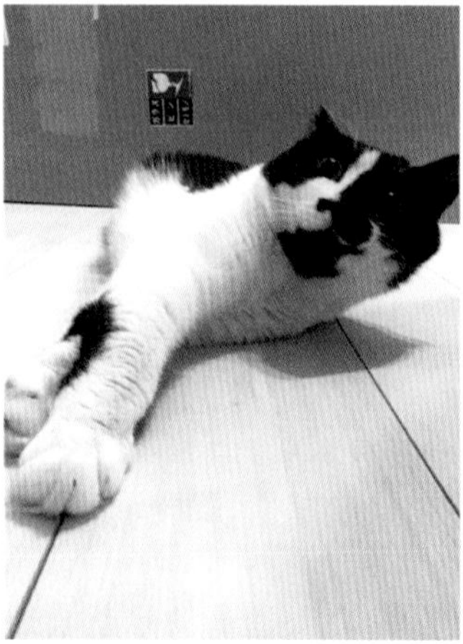

Sorry, It's Not Your Food

I WONDER HOW CATS CAN ACCURATELY RECOGNIZE THE SOUND OF THE CAT FOOD BAG.
RUSTLE
CAT
WHERE'S THE BAG OF MACA-RONI?
RUSTLE
CAT FOOD
WOOSH
TAP
SORRY, IT'S NOT YOUR FOOD.
I'M SORRY.

When Ton-chan senses food, she comes to check it out.

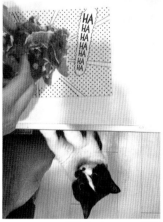

HA HA HA HA HA HA HA HA

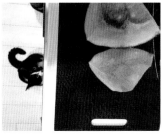

Energy-Saving Ton-chan

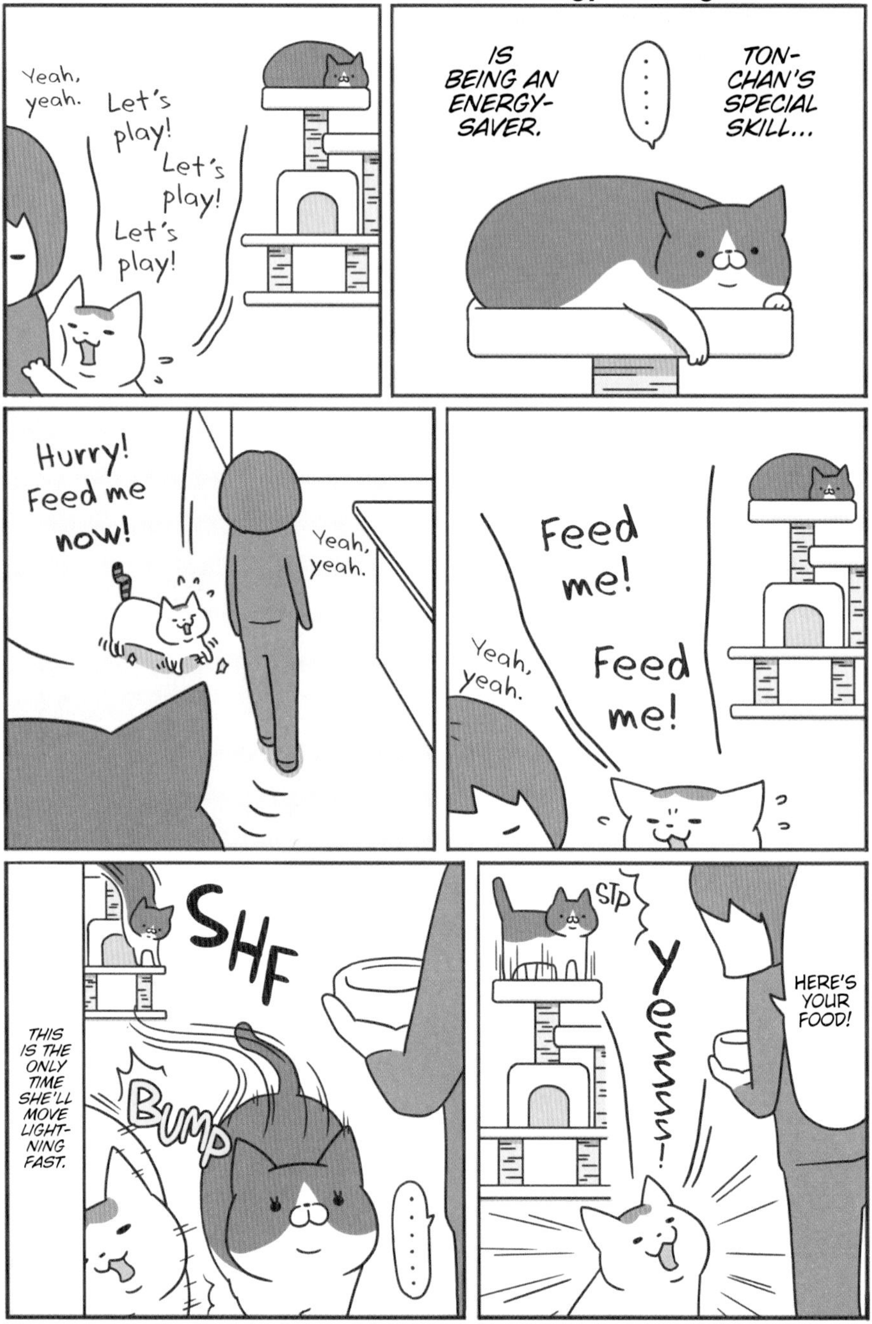
TON-CHAN'S SPECIAL SKILL...
.....
IS BEING AN ENERGY-SAVER.
Let's play!
Let's play!
Let's play!
Yeah, yeah.
Feed me!
Feed me!
Yeah, yeah.
Hurry! Feed me now!
Yeah, yeah.
HERE'S YOUR FOOD!
STP
Yemmm-!
SHF
BUMP
THIS IS THE ONLY TIME SHE'LL MOVE LIGHTNING FAST.
......

The Cause of Her Mess

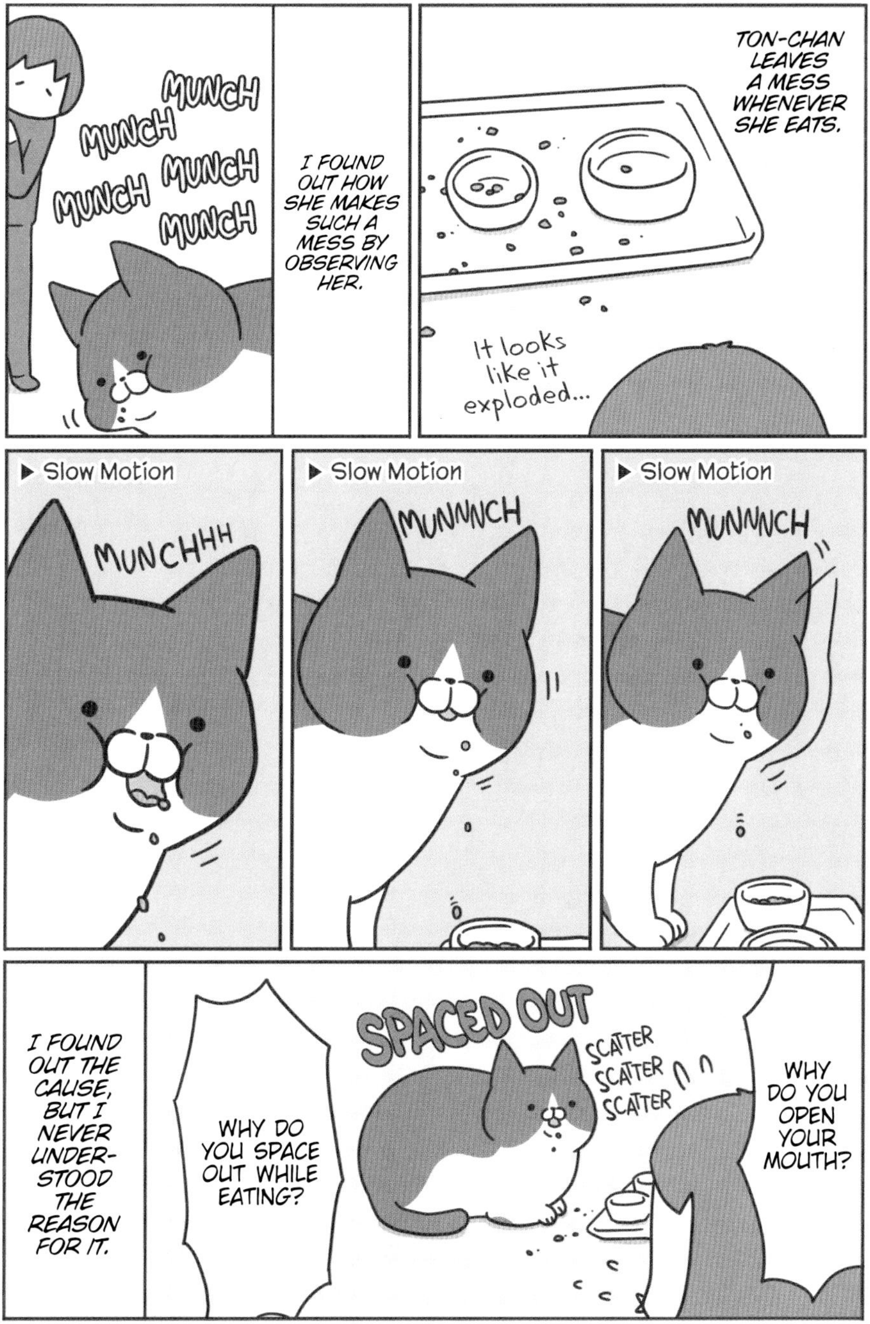
TON-CHAN LEAVES A MESS WHENEVER SHE EATS.
It looks like it exploded...
I FOUND OUT HOW SHE MAKES SUCH A MESS BY OBSERVING HER.
MUNCH
MUNCH
MUNCH
MUNCH
MUNCH
▶ Slow Motion
MUNNNCH
▶ Slow Motion
MUNNNCH
▶ Slow Motion
MUNCHHH
WHY DO YOU OPEN YOUR MOUTH?
SPACED OUT
SCATTER
SCATTER
SCATTER
WHY DO YOU SPACE OUT WHILE EATING?
I FOUND OUT THE CAUSE, BUT I NEVER UNDER-STOOD THE REASON FOR IT.

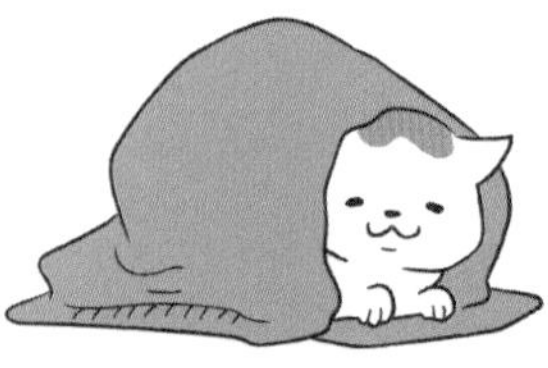

My Cat is Such a Weirdo

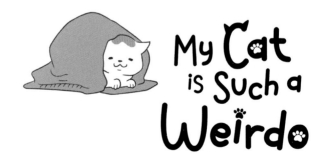

Chapter 4

The Dilemma of Being a Cat Owner

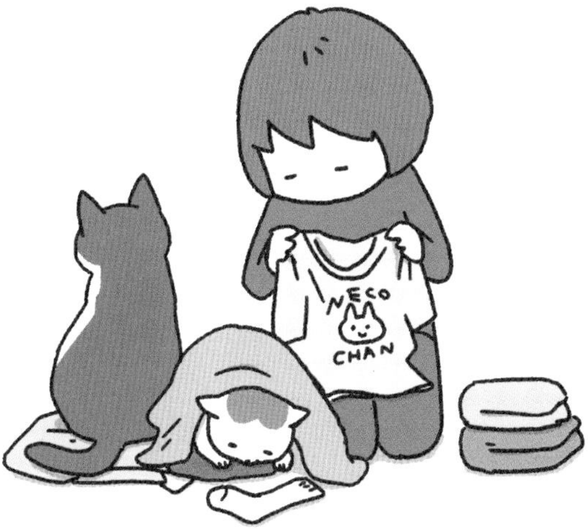
NECO
CHAN

Night after Night after Night

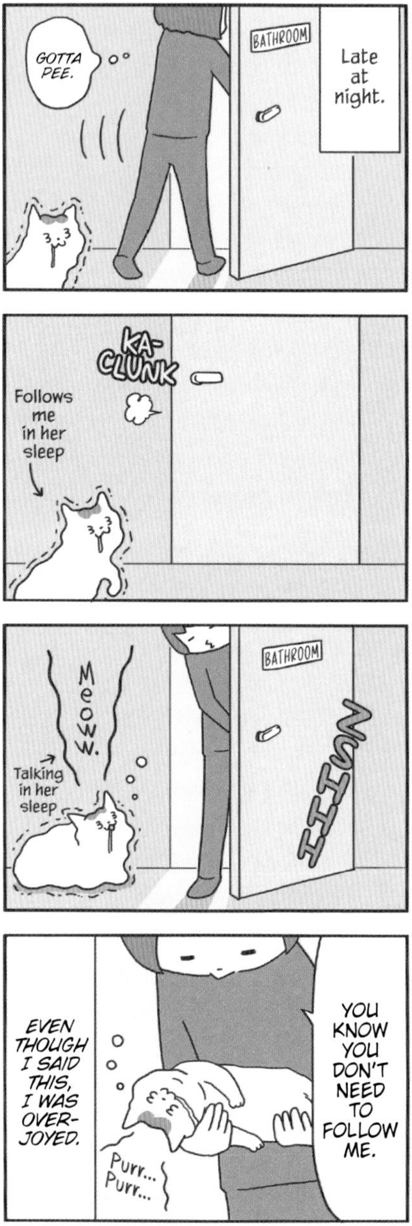
Late at night.
GOTTA PEE.
BATHROOM
KA-CLUNK
Follows me in her sleep
BATHROOM
Meoww.
Talking in her sleep
YOU KNOW YOU DON'T NEED TO FOLLOW ME.
EVEN THOUGH I SAID THIS, I WAS OVERJOYED.
Purr... Purr...

My Cats in the Morning

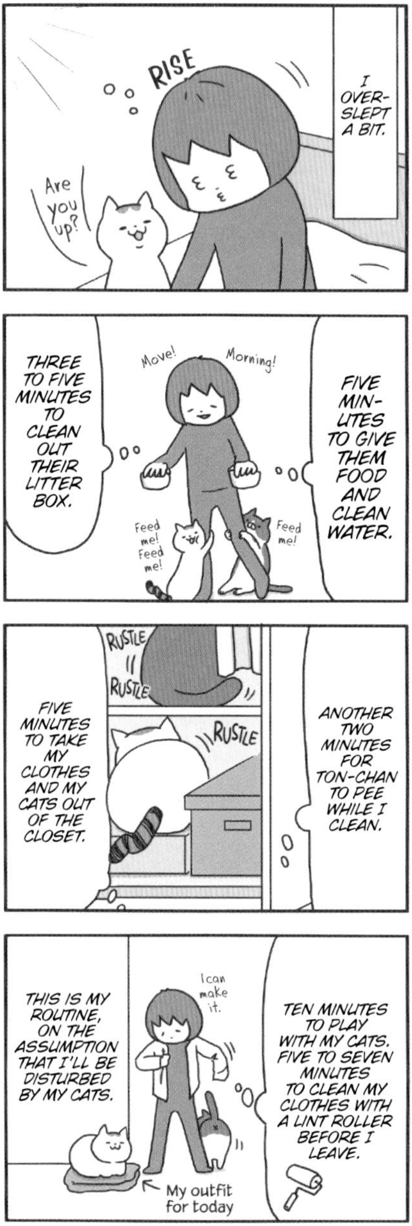
I OVERSLEPT A BIT.
RISE
Are you up?
FIVE MINUTES TO GIVE THEM FOOD AND CLEAN WATER.
Morning!
Move!
THREE TO FIVE MINUTES TO CLEAN OUT THEIR LITTER BOX.
Feed me!
Feed me! Feed me!
ANOTHER TWO MINUTES FOR TON-CHAN TO PEE WHILE I CLEAN.
RUSTLE
RUSTLE
RUSTLE
FIVE MINUTES TO TAKE MY CLOTHES AND MY CATS OUT OF THE CLOSET.
TEN MINUTES TO PLAY WITH MY CATS. FIVE TO SEVEN MINUTES TO CLEAN MY CLOTHES WITH A LINT ROLLER BEFORE I LEAVE.
I can make it.
THIS IS MY ROUTINE, ON THE ASSUMPTION THAT I'LL BE DISTURBED BY MY CATS.
My outfit for today

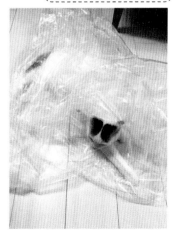

Seeing Things Wrong

TON-CHAN IS WAITING OBEDIENTLY WITHIN MY SIGHT.
How admirable.
Cooking →
TON-CHAN...
FLIP
That's not her.
TRASH BAGS
LATELY ...
Shino-san...
Oh!
I almost pet a bath mat.
I'VE BEEN SEEING THINGS WRONG A LOT.
You're goofy.

This cow toy looks away all the time.

Sometimes it pretends to not be there.

There's a Lot You Don't Need to Know

TON-CHAN LOOKS LIKE
PRR PRR
NOW...
Six months old
BUT SHE LOOKED SHARP WHEN I ADOPTED HER.
She was skinny.
STROKE STROKE
LICK
LICK
LICK
SHE'S LICKING WHERE I PETTED HER! SO ADORABLE! WHAT DOES THIS MEAN?
LICK
Why does your cat lick where you pet them?
It is believed that they don't like or get creepe out by the scent on the and lick themselves to erase it.
MR. GOOGLE

I'm shocked.

Ton-chan was thinner and looked sharp as a kitten.

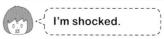

Ton-chan and Summer

LET'S PLAY, TON-CHAN!
Come on!
Come on!
Hey! Come here!
....
Let's play!
Hey!
Come on!
MIIIIN
MIN MIN MIN
MIIIIN
WHEEZE WHEEZE
....
SHE DIDN'T PLAY WITH ME.

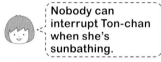

Nobody can interrupt Ton-chan when she's sunbathing.

Even Though They Come To Me

INCH
INCH
EVEN THOUGH THEY COME TO ME...
Don't pet me.
THEY WON'T LET ME PET THEM.
Don't pet me.

Why?

They come to me but keep their distance.

Petting Attentively

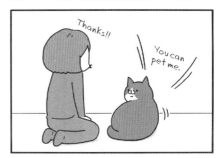

You can pet me.
Thanks!!
STROKE
STROKE
STROKE
PURR...
PURR...
......
STROKE STROKE
← Phone
IF I DON'T PET HER ATTEN-TIVELY...
SHE KNOWS I'M FOCUSED ELSE-WHERE.
LET ME TRY AGAIN!

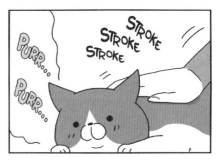

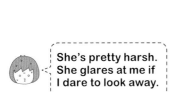

She's pretty harsh. She glares at me if I dare to look away.

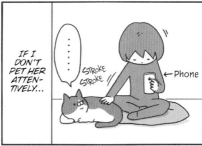

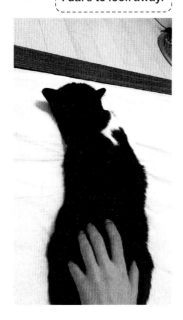

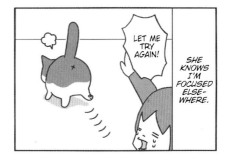

My Thoughts on Sleeping with My Cat

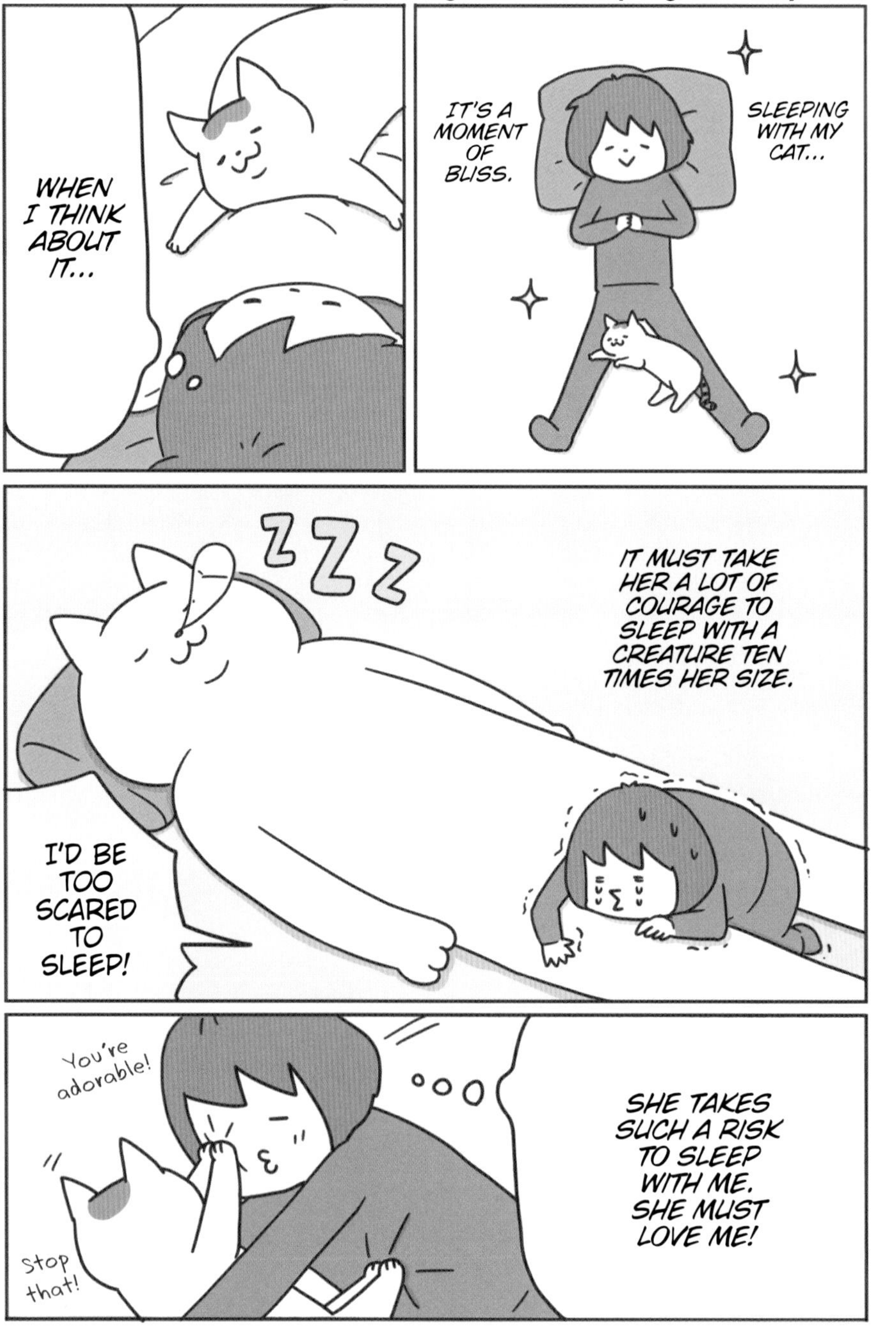
SLEEPING WITH MY CAT...
IT'S A MOMENT OF BLISS.
WHEN I THINK ABOUT IT...
IT MUST TAKE HER A LOT OF COURAGE TO SLEEP WITH A CREATURE TEN TIMES HER SIZE.
I'D BE TOO SCARED TO SLEEP!
ZZZ
SHE TAKES SUCH A RISK TO SLEEP WITH ME. SHE MUST LOVE ME!
You're adorable!
Stop that!

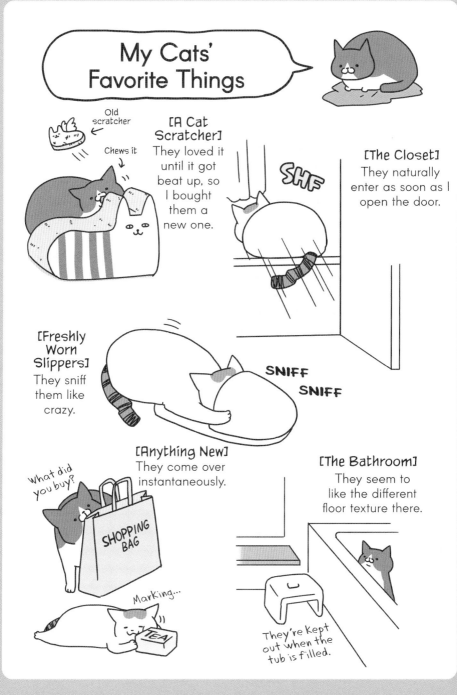

My Cats' Favorite Things

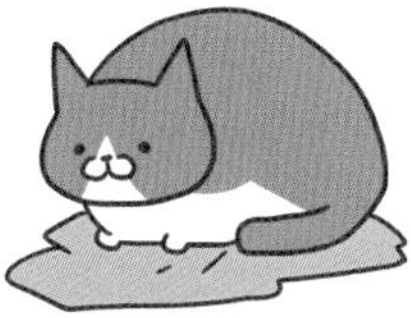

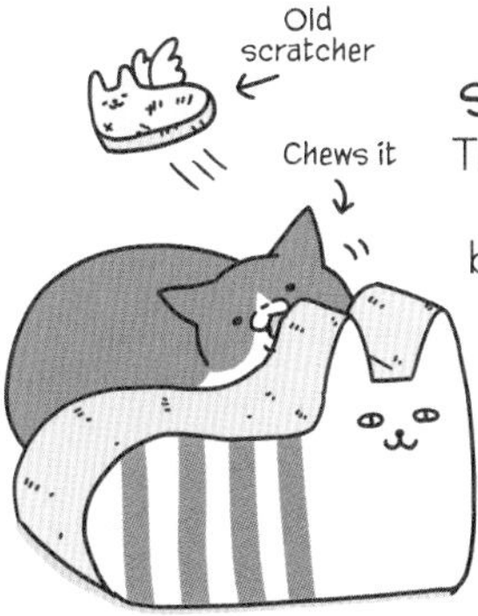
Old scratcher
Chews it

[A Cat Scratcher]
They loved it until it got beat up, so I bought them a new one.

[The Closet]
They naturally enter as soon as I open the door.

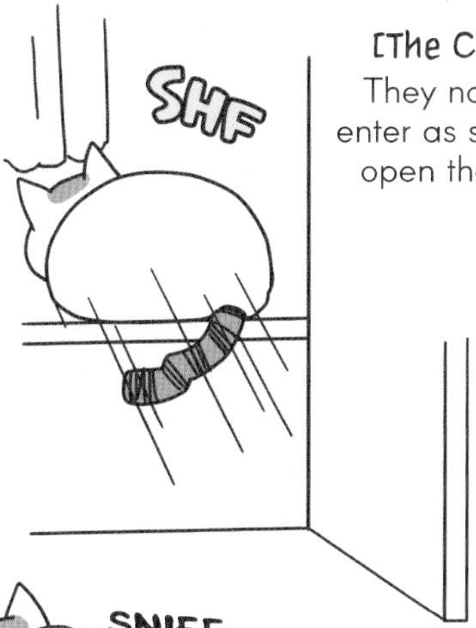
SHF

[Freshly Worn Slippers]
They sniff them like crazy.

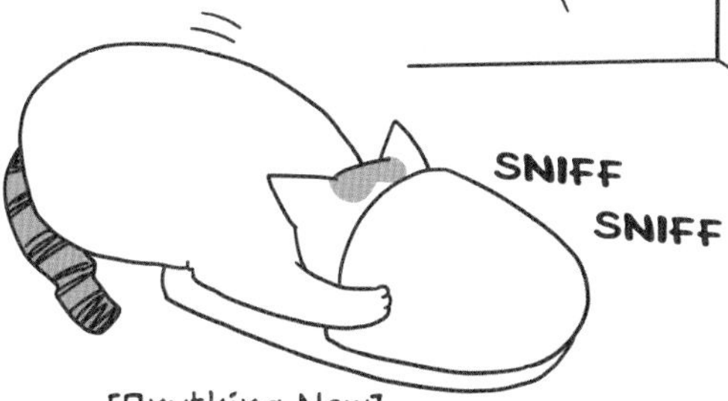
SNIFF
SNIFF

[Anything New]
They come over instantaneously.

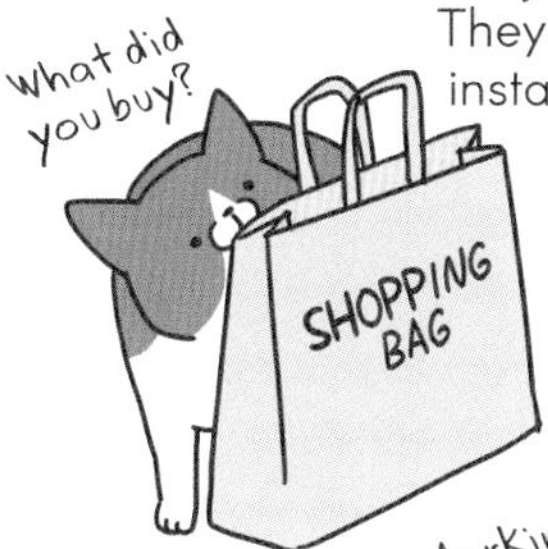
What did you buy?
SHOPPING BAG

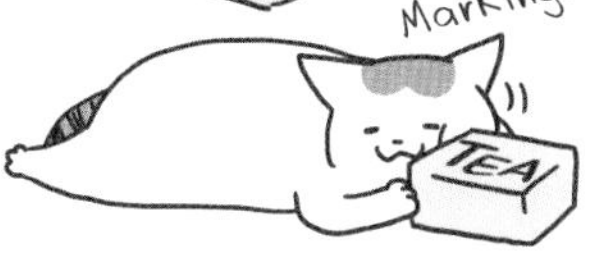
Marking...
TEA

[The Bathroom]
They seem to like the different floor texture there.

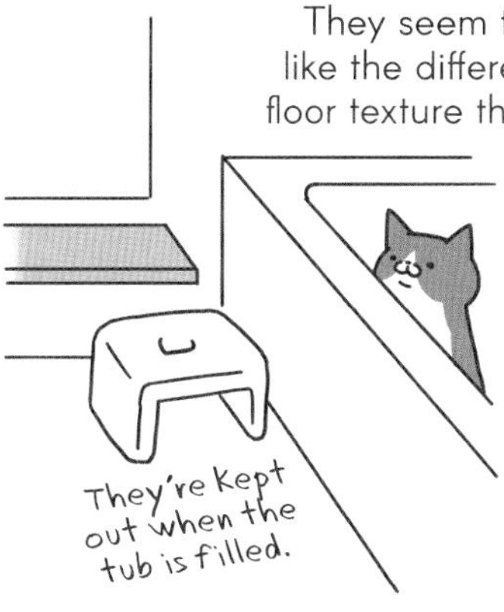
They're kept out when the tub is filled.

I Want to Be a Cat

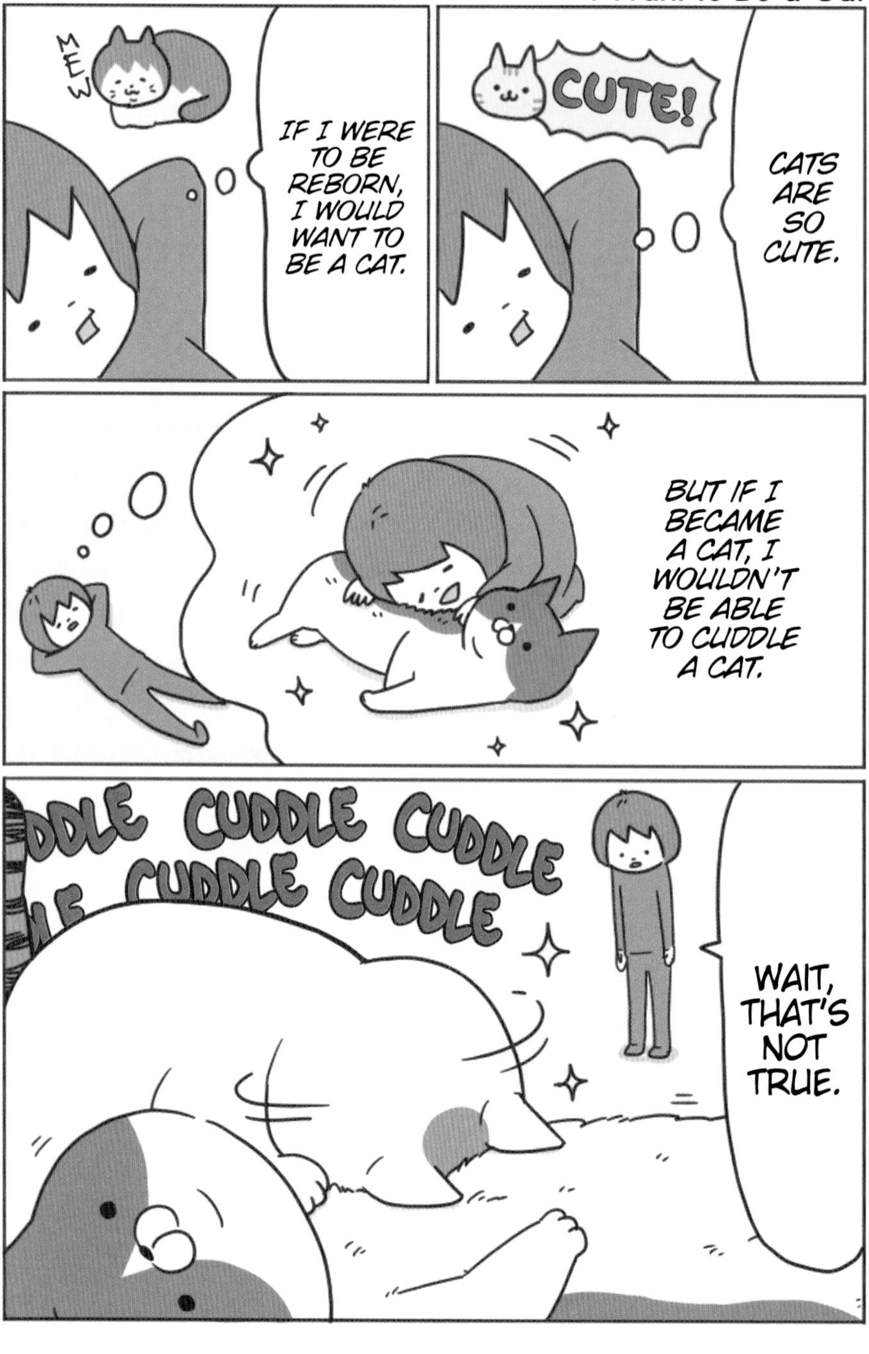
CUTE!
CATS ARE SO CUTE.
MEW
IF I WERE TO BE REBORN, I WOULD WANT TO BE A CAT.
BUT IF I BECAME A CAT, I WOULDN'T BE ABLE TO CUDDLE A CAT.
WAIT, THAT'S NOT TRUE.
DDLE CUDDLE CUDDLE
CUDDLE CUDDLE

Cats Are Really Cute!

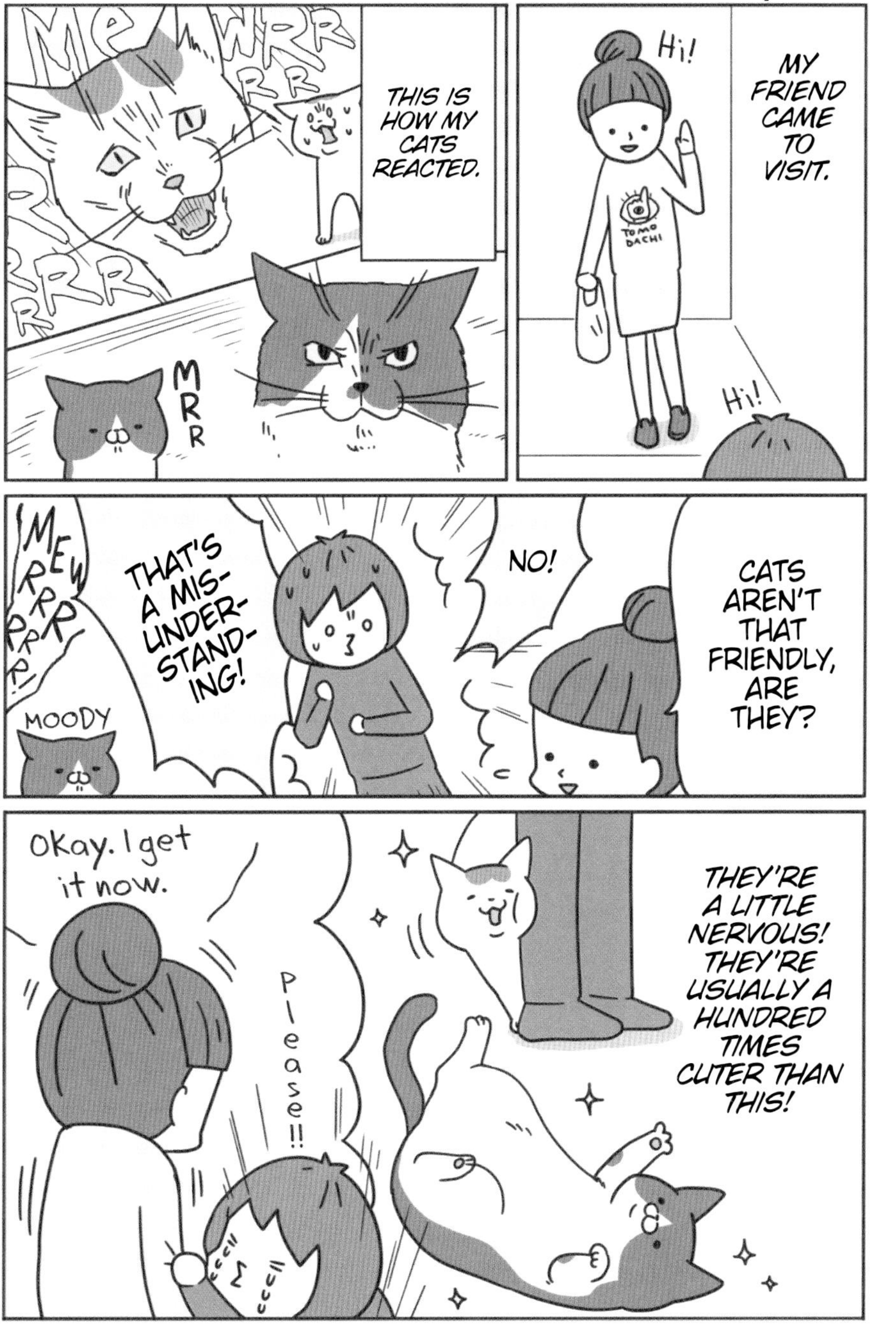

MY FRIEND CAME TO VISIT.
Hi!
Hi!
THIS IS HOW MY CATS REACTED.
MEW
WRRR RR
RRRR R
MRR
CATS AREN'T THAT FRIENDLY, ARE THEY?
NO!
THAT'S A MIS-UNDER-STAND-ING!
MEW RRR RRR R!
MOODY
THEY'RE A LITTLE NERVOUS! THEY'RE USUALLY A HUNDRED TIMES CUTER THAN THIS!
Please!!
Okay. I get it now.

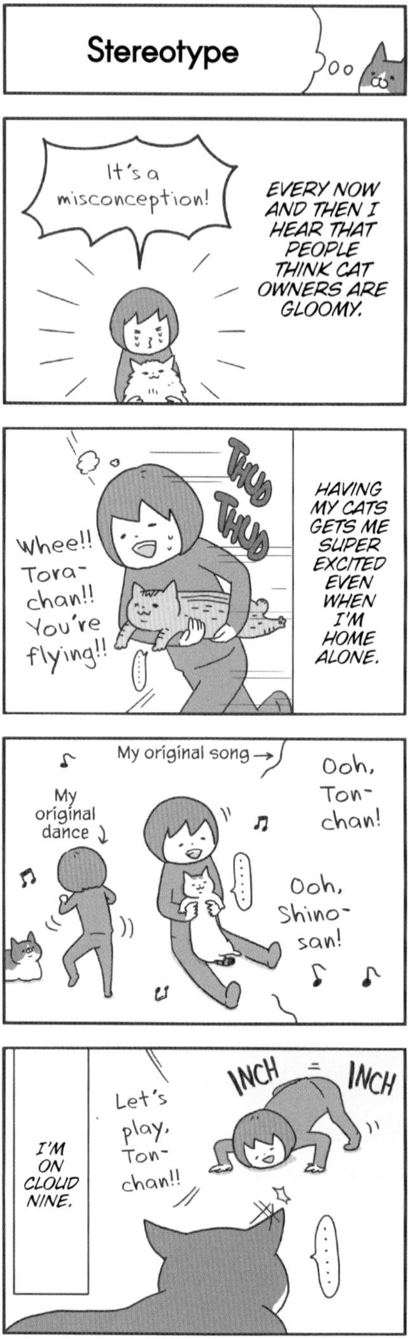
Stereotype
EVERY NOW AND THEN I HEAR THAT PEOPLE THINK CAT OWNERS ARE GLOOMY.
It's a misconception!
HAVING MY CATS GETS ME SUPER EXCITED EVEN WHEN I'M HOME ALONE.
THUD THUD
Whee!! Tora-chan!! You're flying!!
...
Ooh, Ton-chan!
My original song →
Ooh, Shino-san!
......
My original dance
INCH INCH
Let's play, Ton-chan!!
I'M ON CLOUD NINE.
......

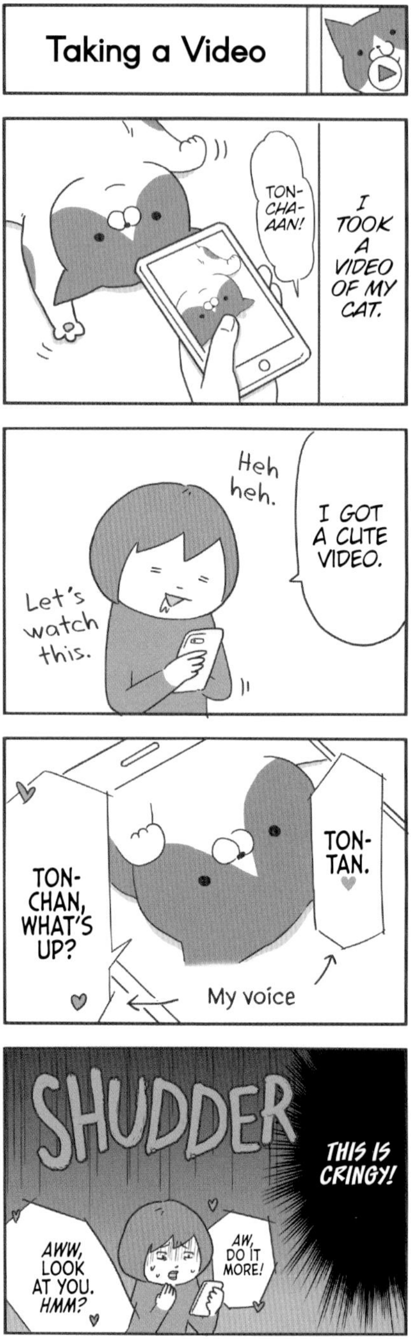
Taking a Video
I TOOK A VIDEO OF MY CAT.
TON-CHA-AAN!
I GOT A CUTE VIDEO.
Heh heh.
Let's watch this.
TON-TAN.
TON-CHAN, WHAT'S UP?
My voice
THIS IS CRINGY!
SHUDDER
AW, DO IT MORE!
AWW, LOOK AT YOU. HMM?

Excellent

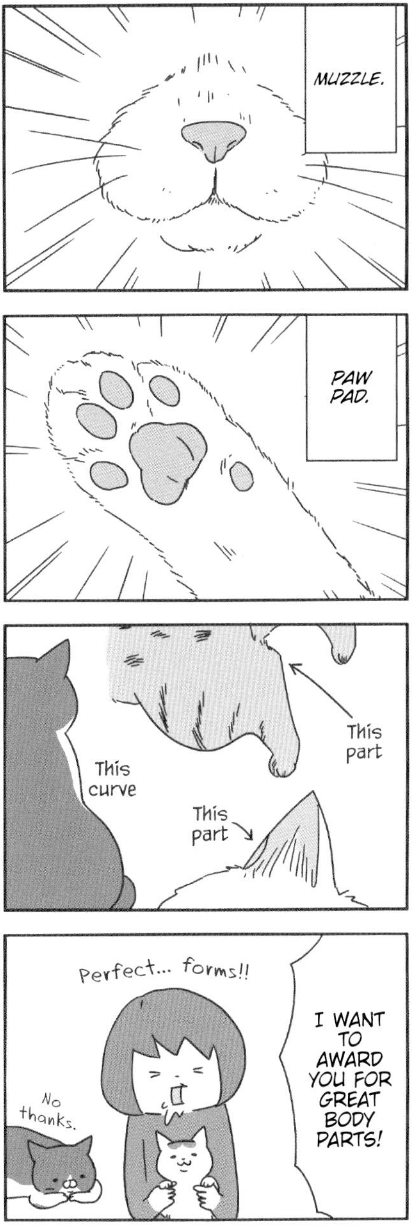
MUZZLE.
PAW PAD.
This part
This curve
This part
I WANT TO AWARD YOU FOR GREAT BODY PARTS!
Perfect... forms!!
No thanks.

Tap a Nose

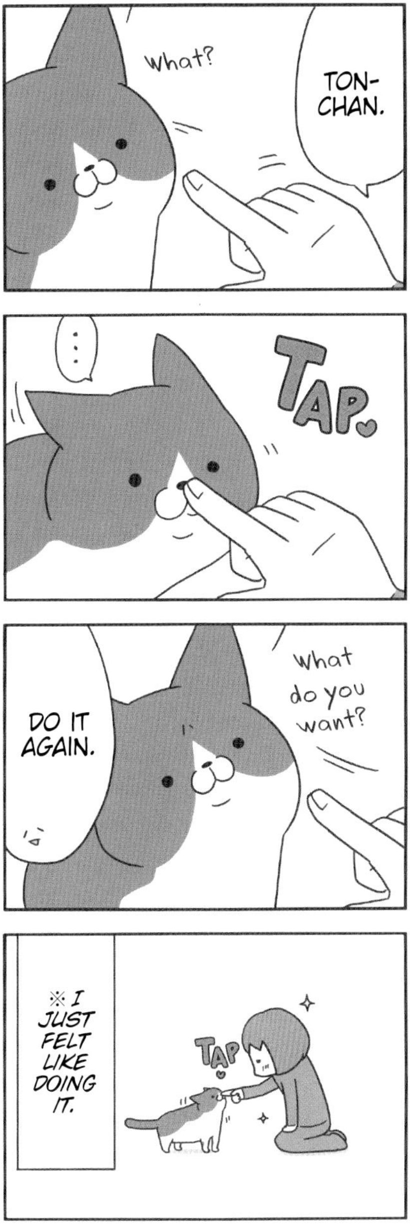
TON-CHAN.
What?
TAP
...
What do you want?
DO IT AGAIN.
TAP
※I JUST FELT LIKE DOING IT.

Caught in a Trap

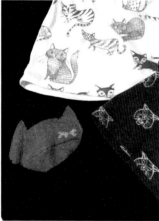

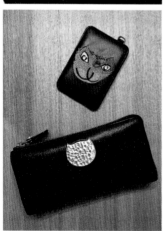

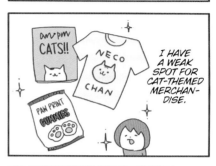

I HAVE A WEAK SPOT FOR CAT-THEMED MERCHAN-DISE.
NECO CHAN
am pm CATS!!
PAW PRINT GUMMIES

poppo cafe
BUSINESS NAMES...
DRIFT
cafe Feline
OPEN
DRIFT

GENERAL GOODS...
KITTY CUSTARD BUN
TRADITIONAL FLAVOR!
AND FOOD, TOO.
BONUS STICKER
I CHOOSE ANYTHING RELATED TO CATS.

YOU CAN'T JUST PUT CATS ON EVERY-THING...
ARGH
BUN
I STILL FALL FOR THEIR MARKET-ING PLOYS.
BUN
RUSTLE

It works like a charm.

I can't help but snag clothes and accessories with cats on them.

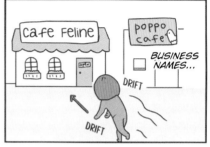

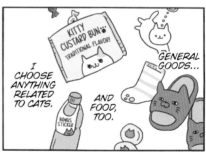

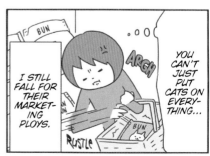

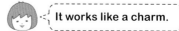

Personal Ranking

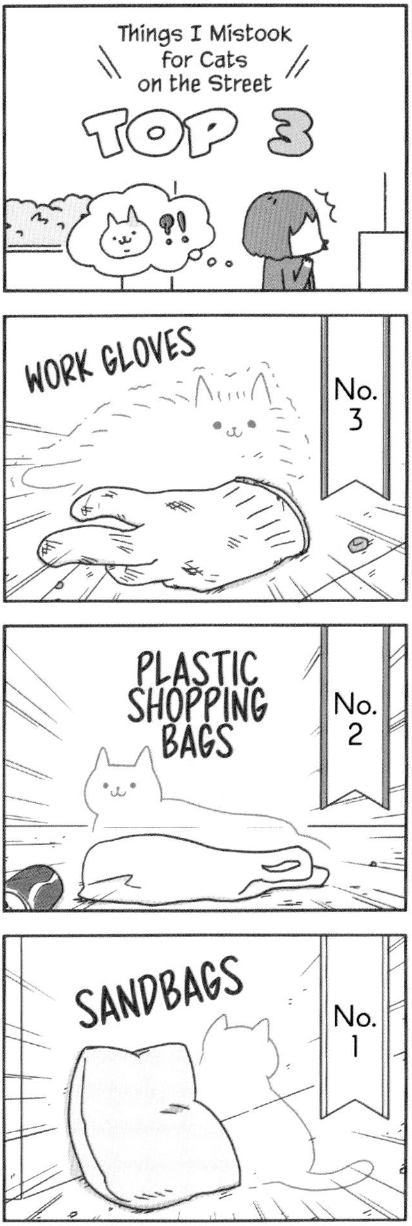
Things I Mistook for Cats on the Street
TOP 3
?!
No. 3
WORK GLOVES
No. 2
PLASTIC SHOPPING BAGS
No. 1
SANDBAGS

Bias for Cats

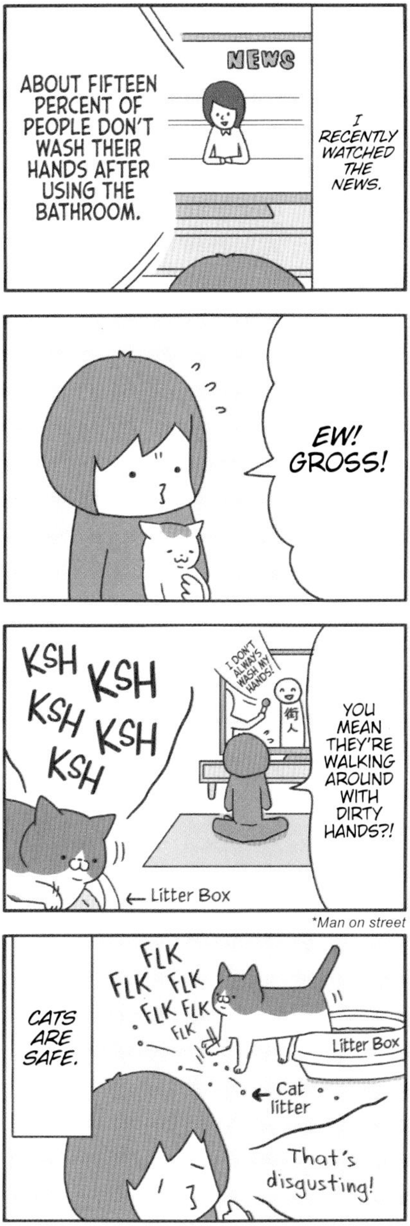
I RECENTLY WATCHED THE NEWS.
NEWS
ABOUT FIFTEEN PERCENT OF PEOPLE DON'T WASH THEIR HANDS AFTER USING THE BATHROOM.
EW! GROSS!
YOU MEAN THEY'RE WALKING AROUND WITH DIRTY HANDS?!
I DON'T ALWAYS WASH MY HANDS!
街人
KSH KSH KSH KSH KSH
← Litter Box
*Man on street
CATS ARE SAFE.
FLK FLK FLK FLK FLK FLK
Litter Box
← Cat litter
That's disgusting!

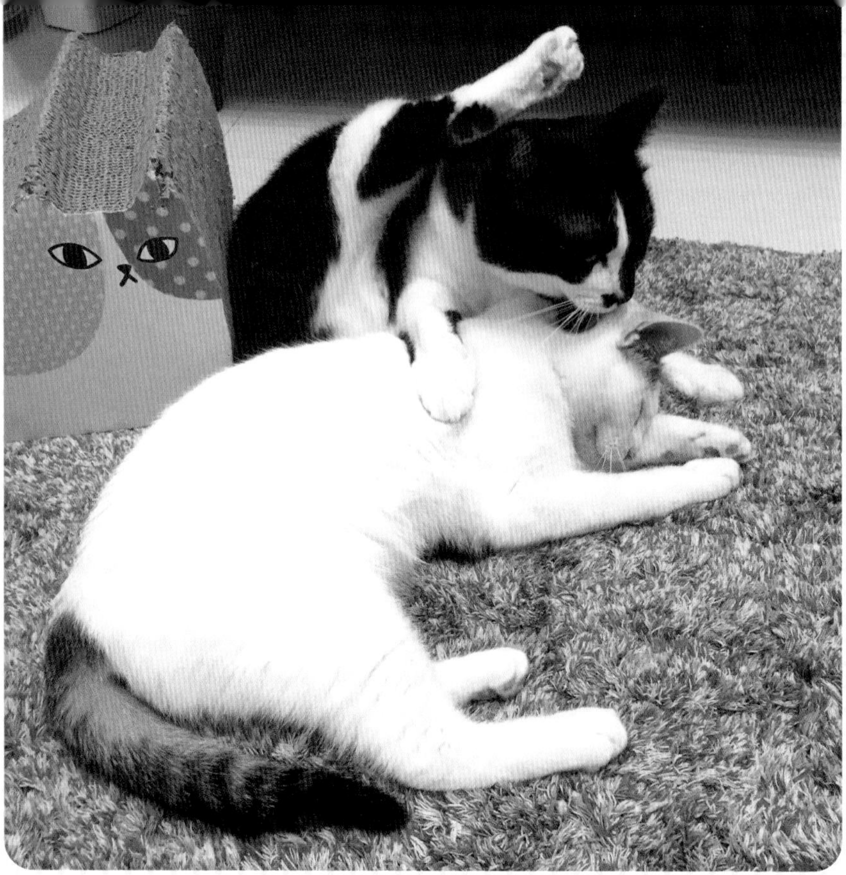

Ton-chan was grooming her friend. I don't think she needed to lift her back leg.

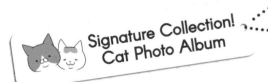

Signature Collection! Cat Photo Album

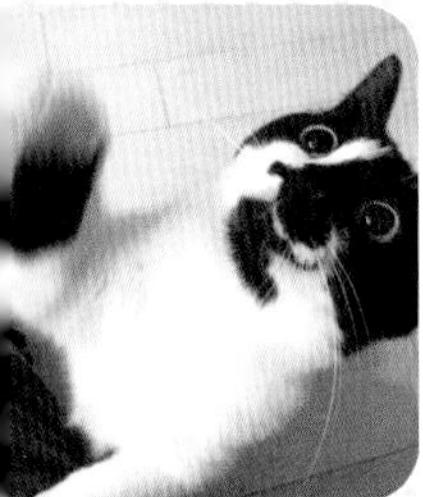

She made this face
for not getting ham.

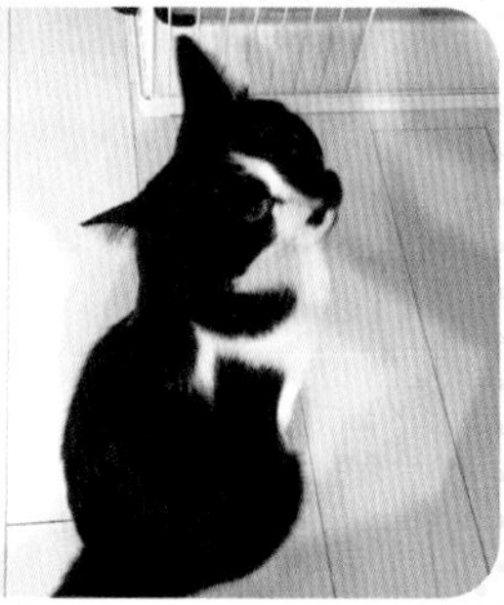

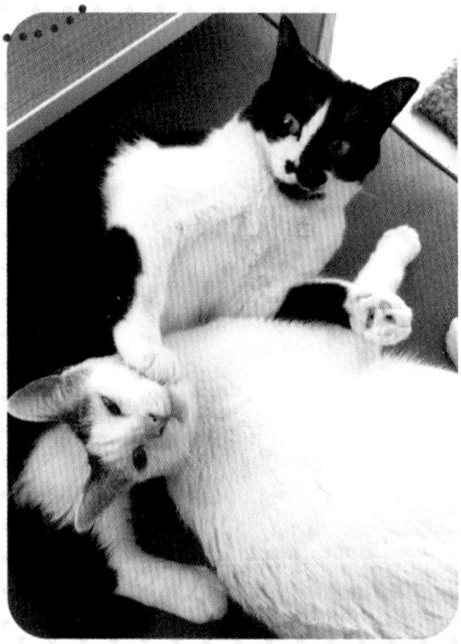

※ They're best friends.

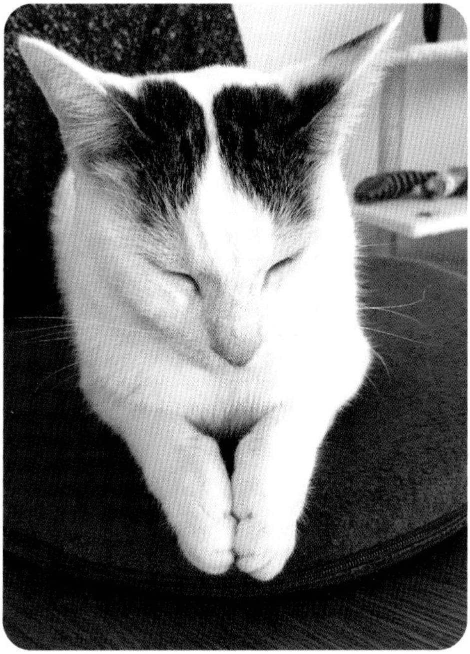

Maybe her paw pads were cold.

Ton-chan was caught off guard by her kiss. Such a comical expression.

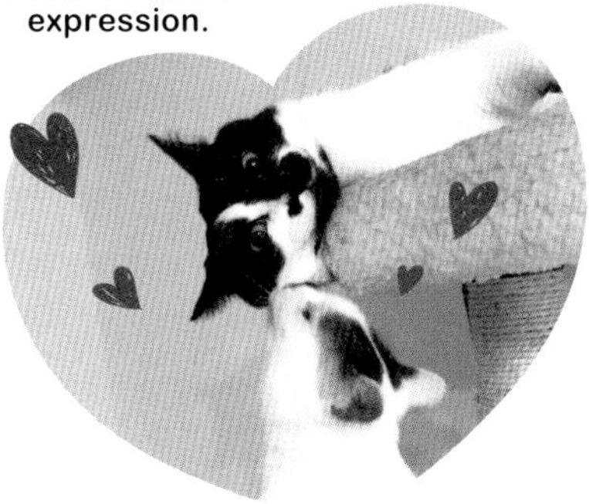

Ton-chan wanted ham.

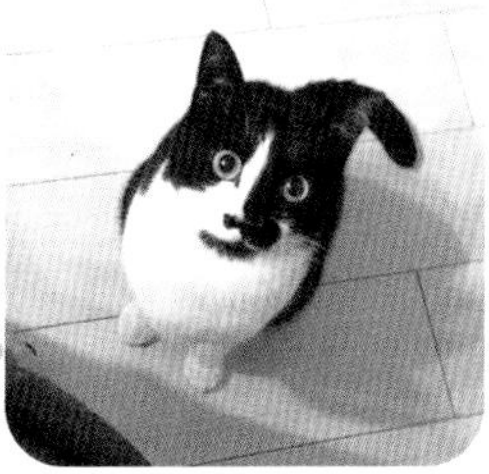

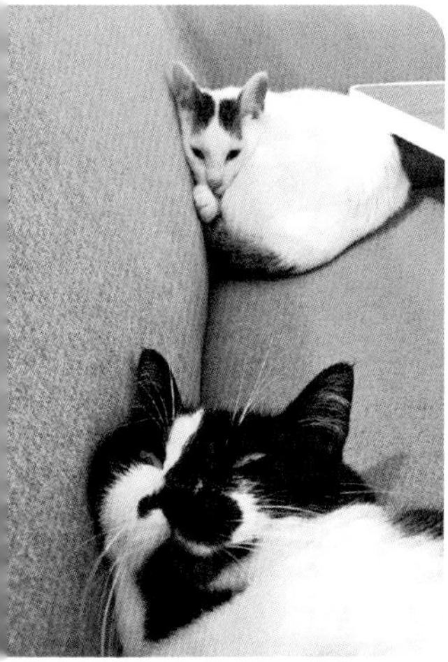

They both look distorted here.

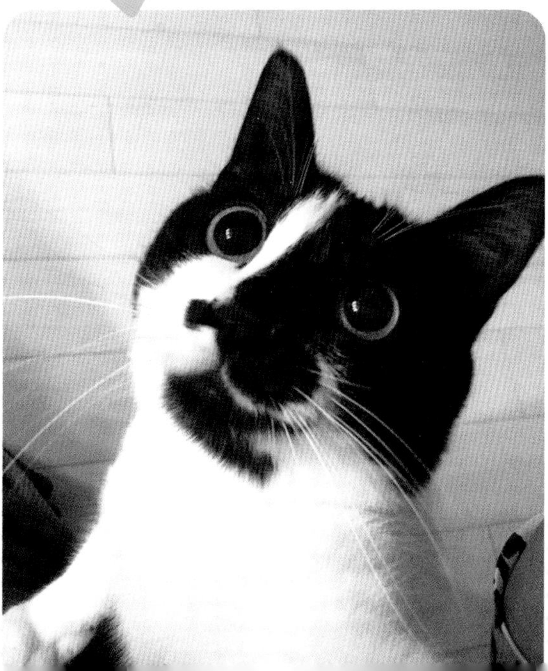

Sharing My Experience

SLOP LICK
I love you. I love you.
SLOP LICK SLOP LICK
Lost interest
......
STINK
ZONED OUT
Husband
SWF
WHAT? PEE-EW!
PEE-EEEWW!!

I sniff it even though I know it stinks.

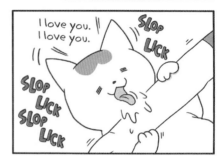

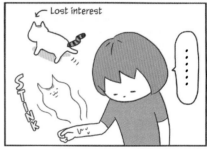

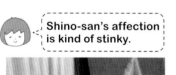

Shino-san's affection is kind of stinky.

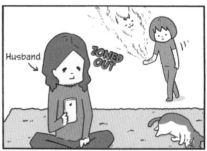

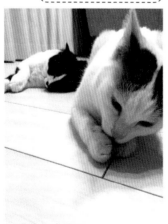

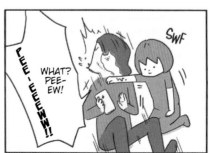

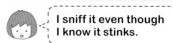

Goal

MY HUSBAND AND MY CATS LIKE TO WATCH SOCCER.
They like to follow the rolling ball
LIVE
YAY! YAY!

Sign: Husband

YAY! YAY!
LIVE
SCRITCH
SCRITCH
SCRITCH
YAY! YAY!

GOAL!!!
YAY!
YAY!
YOU'RE IN THE WAY!

The game ended. Ton-chan seemed content.

Not Convinced

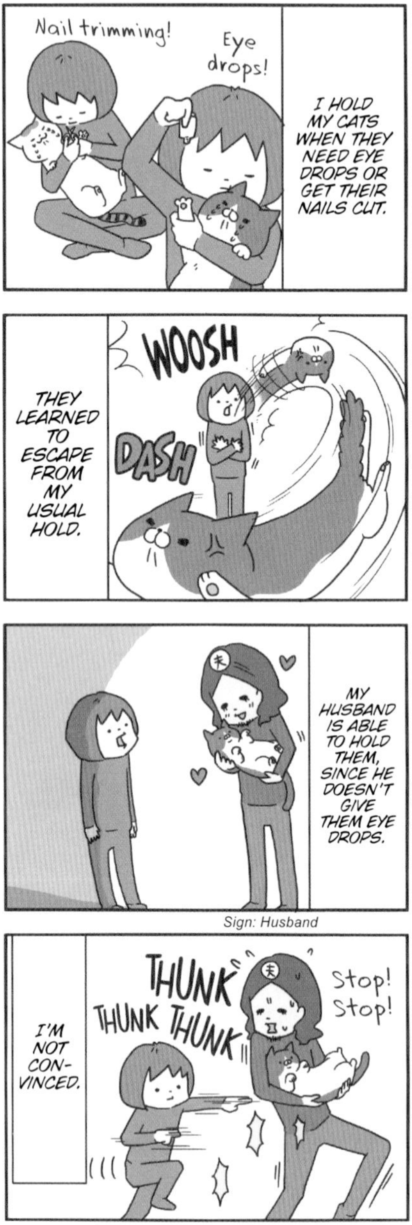
Nail trimming!
Eye drops!
I HOLD MY CATS WHEN THEY NEED EYE DROPS OR GET THEIR NAILS CUT.
WOOSH
DASH
THEY LEARNED TO ESCAPE FROM MY USUAL HOLD.
MY HUSBAND IS ABLE TO HOLD THEM, SINCE HE DOESN'T GIVE THEM EYE DROPS.
Stop! Stop!
THUNK
THUNK THUNK
I'M NOT CONVINCED.

Sign: Husband

Happy to Help

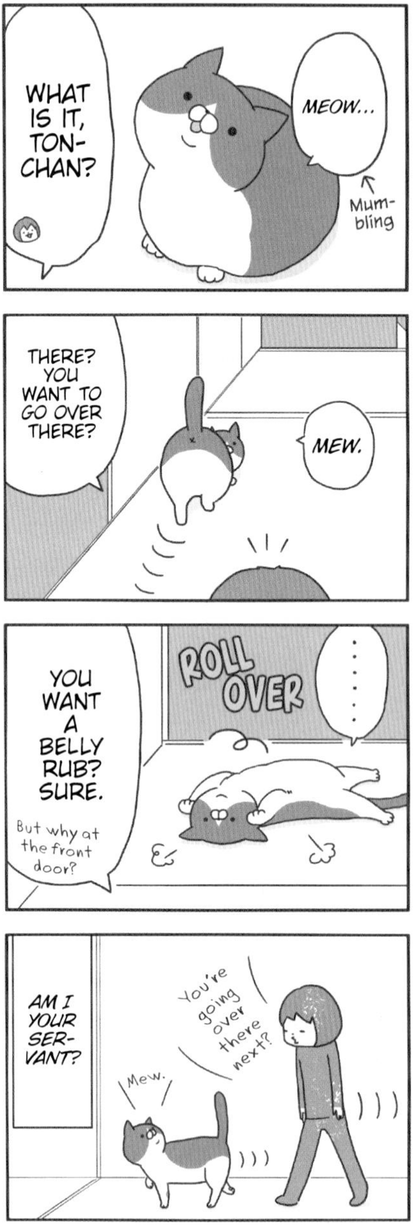
MEOW...
Mumbling
WHAT IS IT, TON-CHAN?
MEW.
THERE? YOU WANT TO GO OVER THERE?
ROLL OVER
....
YOU WANT A BELLY RUB? SURE.
But why at the front door?
You're going over there next?
Mew.
AM I YOUR SERVANT?

Just Before He Leaves

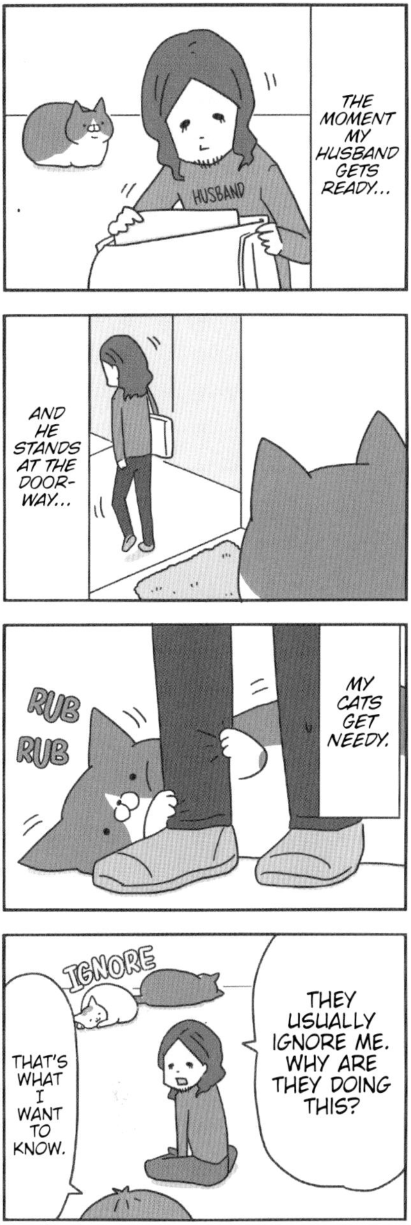
THE MOMENT MY HUSBAND GETS READY...
HUSBAND
AND HE STANDS AT THE DOOR-WAY...
MY CATS GET NEEDY.
RUB RUB
THEY USUALLY IGNORE ME. WHY ARE THEY DOING THIS?
IGNORE
THAT'S WHAT I WANT TO KNOW.

They don't come to my husband that often...but are they marking him as they part?

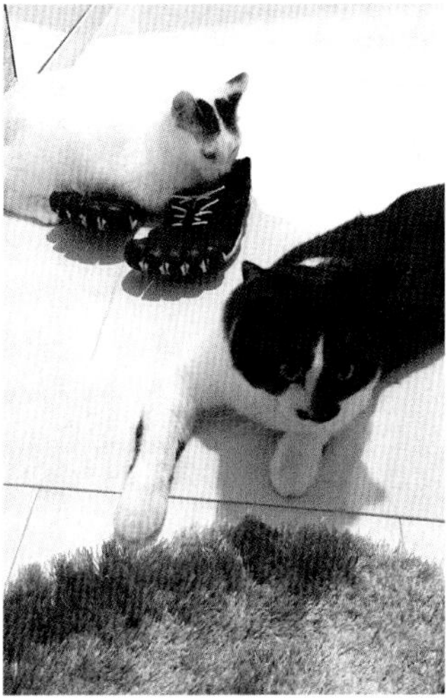

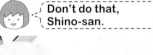

Don't do that, Shino-san.

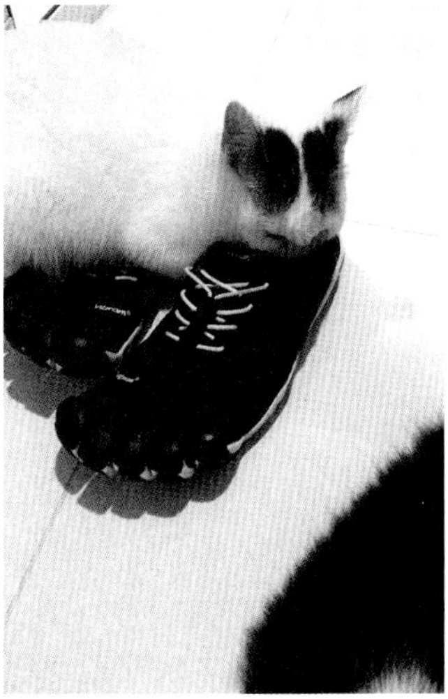

Morning Cuddle

THIS IS TON-CHAN'S MORNING ROUTINE.
CHIRP
CHIRP
Morning.
LOW BLOOD PRESSURE
ON THE...
ENTRY-WAY TILE...
THMP
THMP
THMP
THMP
SHE DEMANDS A BELLY RUB FROM ME.
SPRAWL
YOU'RE BEING CUTE EARLY IN THE DAY, BUT...
CAN'T WE DO THIS SOMEWHERE WARM DURING THE WINTER?
Pajamas
BRR
BRR
PURR
PURR

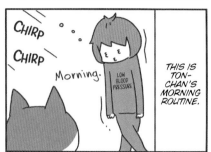

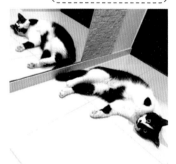

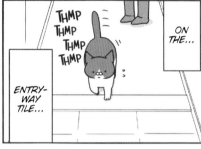

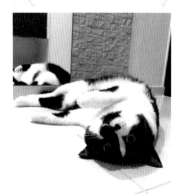

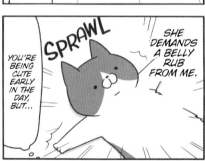

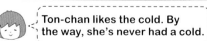

Ton-chan likes the cold. By the way, she's never had a cold.

She always lies around on the tile floor when it's hot.

My Cat Is So Sweet

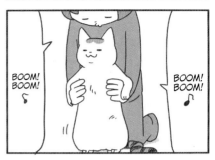

BOOM! BOOM!
BOOM! BOOM!
PAA PAA PAPPA PAPPA PAA
PAPPA PAA PAPPA PAPPA PAA PAPPA PAPPA PAPPA PAA
WSH
WE'RE DOING THE DANCE FROM THE RIZAP COMMERCIAL.
Boom! Boom!
Boom! Boom!
SHINO-SAN JUST GOES ALONG WITH IT.
Good girl
BUT SHE LOOKED AS IF IT WAS THE END OF THE WORLD WHEN I LOOKED CLOSELY.
The End of the World

Shino-san quietly goes along with me. She's so sweet.

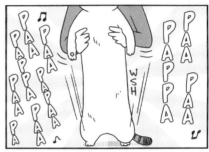

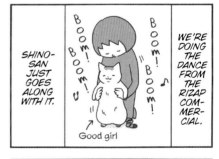

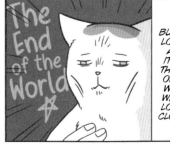

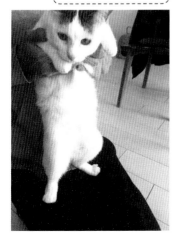

Be Careful

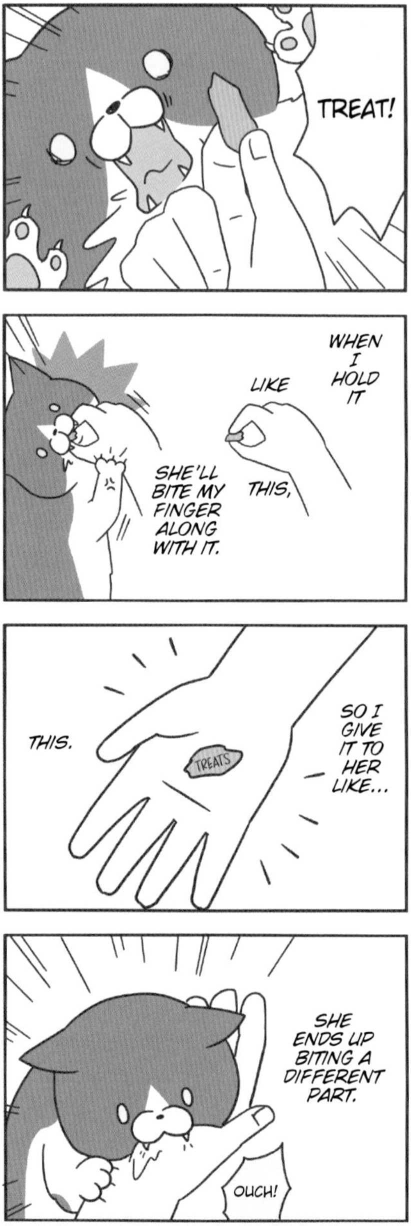
TREAT!
WHEN I HOLD IT
LIKE
THIS,
SHE'LL BITE MY FINGER ALONG WITH IT.
SO I GIVE IT TO HER LIKE...
TREATS
THIS.
SHE ENDS UP BITING A DIFFERENT PART.
OUCH!

Ton-chan's Maturity

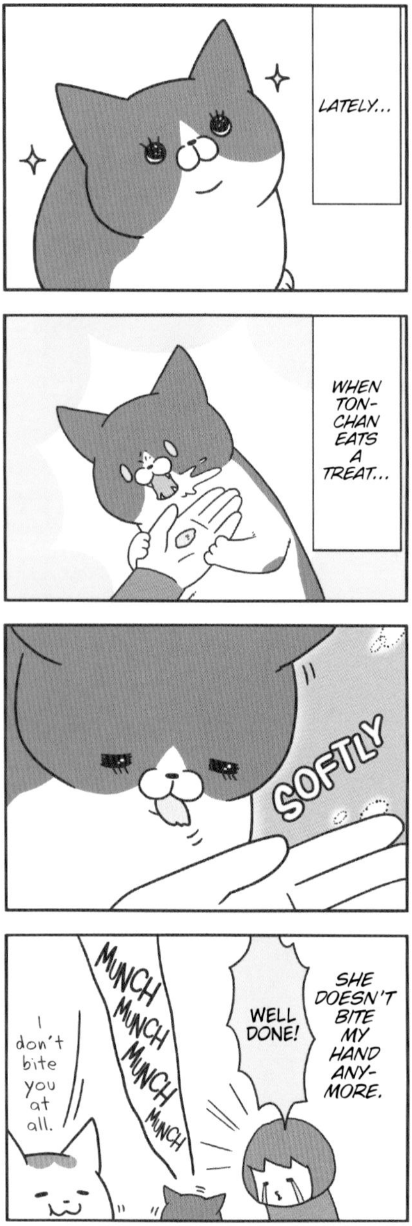
LATELY...
WHEN TON-CHAN EATS A TREAT...
SOFTLY
SHE DOESN'T BITE MY HAND ANYMORE.
WELL DONE!
MUNCH MUNCH MUNCH MUNCH
I don't bite you at all.

Shino-san's Maturity

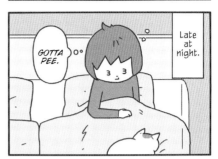

Late at night.
GOTTA PEE.
BATHROOM
FSHHH
OH!
SHINO-SAN HAS... STOPPED FOLLOWING ME TO THE BATHROOM.
SNORE SNORE

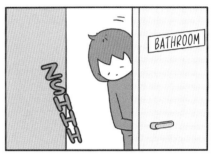

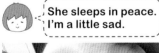

She sleeps in peace. I'm a little sad.

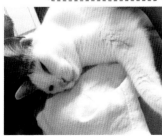

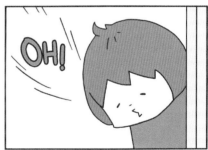

My Cat
is Such a
Weirdo

Chapter 5

A Peaceful Life with My Cats

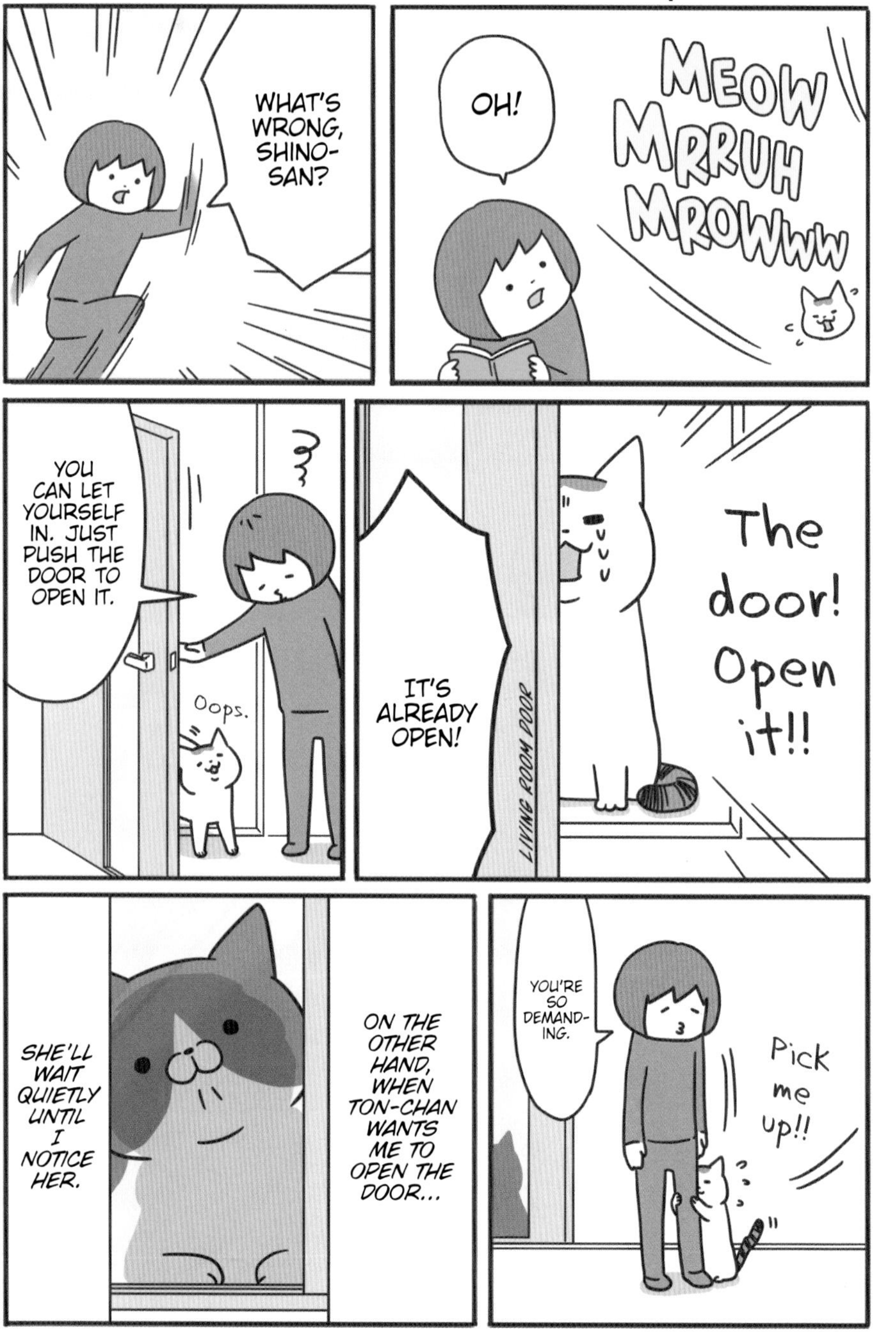
OH!
MEOW MRRUH MROWWW
WHAT'S WRONG, SHINO-SAN?
The door! Open it!!
IT'S ALREADY OPEN!
LIVING ROOM DOOR
YOU CAN LET YOURSELF IN. JUST PUSH THE DOOR TO OPEN IT.
Oops.
Pick me up!!
YOU'RE SO DEMAND-ING.
ON THE OTHER HAND, WHEN TON-CHAN WANTS ME TO OPEN THE DOOR...
SHE'LL WAIT QUIETLY UNTIL I NOTICE HER.

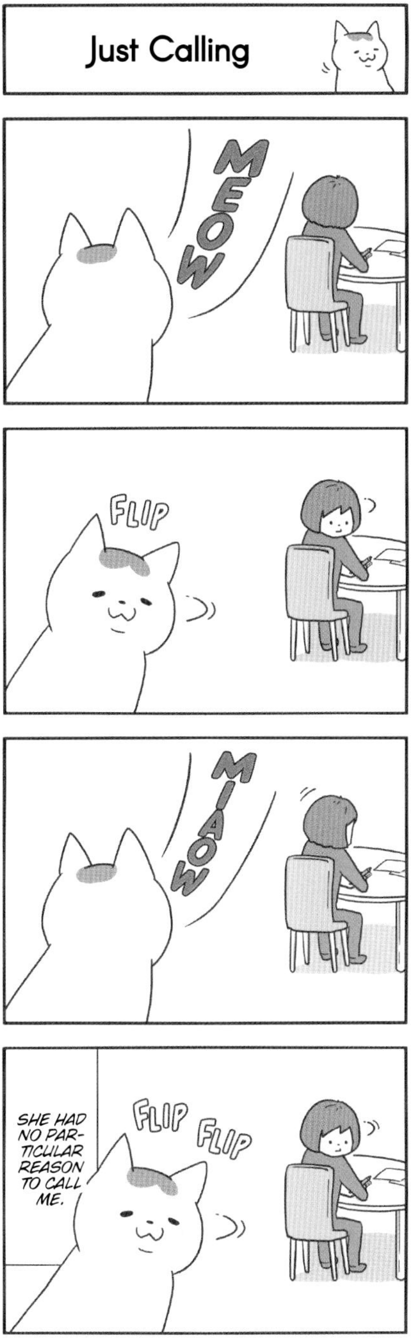
Just Calling
MEOW
FLIP
MIAOW
FLIP FLIP
SHE HAD NO PARTICULAR REASON TO CALL ME.
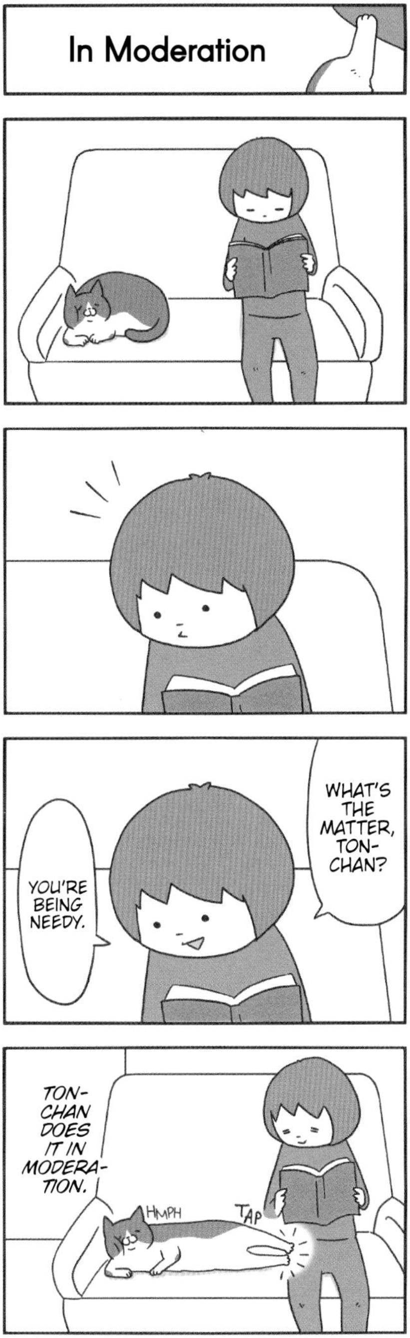
In Moderation
WHAT'S THE MATTER, TON-CHAN?
YOU'RE BEING NEEDY.
TON-CHAN DOES IT IN MODERATION.
TAP
HMPH

My Cats and Measures

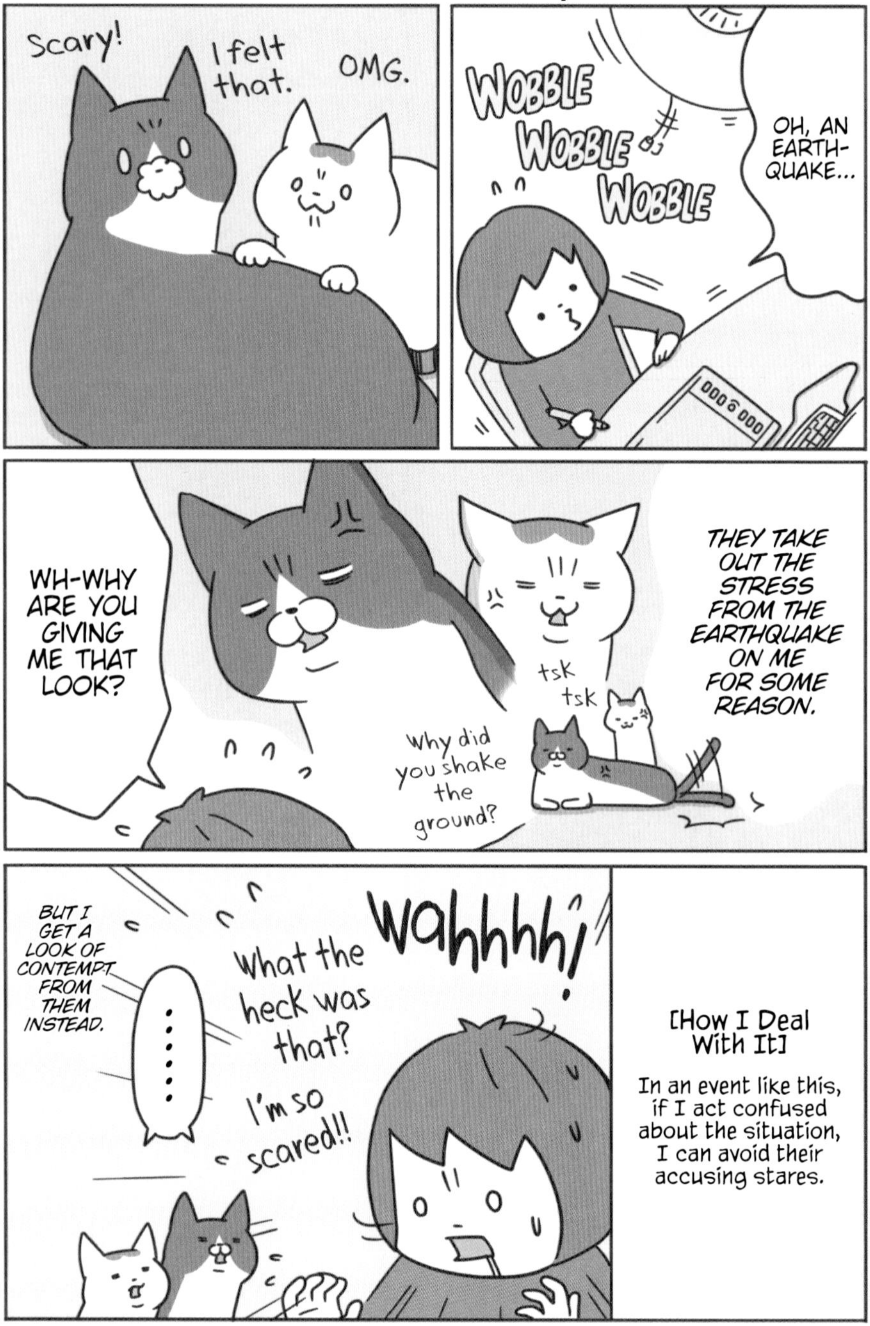

OH, AN EARTH-QUAKE...
WOBBLE
WOBBLE
WOBBLE
OMG.
I felt that.
Scary!
THEY TAKE OUT THE STRESS FROM THE EARTHQUAKE ON ME FOR SOME REASON.
tsk tsk
Why did you shake the ground?
WH-WHY ARE YOU GIVING ME THAT LOOK?
[How I Deal With It]
In an event like this, if I act confused about the situation, I can avoid their accusing stares.
Wahhhh!
What the heck was that?
I'm so scared!!
......
BUT I GET A LOOK OF CONTEMPT FROM THEM INSTEAD.

The Snuggler

SHINO-SAN WANTS TO SNUGGLE WITH TON-CHAN.
......
ZZZ ZZZ
BUT IF SHE TRIED TO DO IT DIRECTLY, THIS ← WOULD HAPPEN.
SHOVE
SHE QUICKLY GETS BEHIND HER AND...
LICK LICK LICK
LICK LICK LICK LICK
Hey!
It's fine.
It's fine.
It's fine.
It's fine.
Stop!
I GUESS WHAT COUNTS IS THE MOMENTUM.

This was her failed attempt. Ton-chan retaliated.

My Cats' Reactions

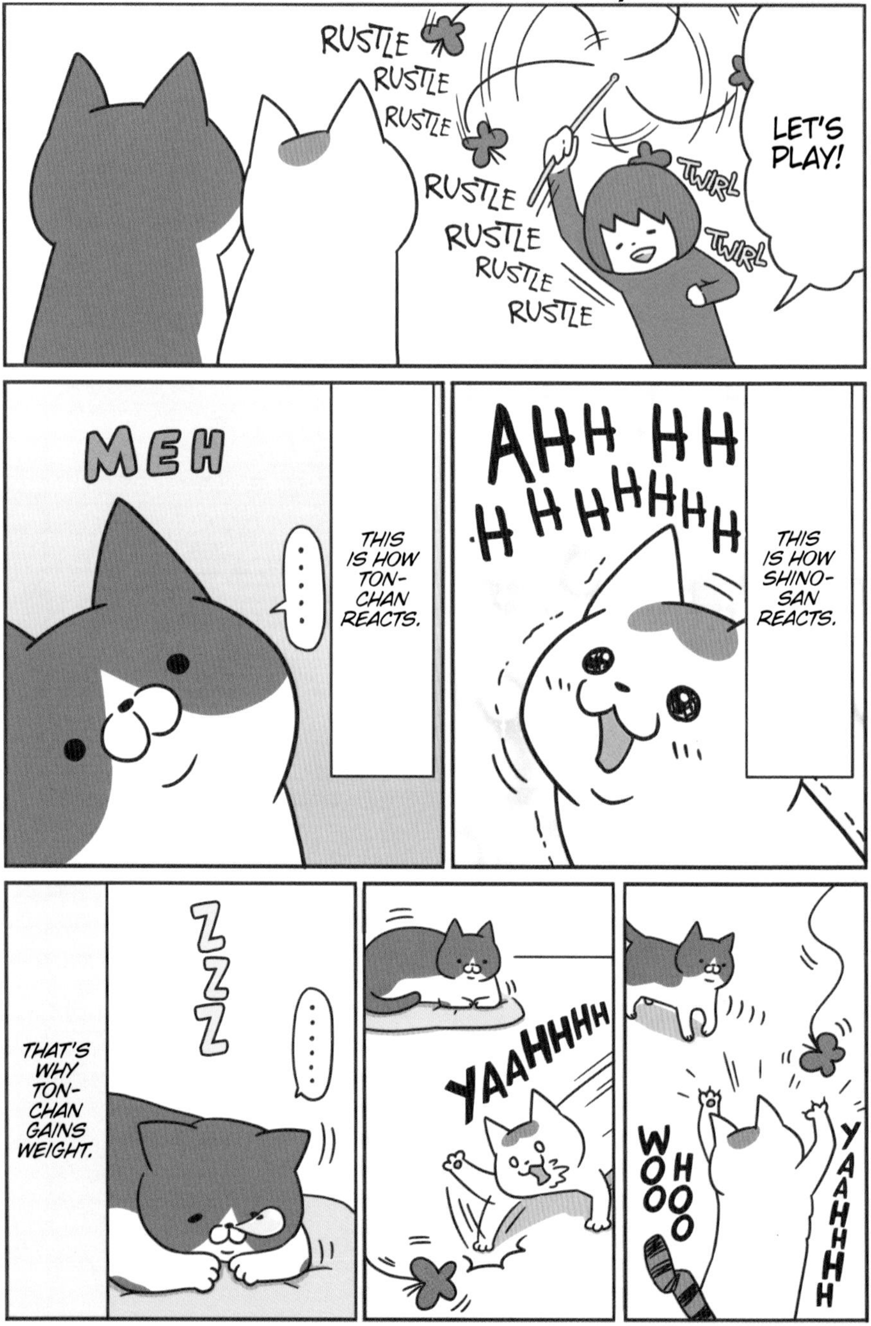
LET'S PLAY!
TWIRL
TWIRL
RUSTLE
RUSTLE
RUSTLE
RUSTLE
RUSTLE
RUSTLE
RUSTLE
AHHHHHHHHHHH
THIS IS HOW SHINO-SAN REACTS.
MEH
……
THIS IS HOW TON-CHAN REACTS.
YAAHHHHHH
WOOHOO
YAAHHHH
ZZZ
……
THAT'S WHY TON-CHAN GAINS WEIGHT.

Whisper Meows

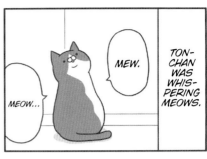

TON-CHAN WAS WHISPERING MEOWS.
MEW.
MEOW...
HEY! TONNIE! LOOKING CUTE TODAY!
Where did Shino-san go?
MEW...
Shino-saaan!
Hello?
MEW, MEW...
MEW ...
SHINO-SAN HAD SNUCK INTO THIS CUPBOARD.
IN!
MEOW ...
RUSTLE RUSTLE
← She was trying to tell me

She doesn't really meow loudly except for food.

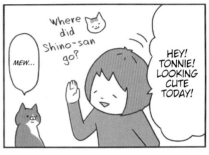

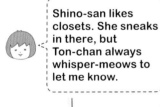

Shino-san likes closets. She sneaks in there, but Ton-chan always whisper-meows to let me know.

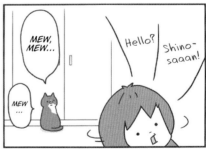

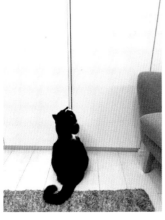

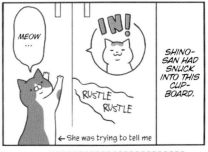

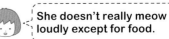

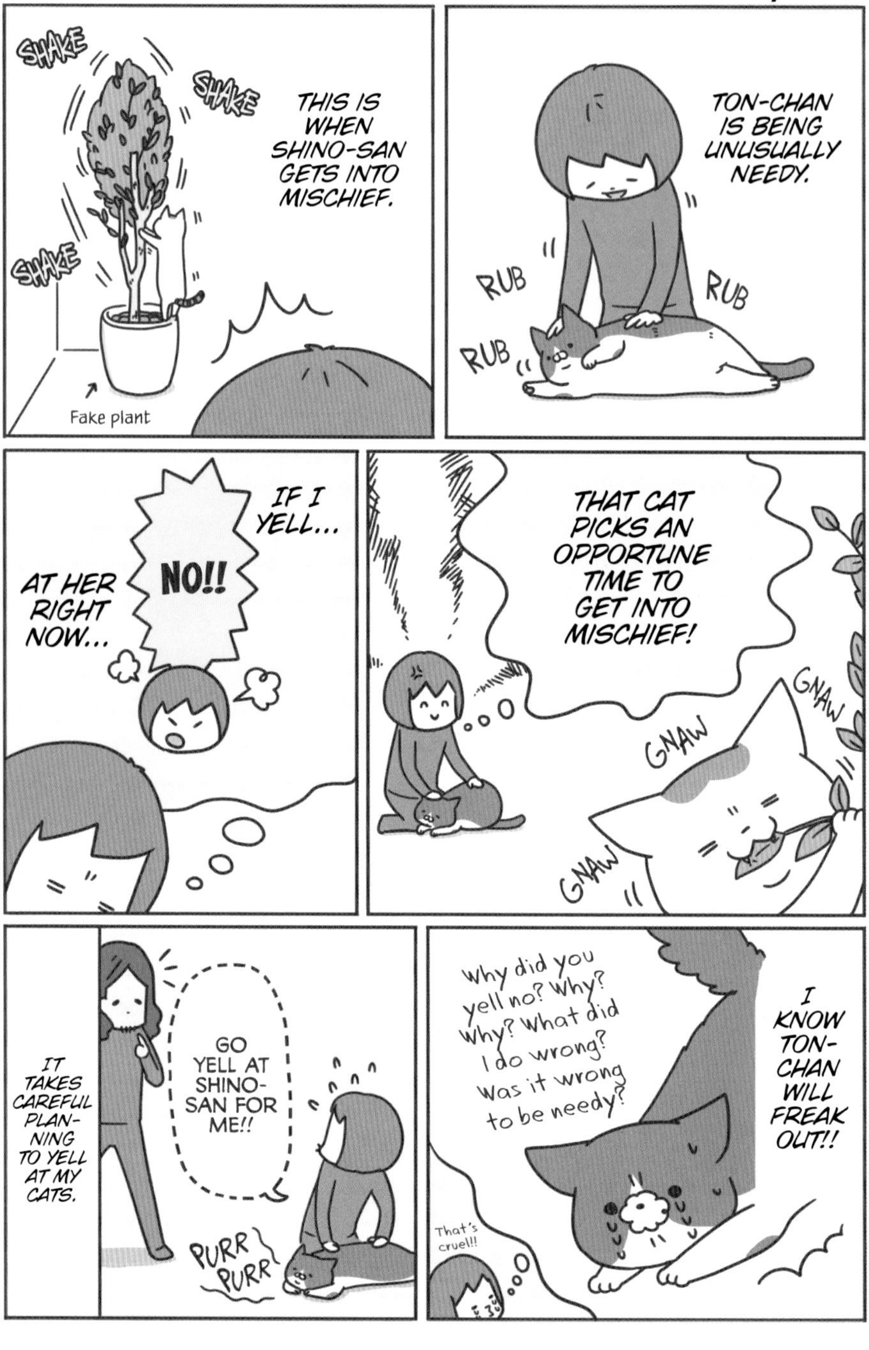
TON-CHAN IS BEING UNUSUALLY NEEDY.
RUB
RUB
RUB
SHAKE
SHAKE
THIS IS WHEN SHINO-SAN GETS INTO MISCHIEF.
SHAKE
Fake plant
THAT CAT PICKS AN OPPORTUNE TIME TO GET INTO MISCHIEF!
GNAW
GNAW
GNAW
IF I YELL...
NO!!
AT HER RIGHT NOW...
I KNOW TON-CHAN WILL FREAK OUT!!
Why did you yell no? Why? Why? What did I do wrong? Was it wrong to be needy?
That's cruel!!
GO YELL AT SHINO-SAN FOR ME!!
IT TAKES CAREFUL PLAN-NING TO YELL AT MY CATS.
PURR
PURR

Very Popular Drawers

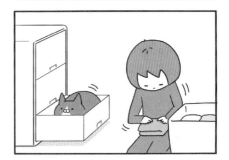

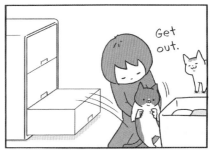

Get out.
EXCITED!
RINSE AND REPEAT.
Get out.

We had a good time.
Sheesh.
You're hope-less.

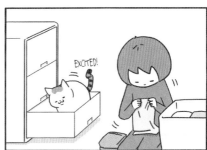

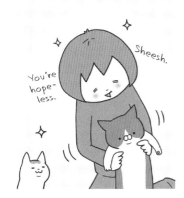

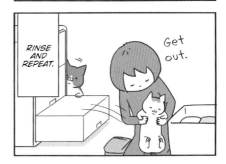

Cleaning

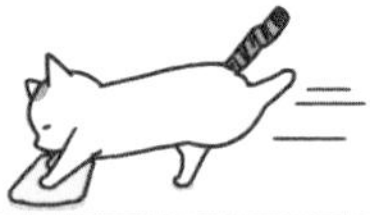

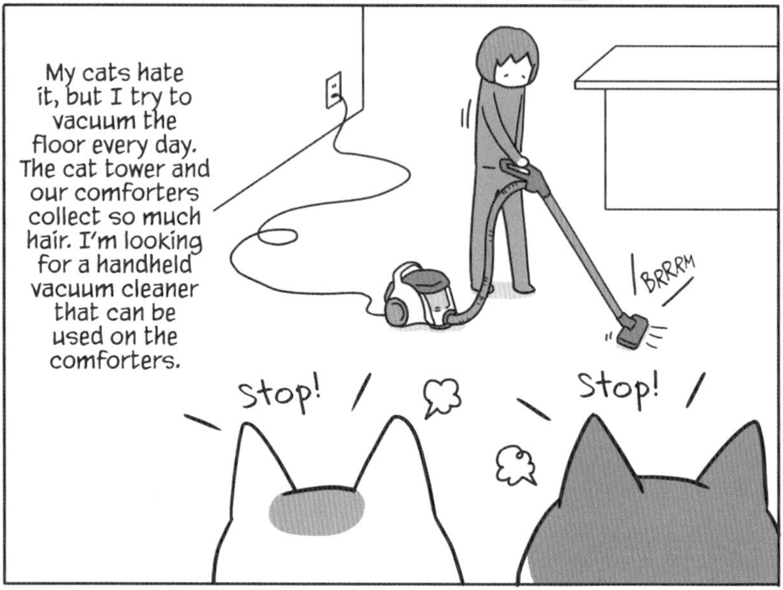

My cats hate it, but I try to vacuum the floor every day. The cat tower and our comforters collect so much hair. I'm looking for a handheld vacuum cleaner that can be used on the comforters.
BRRRM
Stop!
Stop!

We have a minimum amount of furniture to make the cleaning easier.

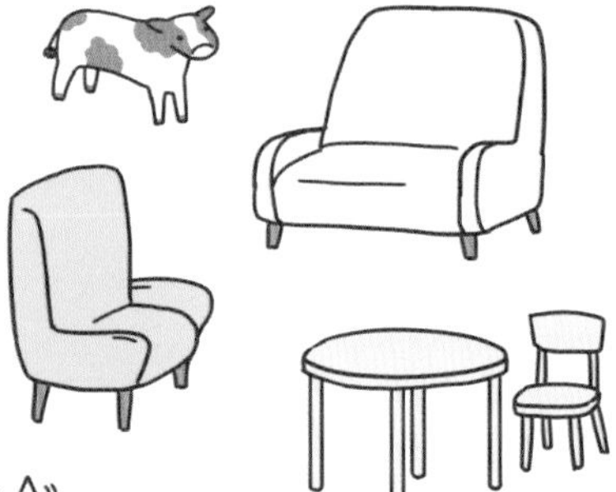

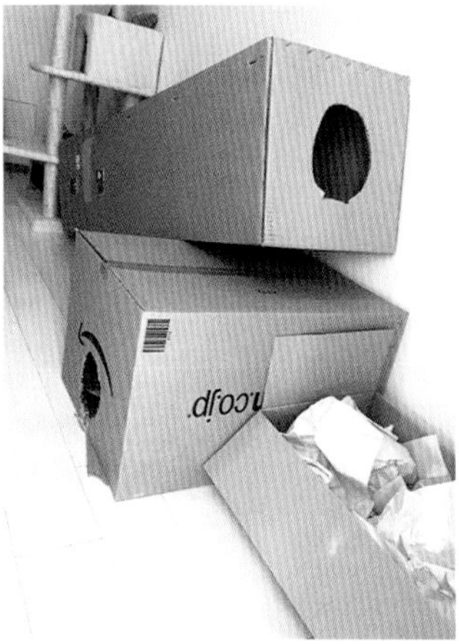

We try not to keep many things around, but we have trouble throwing out this pile of cardboard boxes that my cats like.

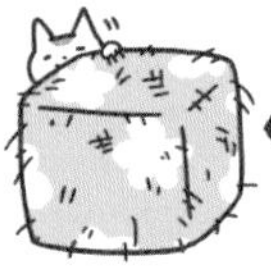

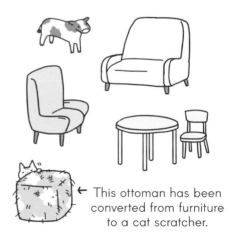

← This ottoman has been converted from furniture to a cat scratcher.

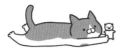

Interior Decorating

We wish we could have some knick-knacks.
My cats would chew them up, so we don't keep many.

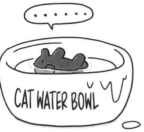

I've had a small plushie dropped in a bowl of water.

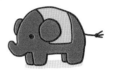

Elephant

CAT WATER BOWL

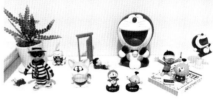

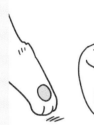

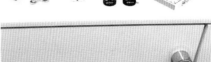

Most of our figurines are displayed in the bathroom.

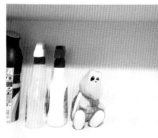

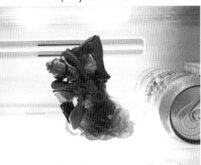

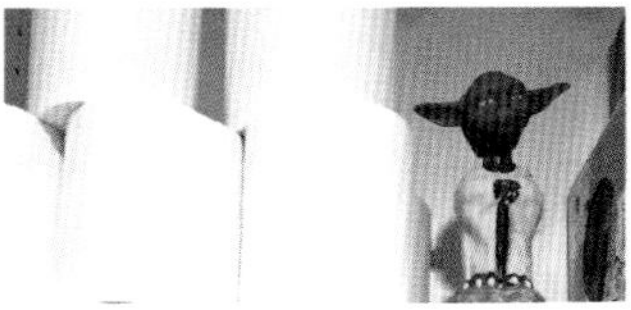

Some of our figurines and toys are hidden out of my cats' reach throughout the house, like inside the fridge.

The Cat Tower

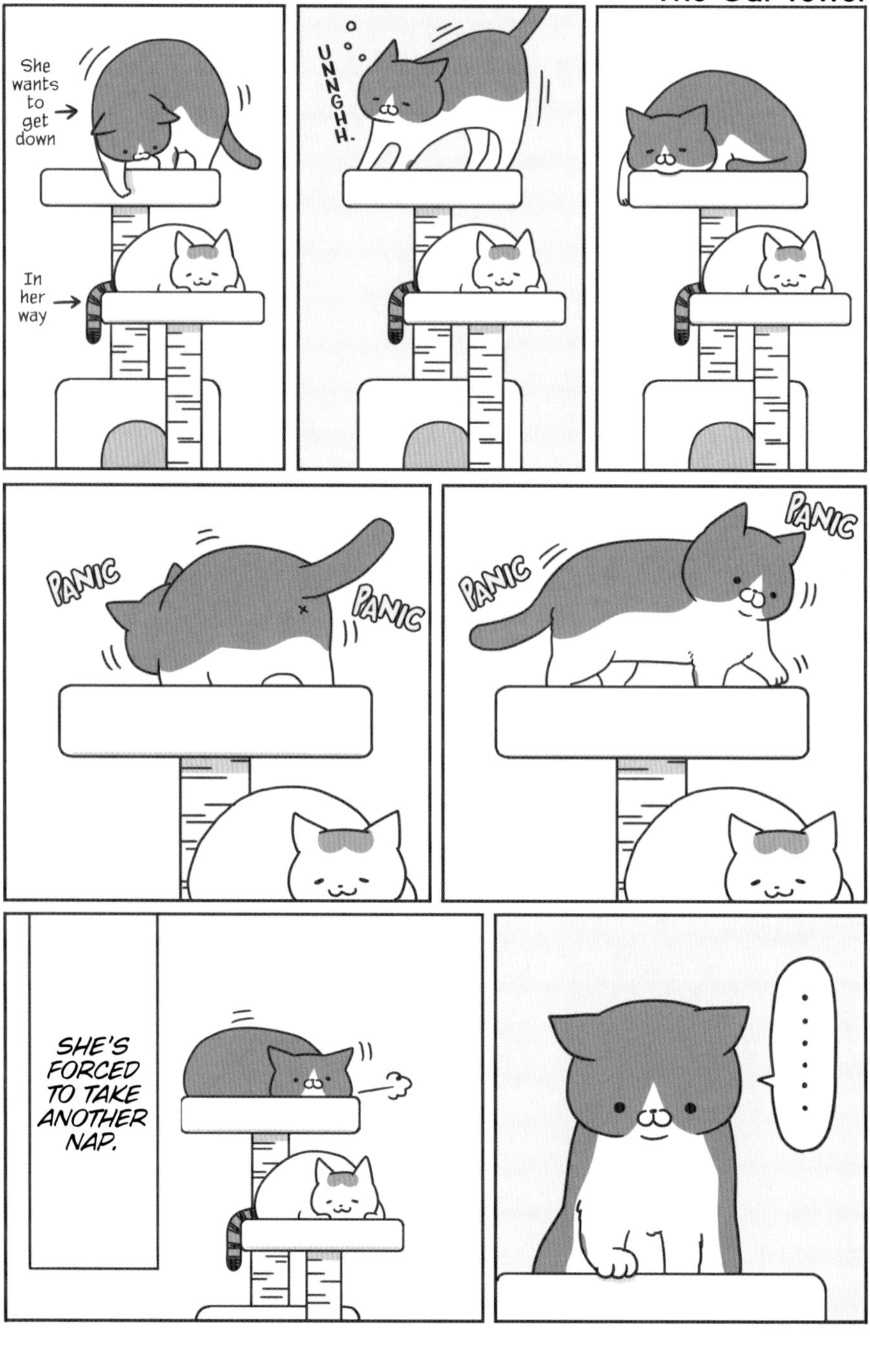
UNNGHH.
She wants to get down
In her way
PANIC
PANIC
PANIC
PANIC
......
SHE'S FORCED TO TAKE ANOTHER NAP.

Just a Marking

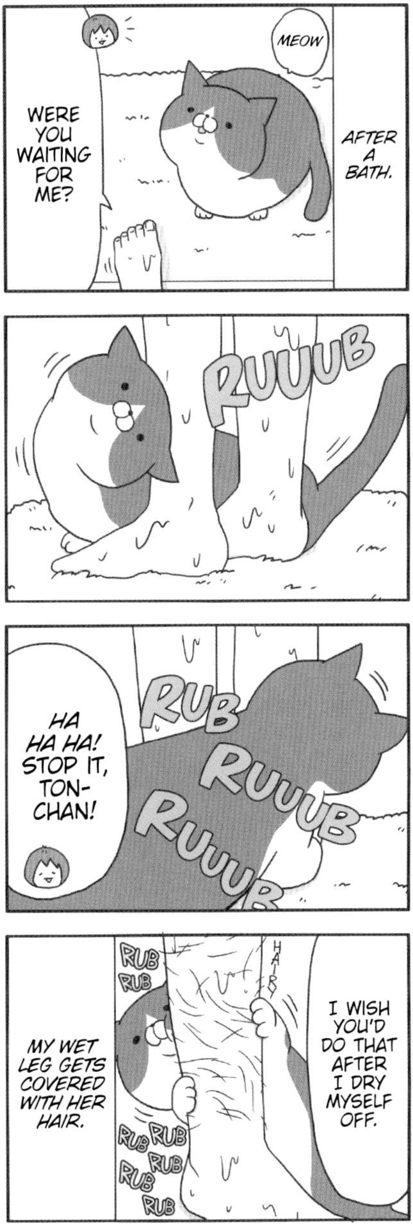
AFTER A BATH.
MEOW
WERE YOU WAITING FOR ME?
RUUUB
RUB
RUUUB
RUUUR
HA HA HA! STOP IT, TON-CHAN!
I WISH YOU'D DO THAT AFTER I DRY MYSELF OFF.
HAIRY
RUB RUB
MY WET LEG GETS COVERED WITH HER HAIR.
RUB RUB RUB RUB RUB

Totally Bummed Out

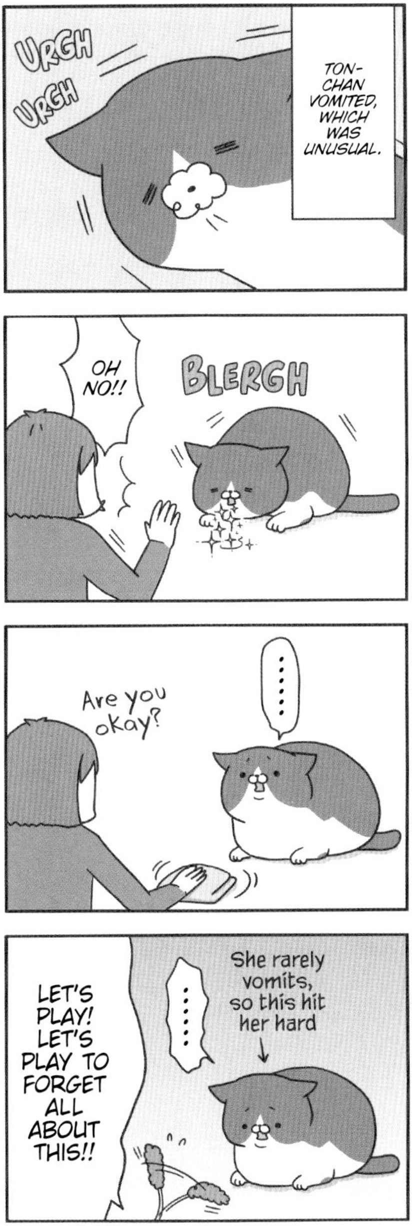
TON-CHAN VOMITED, WHICH WAS UNUSUAL.
URGH
URGH
BLERGH
OH NO!!
......
Are you okay?
She rarely vomits, so this hit her hard
......
LET'S PLAY! LET'S PLAY TO FORGET ALL ABOUT THIS!!

Within Three Seconds

TON-CHAN, LET ME HOLD YOU.

`00:00:14`

Here we go.

`00:01:27`

She might have learned that holding means I'm going to cut her nails. I regret it.

FLAIL FLAIL FLAIL FLAIL

`00:02:40`

WHUMP

`00:03:34`

The Mystery of Throwing Litter Around

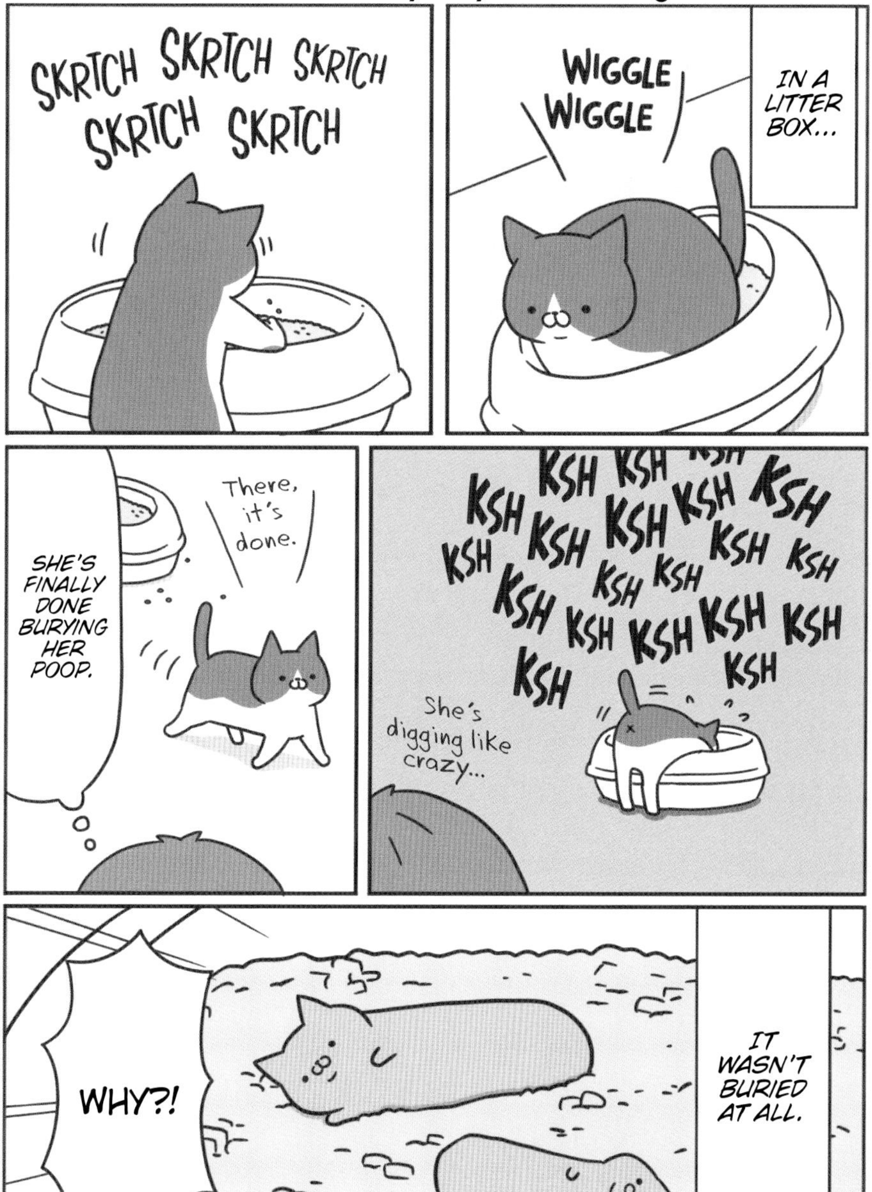
IN A LITTER BOX...
WIGGLE WIGGLE
SKRTCH SKRTCH SKRTCH
SKRTCH SKRTCH
KSH KSH KSH KSH
KSH KSH KSH KSH KSH
KSH KSH KSH KSH
KSH KSH KSH KSH KSH
KSH KSH
She's digging like crazy...
There, it's done.
SHE'S FINALLY DONE BURYING HER POOP.
IT WASN'T BURIED AT ALL.
WHY?!

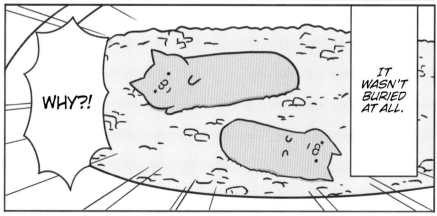

Stretching Longer Than Expected

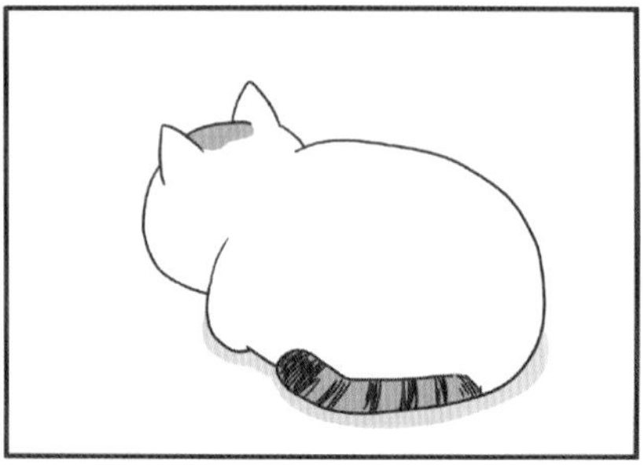

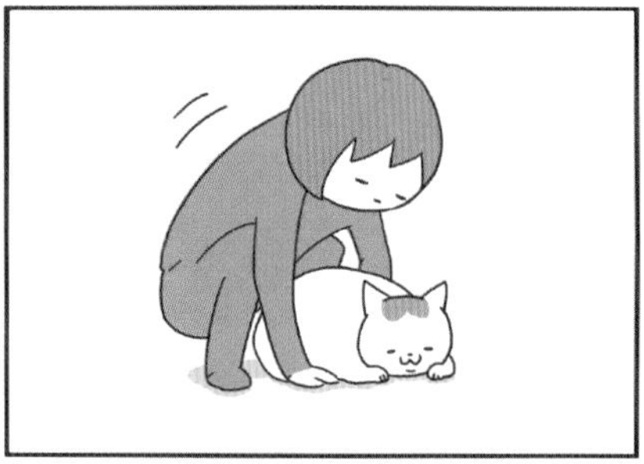

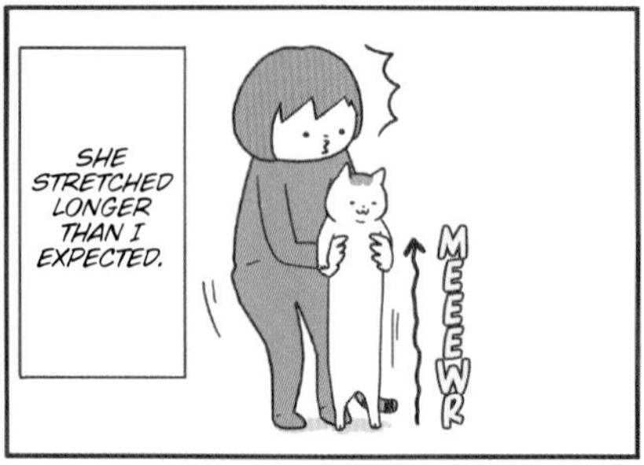
MEEEEWR
SHE STRETCHED LONGER THAN I EXPECTED.

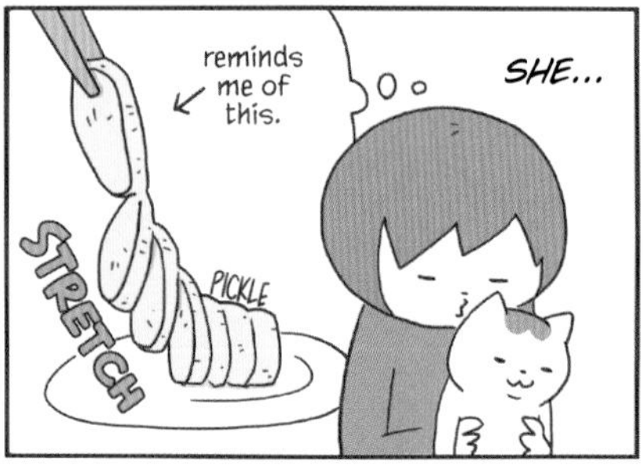
SHE...
reminds me of this.
PICKLE
STRETCH

Cats are always unpredictable.

There are "round" and "stick" types.

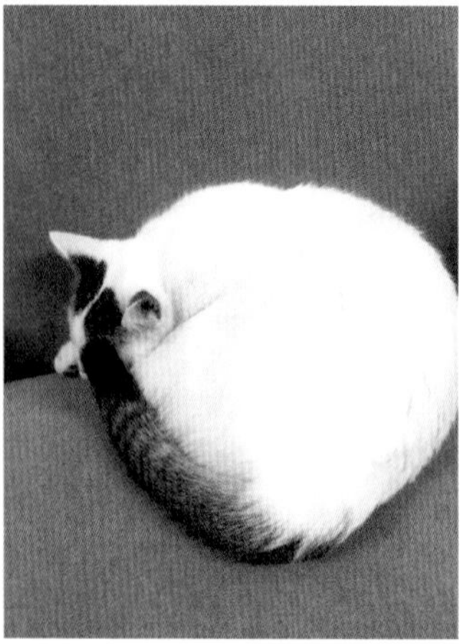

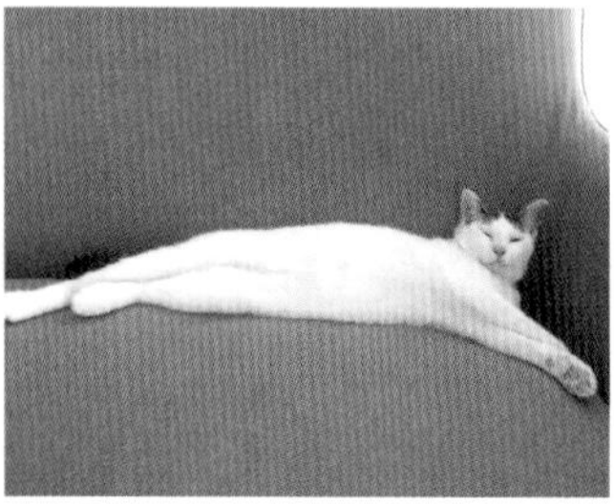

Be Quiet

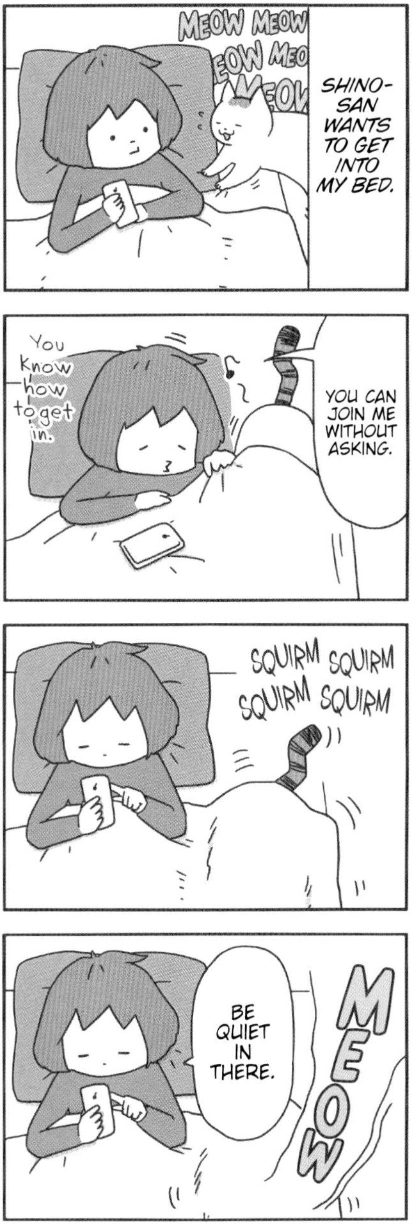
SHINO-SAN WANTS TO GET INTO MY BED.
MEOW MEOW
MEOW MEO
MEOW
YOU CAN JOIN ME WITHOUT ASKING.
You know how to get in.
SQUIRM SQUIRM
SQUIRM SQUIRM
MEOW
BE QUIET IN THERE.

I don't know who she's talking to, but she meows inside the bed too.

Shino-san likes to crawl into things. She probably thinks she's hiding.

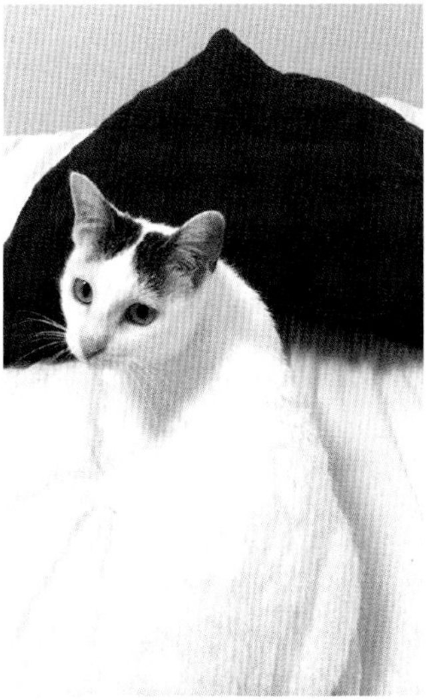

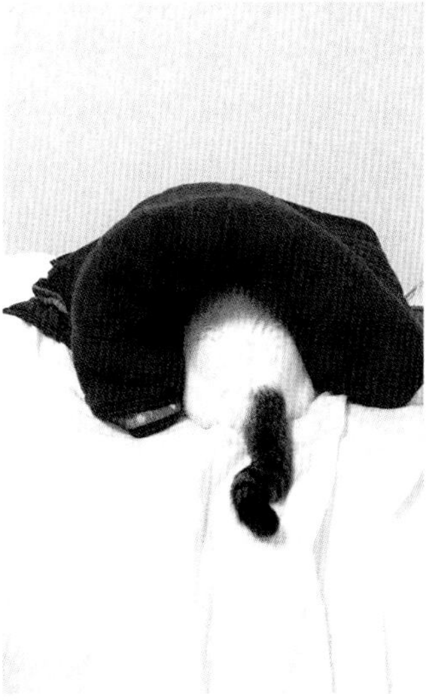

Hold It
UHH
UHH
WHAT'S THE MATTER? YOU NEED TO VOMIT?
UHH
UHH
UHH
UHH
......
UHH
UHH
Hold it!
ARE YOU TRYING TO VOMIT ON MY FACE?

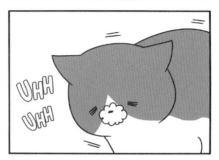

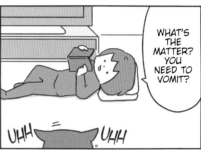

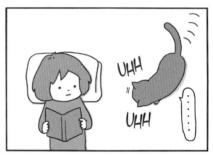

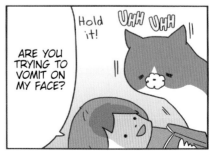

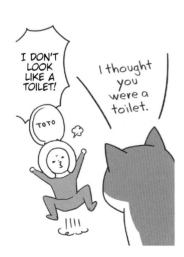

I thought you were a toilet.
I DON'T LOOK LIKE A TOILET!
TOTO

Pride

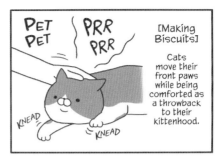

[Making Biscuits]
Cats move their front paws while being comforted as a throwback to their kittenhood.
PRR PRR
PET PET
KNEAD
KNEAD
PET PET PET PET PET
......
ARGH
PAUSE
PET PET PET PET PET
PRR PRR PRR
KNEAD
KNEAD
ARGH
PET PET PET
SHE'S HOLDING BACK.
PAUSE

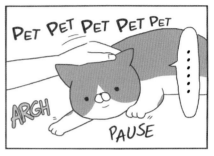

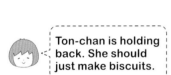

Ton-chan is holding back. She should just make biscuits.

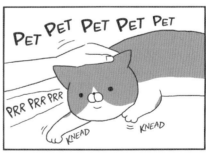

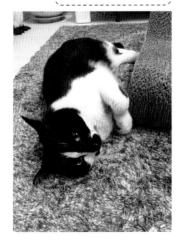

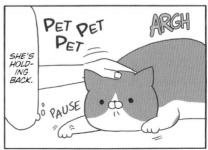

Personifying My Cats

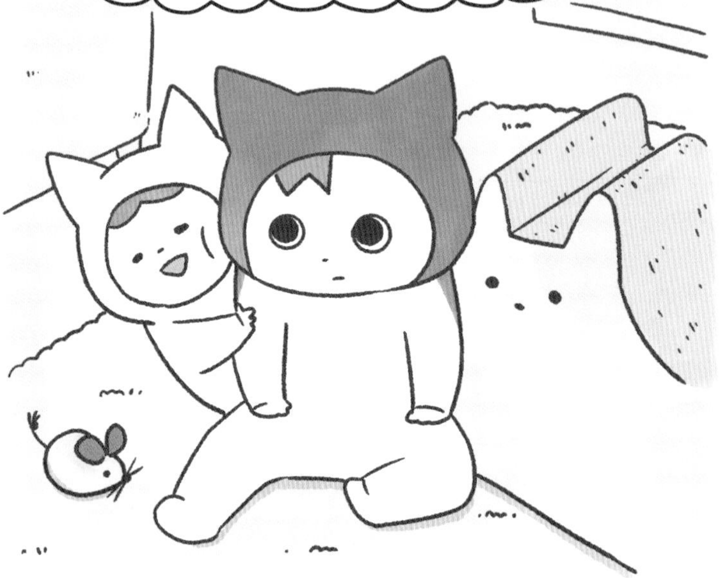

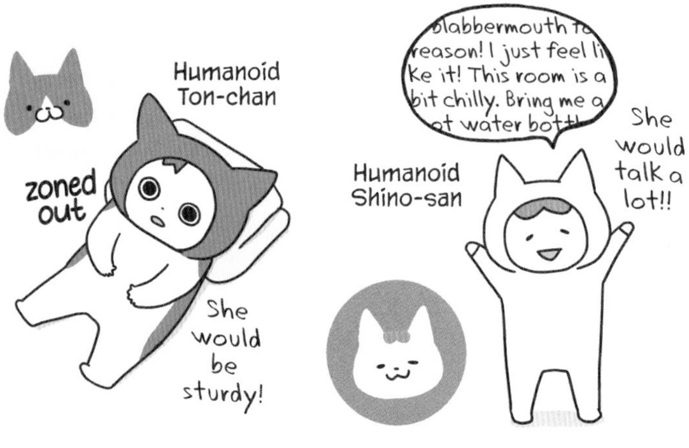
blabbermouth fo reason! I just feel like it! This room is a bit chilly. Bring me a ot water bott
She would talk a lot!!
Humanoid Shino-san
Humanoid Ton-chan
zoned out
She would be sturdy!

Human Ton-chan

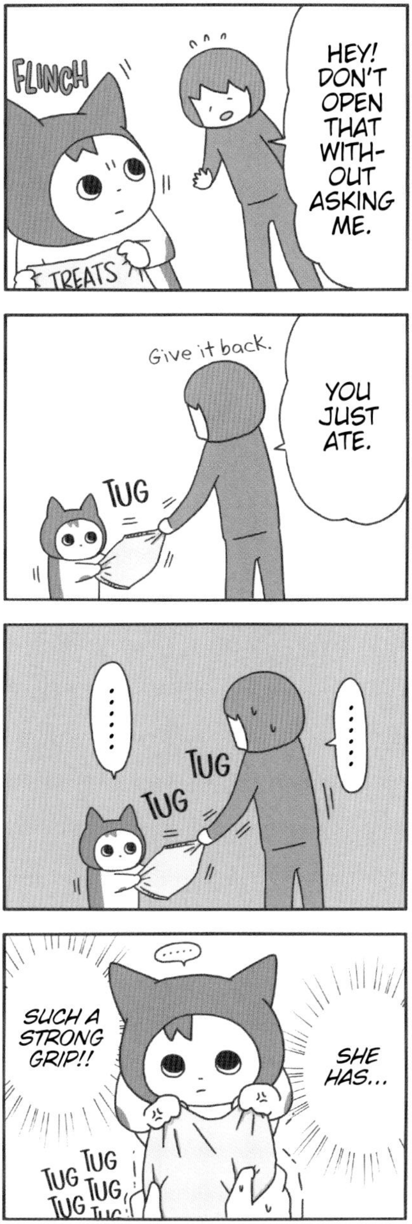
HEY! DON'T OPEN THAT WITH-OUT ASKING ME.
FLINCH
TREATS
YOU JUST ATE.
Give it back.
TUG
......
TUG
TUG
......
.....
SHE HAS...
SUCH A STRONG GRIP!!
TUG TUG
TUG TUG
TUG

Human Shino-san

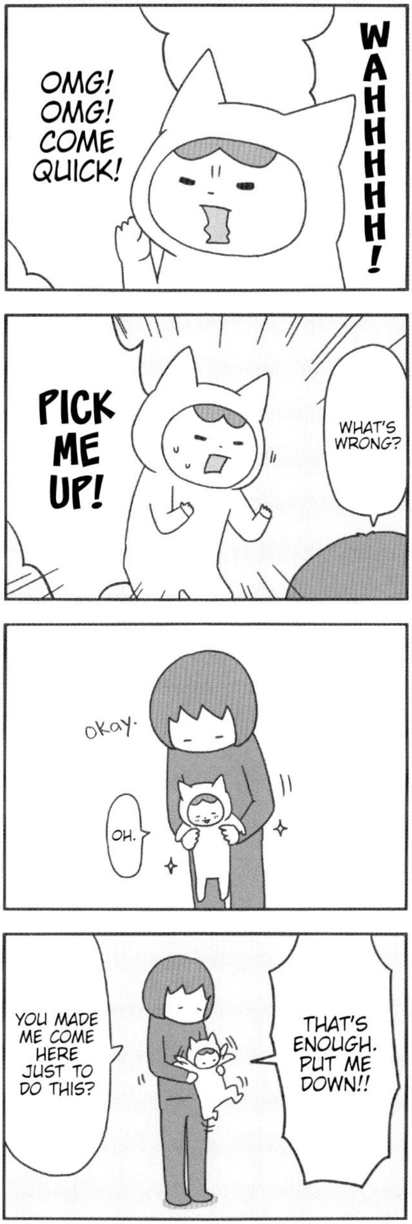
WAHHHHHH!
OMG! OMG! COME QUICK!
WHAT'S WRONG?
PICK ME UP!
okay.
OH.
THAT'S ENOUGH. PUT ME DOWN!!
YOU MADE ME COME HERE JUST TO DO THIS?

Autumn Cuddling

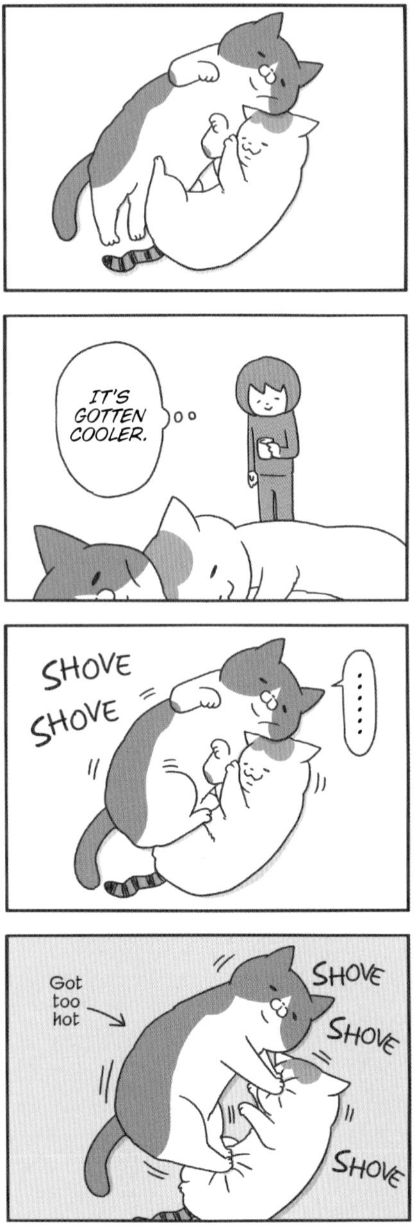
IT'S GOTTEN COOLER.
SHOVE
SHOVE
......
SHOVE
SHOVE
SHOVE
Got too hot

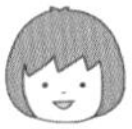

I enjoy seeing the kitties cuddling in their sleep. I hope Shino-san will keep at it.

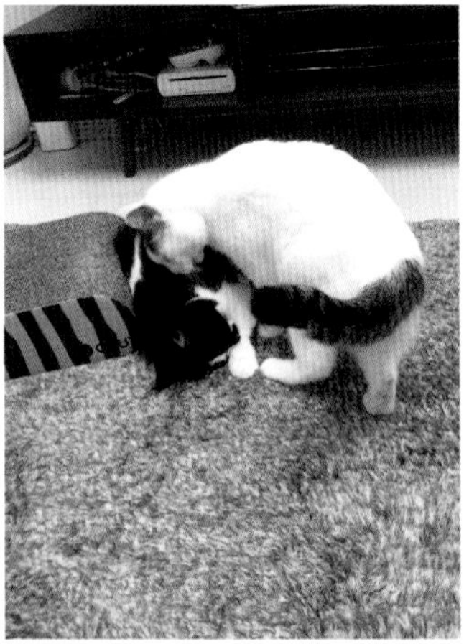

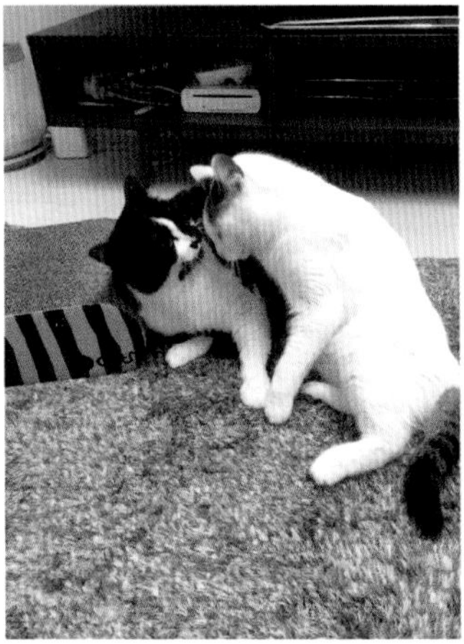

Admirable Shino-san

SHINO-SAN WANTS TO SNUGGLE WITH TON-CHAN.

INCH INCH

REJECTED.

stay away!

DEJECTED

Ton-chan's favorite bed ↓

TEARY

GLOOM

IT MUST SMELL LIKE TON-CHAN!!

Sometimes Ton-chan shows her appreciation.

PRR PRR PRR

Bite-worthy Back

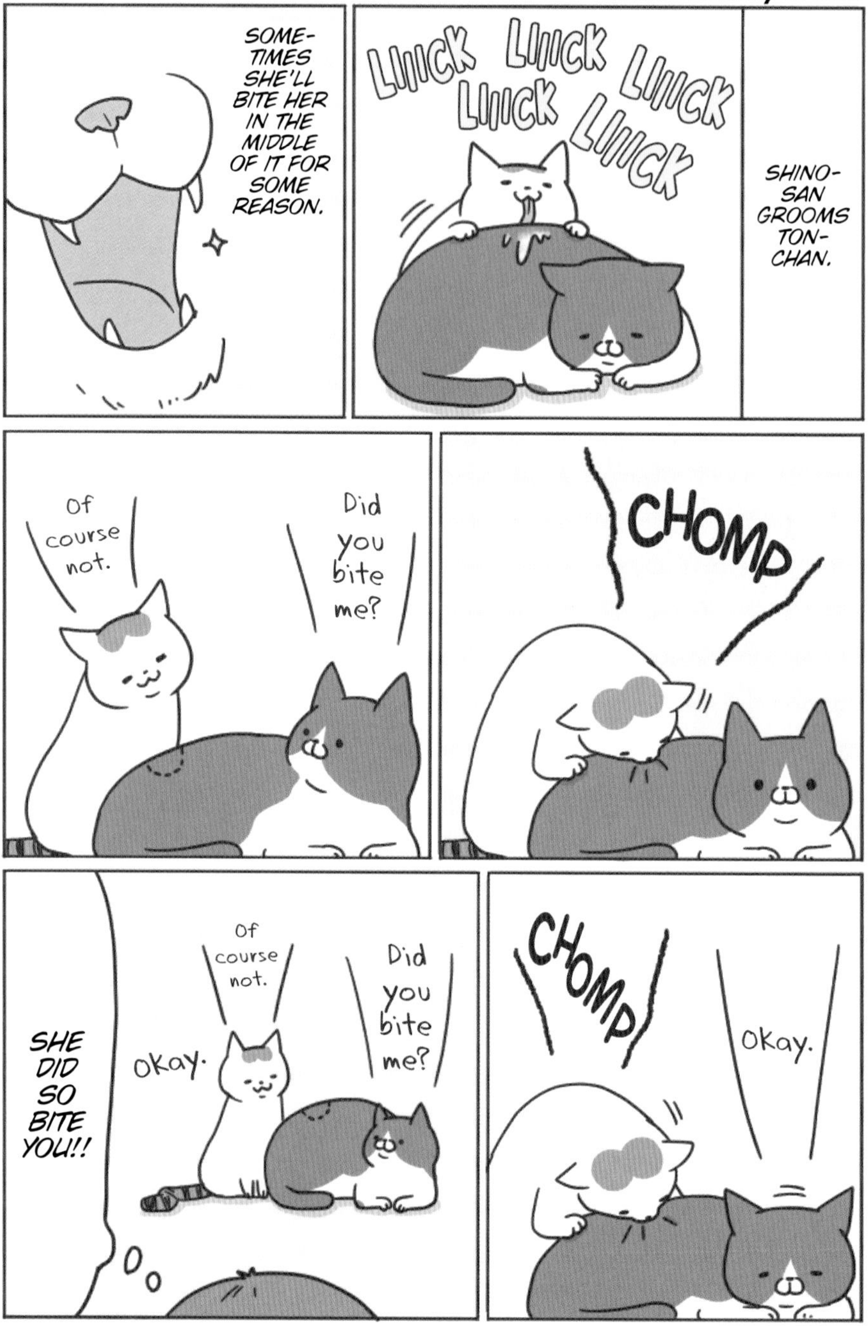
SHINO-SAN GROOMS TON-CHAN.
LIIICK LIIICK LIIICK LIIICK LIIICK
SOMETIMES SHE'LL BITE HER IN THE MIDDLE OF IT FOR SOME REASON.
CHOMP
Did you bite me?
Of course not.
CHOMP
Okay.
Did you bite me?
Of course not.
Okay.
SHE DID SO BITE YOU!!

Next to My Cat

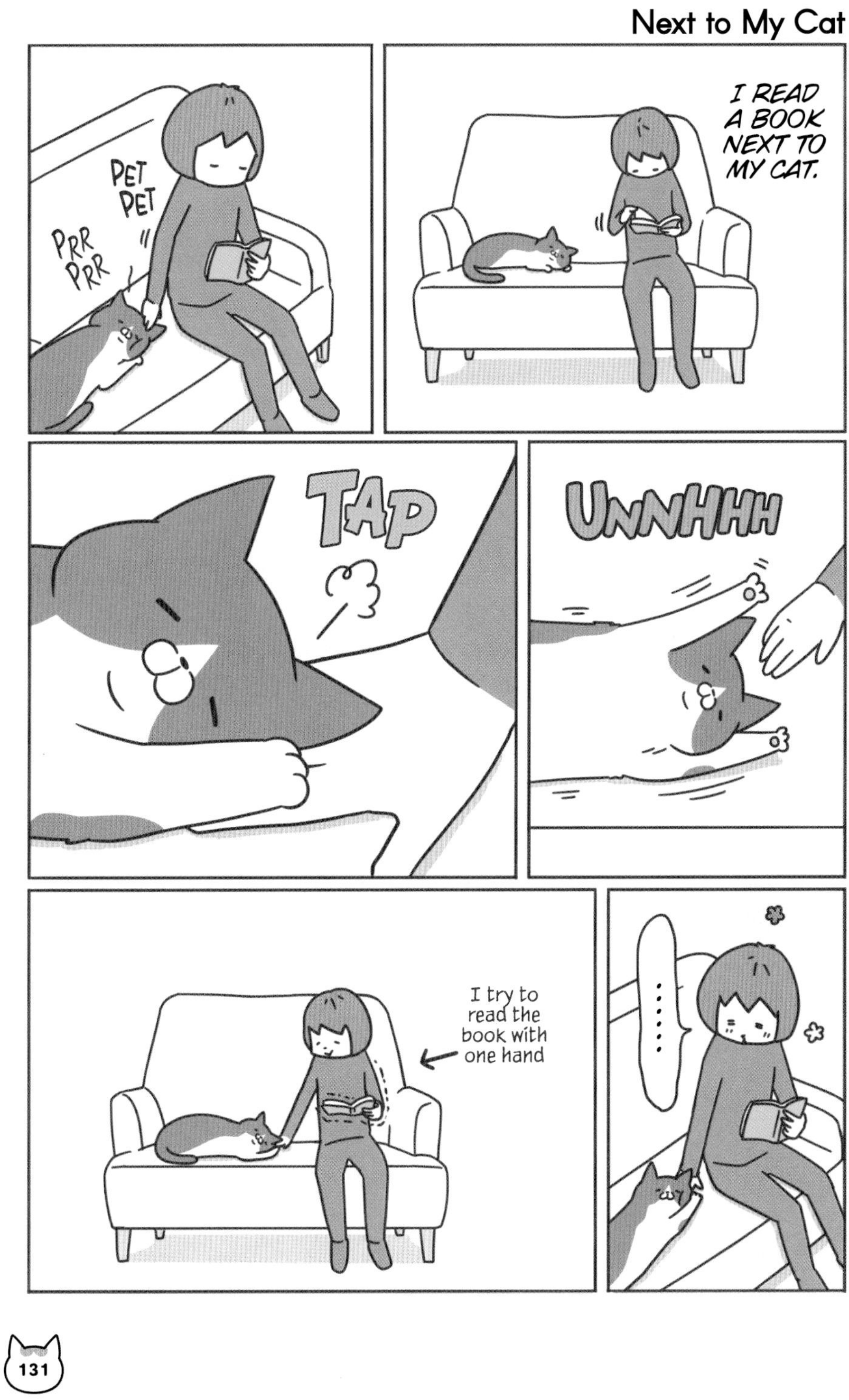
I READ A BOOK NEXT TO MY CAT.
PET PET
PRR PRR
UNNHHH
TAP
......
I try to read the book with one hand

Making Faces

THERE ARE SNOTS ON SHINO-SAN'S NOSE.
I'LL CLEAN THEM OFF WITH A WIPE.
Can you hold her?
Sure.
NO!
THAT FACE!
PFFT
uh-oh!
MAKING THAT FACE HELPED HER ESCAPE.
DASH

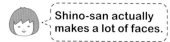

Shino-san actually makes a lot of faces.

A Feint

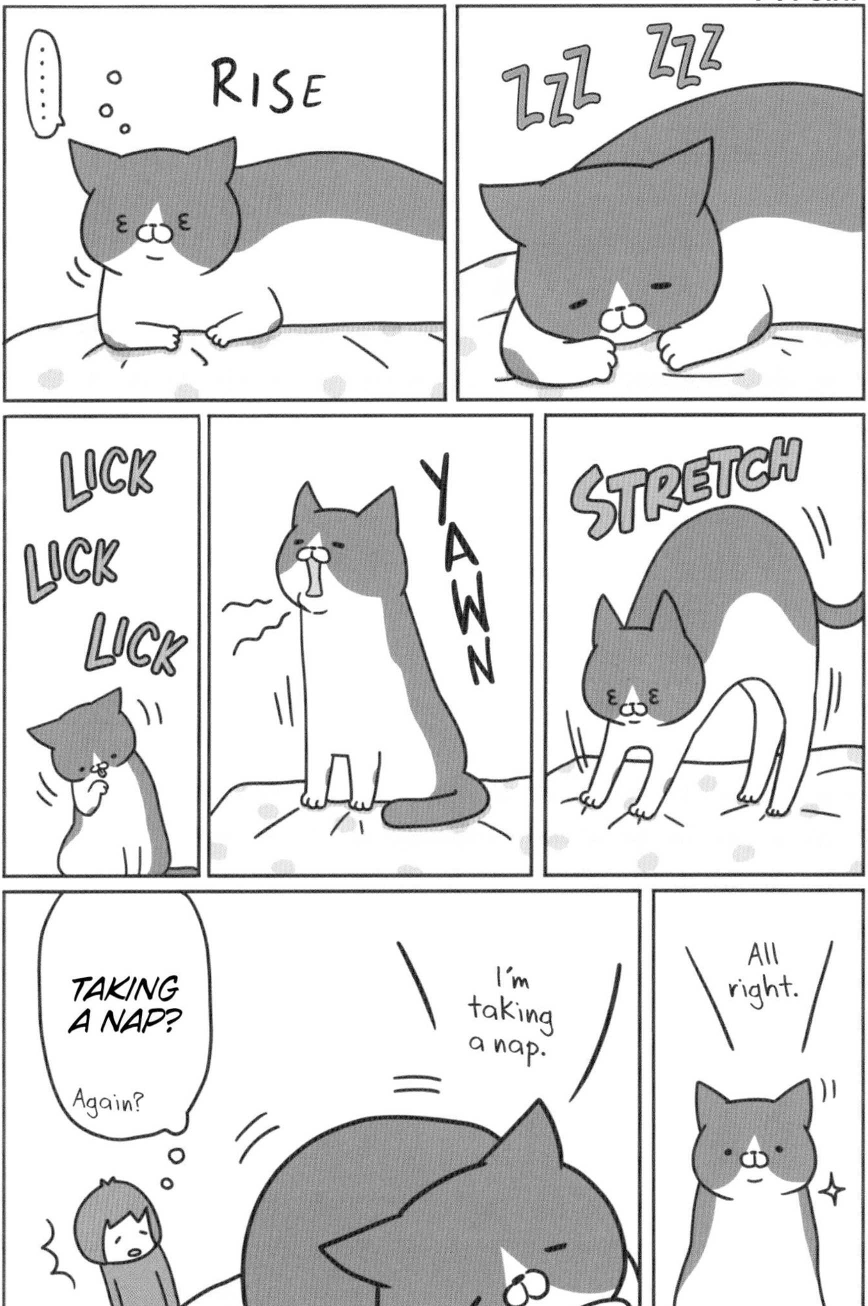

ZZZ ZZZ
……
RISE
STRETCH
YAWN
LICK
LICK
LICK
All right.
I'm taking a nap.
TAKING A NAP?
Again?

Unbearable

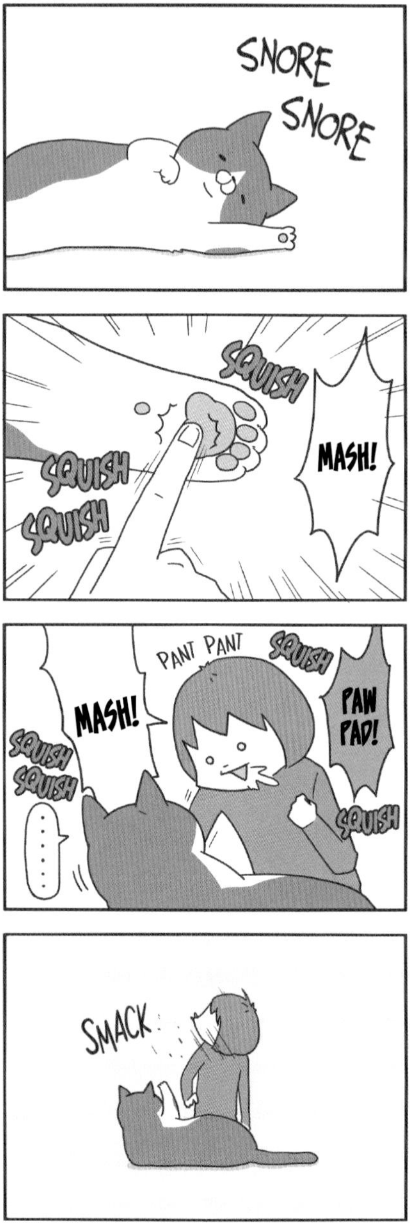
SNORE
SNORE
MASH!
SQUISH
SQUISH
SQUISH
PAW PAD!
SQUISH
PANT PANT
MASH!
SQUISH
SQUISH SQUISH
......
SMACK

Both Being Hyper

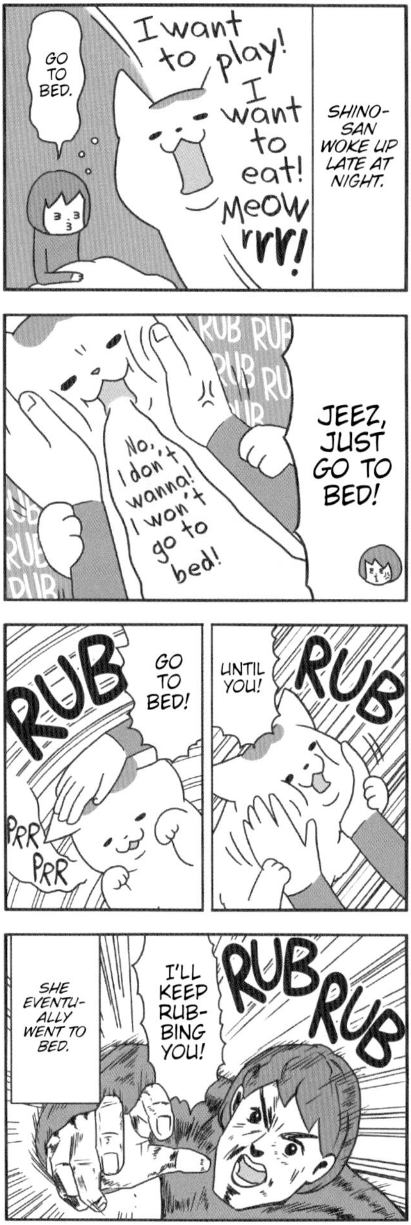
SHINO-SAN WOKE UP LATE AT NIGHT.
I want to play! I want to eat! Meowrrr!
GO TO BED.
JEEZ, JUST GO TO BED!
RUB RUB RUB RUB RUB
No, I don't wanna! I won't go to bed!
RUB RUB RUB
RUB
UNTIL YOU!
GO TO BED!
RUB
PRR PRR
RUB RUB
I'LL KEEP RUB-BING YOU!
SHE EVENTU-ALLY WENT TO BED.

Bliss

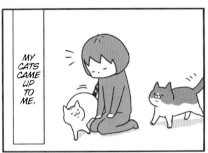

MY CATS CAME UP TO ME.
......
I WANT TO...
FREEZE TIME!!

I got this bonus time unexpectedly.

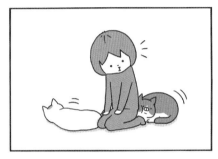

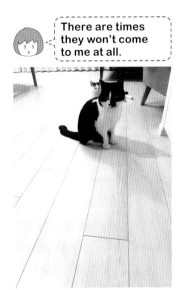

There are times they won't come to me at all.

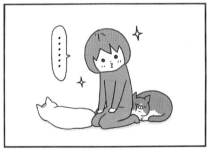

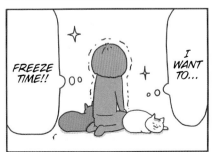

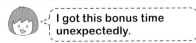

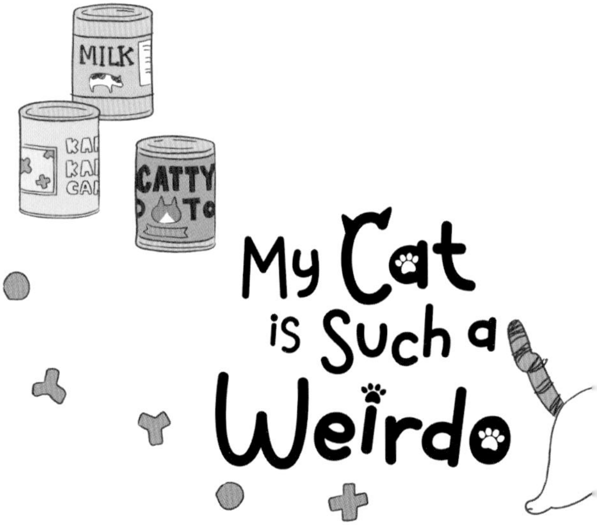
MILK
CATTY
My Cat is Such a Weirdo

Chapter 6

My Parents' Cats

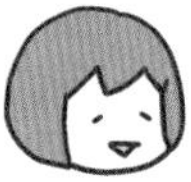

This chapter is about the two cats my parents used to care for.

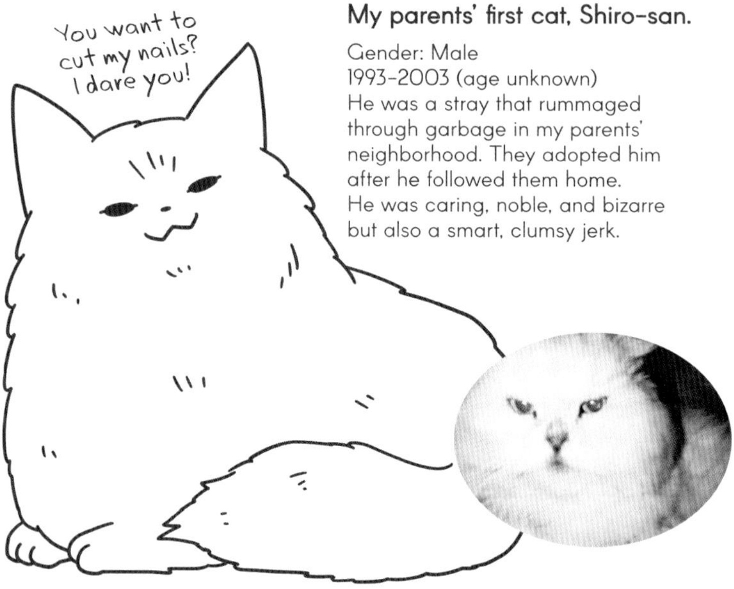
You want to cut my nails? I dare you!

My parents' first cat, Shiro-san.

Gender: Male
1993-2003 (age unknown)
He was a stray that rummaged through garbage in my parents' neighborhood. They adopted him after he followed them home.
He was caring, noble, and bizarre but also a smart, clumsy jerk.

My parents' second cat, Tora-chan.

Gender: Male
2006-2015 (age unknown)
A former stray. He was caring, energetic, and innocent. If I were to describe him in one word, he was an angel. He loved my dad so much that he stalked him. He had a mild congenital defect in his right eye, but it was his most charming characteristic.

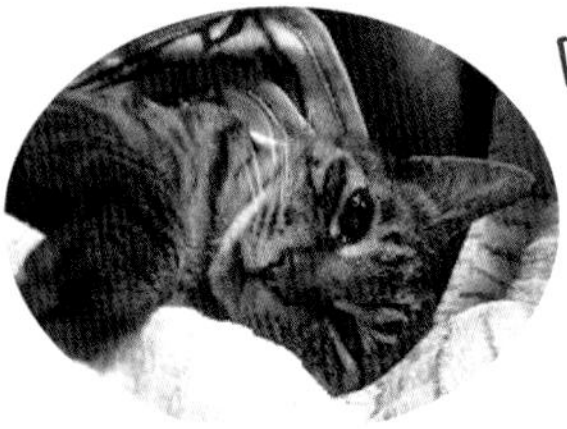

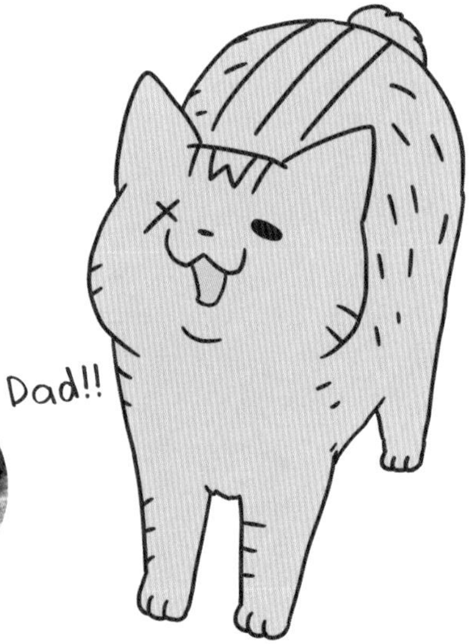
Dad!!

The Man Named Shiro

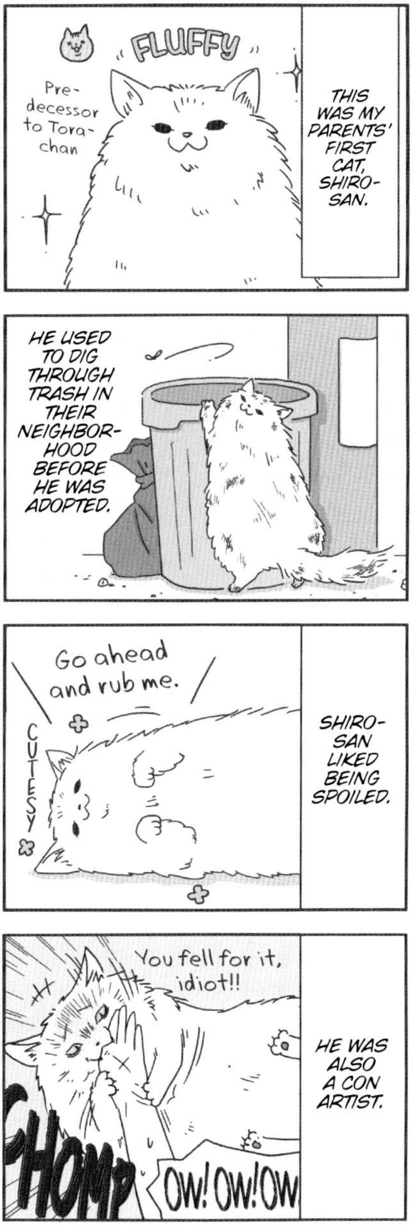
THIS WAS MY PARENTS' FIRST CAT, SHIRO-SAN.
FLUFFY
Pre-decessor to Tora-chan
HE USED TO DIG THROUGH TRASH IN THEIR NEIGHBOR-HOOD BEFORE HE WAS ADOPTED.
SHIRO-SAN LIKED BEING SPOILED.
Go ahead and rub me.
CUTESY
HE WAS ALSO A CON ARTIST.
You fell for it, idiot!!
CHOMP
OW! OW! OW

Summer Haircut

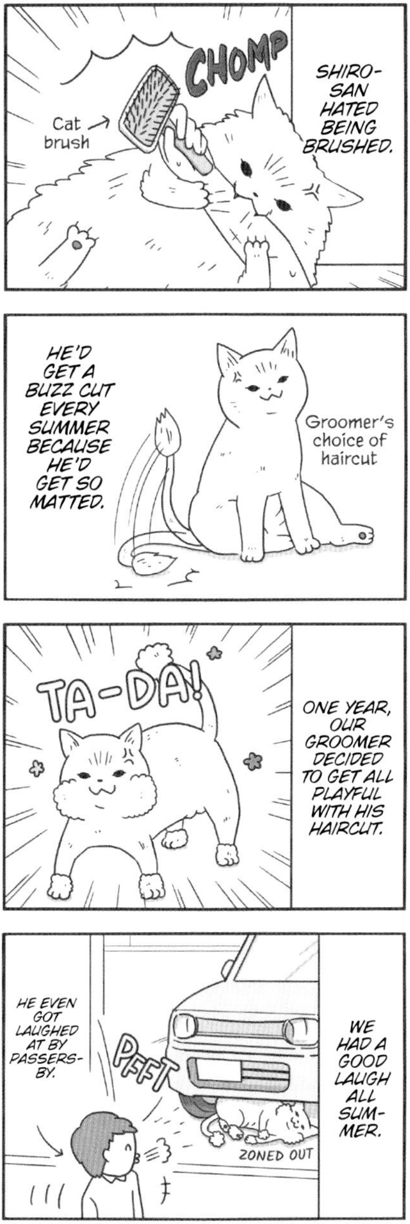
SHIRO-SAN HATED BEING BRUSHED.
CHOMP
Cat brush
Groomer's choice of haircut
HE'D GET A BUZZ CUT EVERY SUMMER BECAUSE HE'D GET SO MATTED.
ONE YEAR, OUR GROOMER DECIDED TO GET ALL PLAYFUL WITH HIS HAIRCUT.
TA-DA!
WE HAD A GOOD LAUGH ALL SUM-MER.
PFFT
HE EVEN GOT LAUGHED AT BY PASSERS-BY.
ZONED OUT

The Unforgettable Comment

Stocky and weighed nine kilograms

The size of a small dog

SHIRO-SAN MIGHT HAVE BEEN A FOREIGN BREED. HE WAS A BIG CAT.

Nice seeing you.

WHEN PEOPLE FIRST SAW HIM.

SO BIG!!

HE'D ALWAYS GET A COMMENT...

A stranger

WE GOT AT THE VET.

THERE WAS ONE UNFORGETTABLE COMMENT...

Oh my god! This is amazing!!

WRRRMRRO WRRRMRRO

It's a cat. ♡

WHAT THE HECK IS *THIS*?!!

Shocked

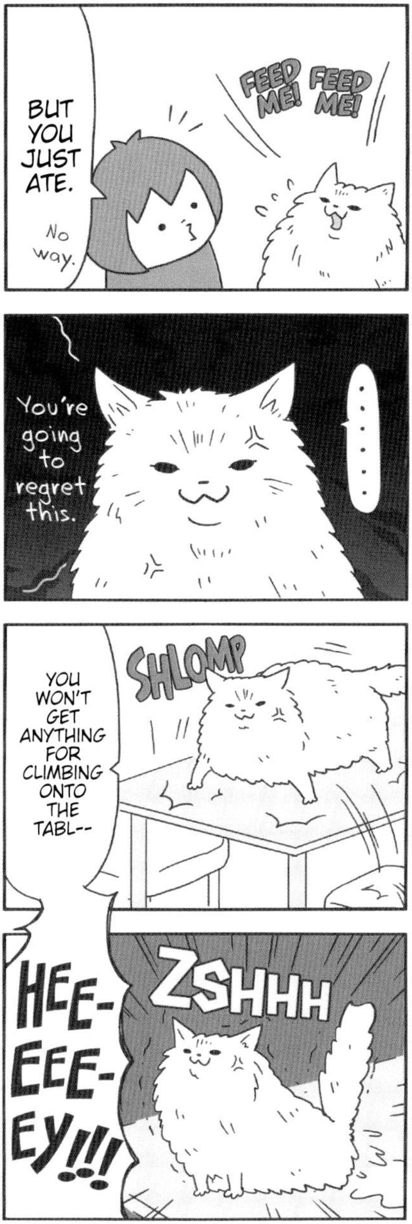
FEED ME! FEED ME!
BUT YOU JUST ATE.
No way.
......
You're going to regret this.
SHLOMP
YOU WON'T GET ANYTHING FOR CLIMBING ONTO THE TABL--
ZSHHH
HEE-EEE-EY!!!

Dangerous Play

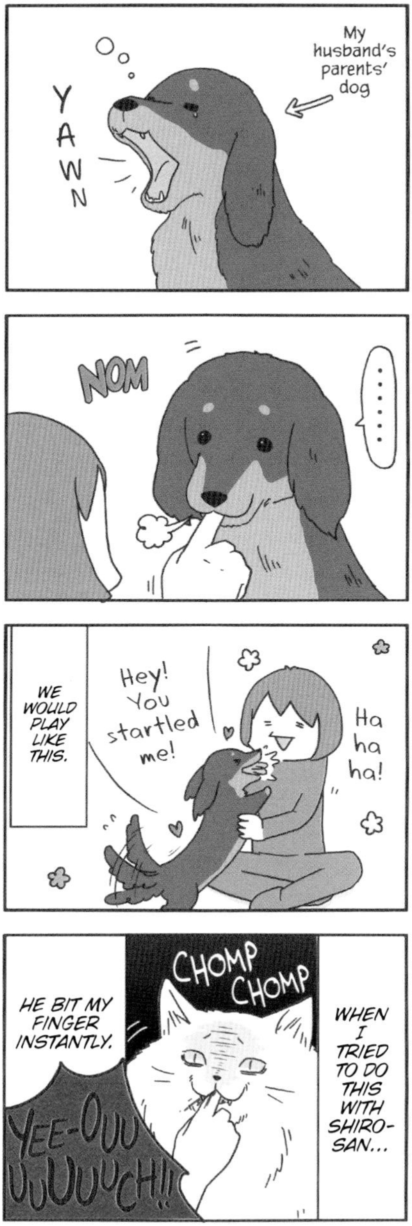
My husband's parents' dog
YAWN
......
NOM
Ha ha ha!
Hey! You startled me!
WE WOULD PLAY LIKE THIS.
WHEN I TRIED TO DO THIS WITH SHIRO-SAN...
CHOMP CHOMP
HE BIT MY FINGER INSTANTLY.
YEE-OUUUUUUUCH!!

Old Habits Never Die

HEY!
HEY!
KITCHEN
TRASH
......
SOMETIMES SHIRO-SAN, THE FORMER STRAY, WOULD RUMMAGE THROUGH OUR TRASH.
STOP IT!
DASH

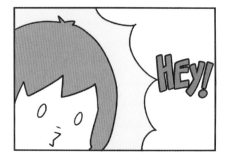

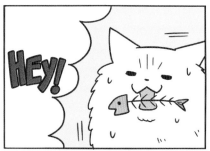

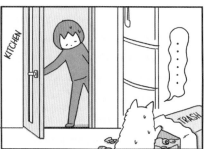

He was able to open our lidded trash can too.

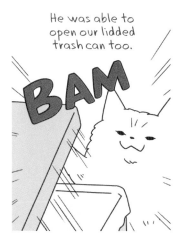

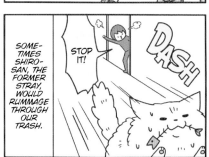

BAM

Kotatsu* Fantasy

*A kotatsu is a heated table.

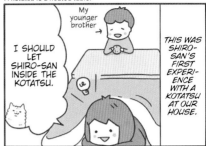

THIS WAS SHIRO-SAN'S FIRST EXPERIENCE WITH A KOTATSU AT OUR HOUSE.
My younger brother
I SHOULD LET SHIRO-SAN INSIDE THE KOTATSU.
ISN'T THIS EXCITING, SHIRO-SAN?
SHOVE
SHOVE
Stop it, Kids!
BUT CATS LIKE TO CURL UP UNDER A KOTATSU...
WSH
NOT HIM!!
Got too hot
WUMP
SHIRO-SAN WOULD LAY STRETCHED OUT IN THE HALLWAY.

← Next is about my parents' second cat, Tora-chan!

SECOND

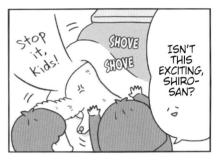

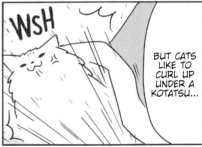

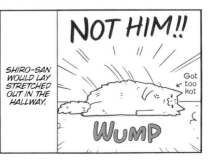

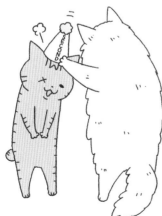

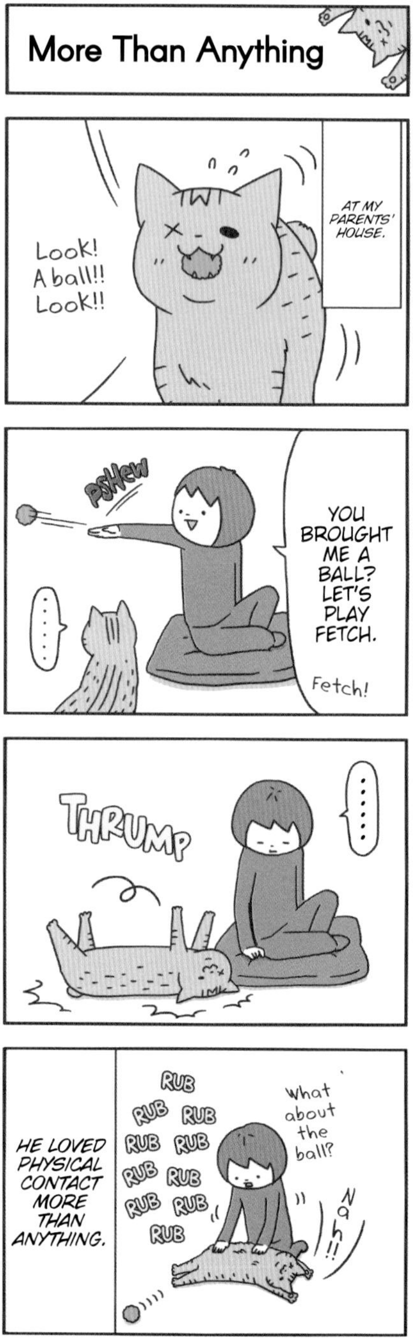
More Than Anything
AT MY PARENTS' HOUSE.
Look! A ball!! Look!!
YOU BROUGHT ME A BALL? LET'S PLAY FETCH.
Fetch!
PSHEW
......
THRUMP
......
What about the ball?
Nah!!
RUB
RUB
RUB
RUB
RUB
RUB
RUB
RUB
RUB
RUB
HE LOVED PHYSICAL CONTACT MORE THAN ANYTHING.

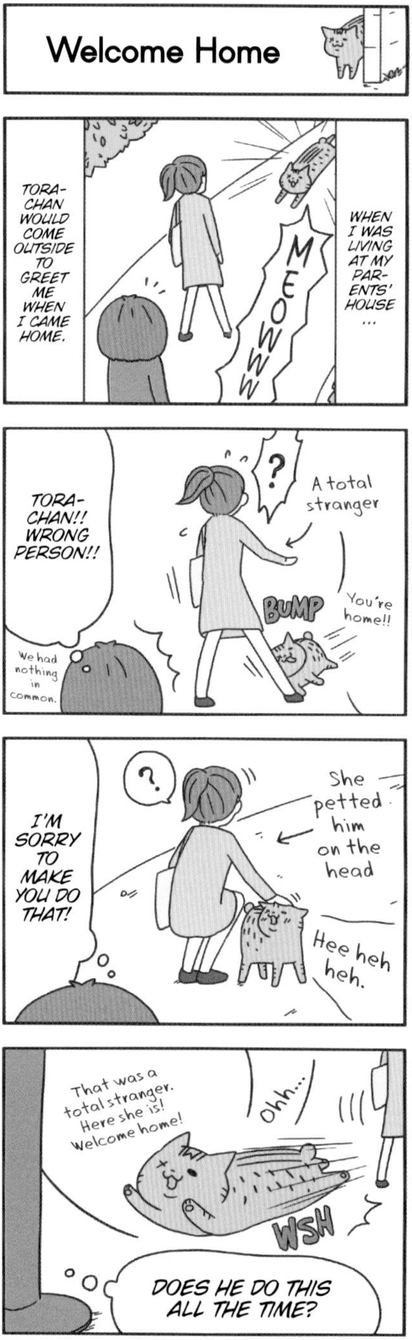
Welcome Home
WHEN I WAS LIVING AT MY PARENTS' HOUSE...
MEOWWW
TORA-CHAN WOULD COME OUTSIDE TO GREET ME WHEN I CAME HOME.
?
A total stranger
You're home!!
BUMP
TORA-CHAN!! WRONG PERSON!!
We had nothing in common.
?
She petted him on the head
Hee heh heh.
I'M SORRY TO MAKE YOU DO THAT!
Ohh...
That was a total stranger. Here she is! Welcome home!
WSH
DOES HE DO THIS ALL THE TIME?

The House Rule

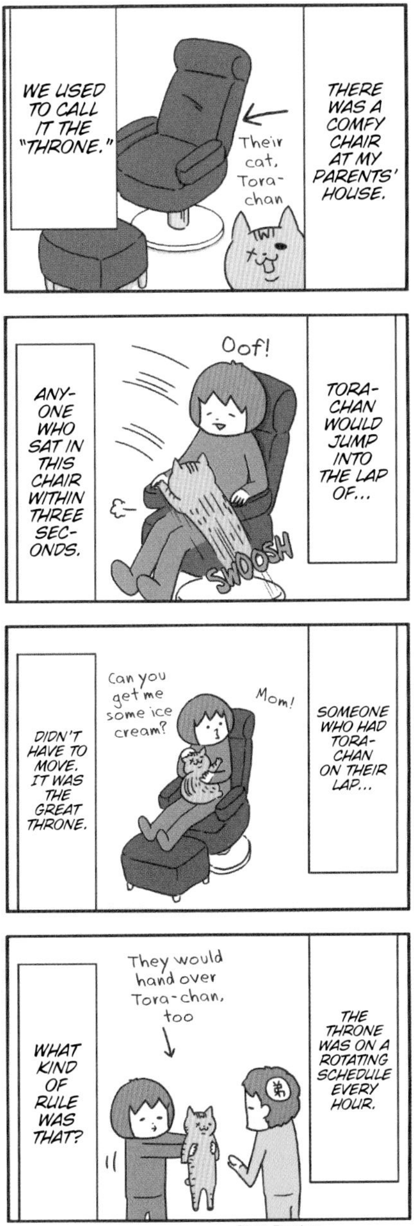
THERE WAS A COMFY CHAIR AT MY PARENTS' HOUSE.
Their cat, Tora-chan
WE USED TO CALL IT THE "THRONE."
TORA-CHAN WOULD JUMP INTO THE LAP OF...
Oof!
SWOOSH
ANYONE WHO SAT IN THIS CHAIR WITHIN THREE SECONDS.
SOMEONE WHO HAD TORA-CHAN ON THEIR LAP...
Mom!
Can you get me some ice cream?
DIDN'T HAVE TO MOVE. IT WAS THE GREAT THRONE.
THE THRONE WAS ON A ROTATING SCHEDULE EVERY HOUR.
They would hand over Tora-chan, too
弟
WHAT KIND OF RULE WAS THAT?

Sign: Brother

Impossible to Hate

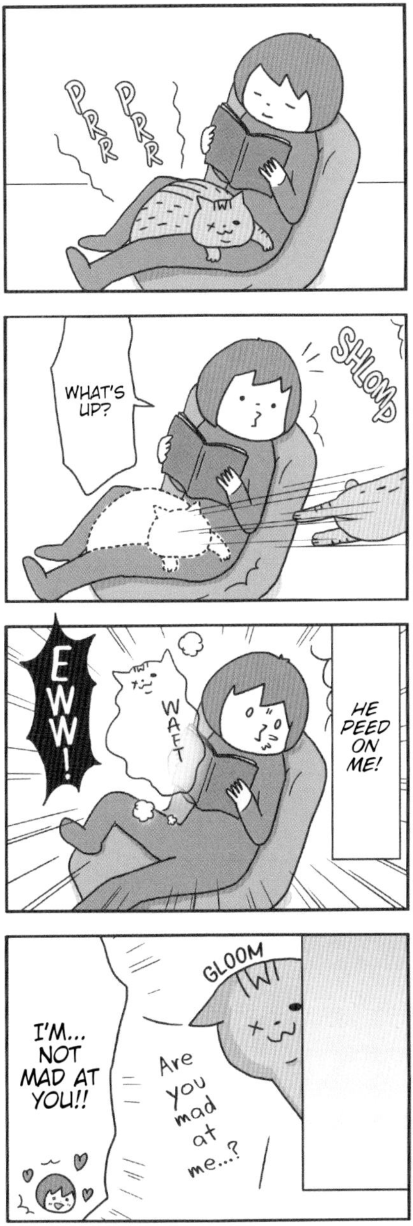
PRRR
PRRR
SHLOMP
WHAT'S UP?
HE PEED ON ME!
WAFT
EWW!
GLOOM
Are you mad at me...?
I'M... NOT MAD AT YOU!!

Tora-chan and My Dad

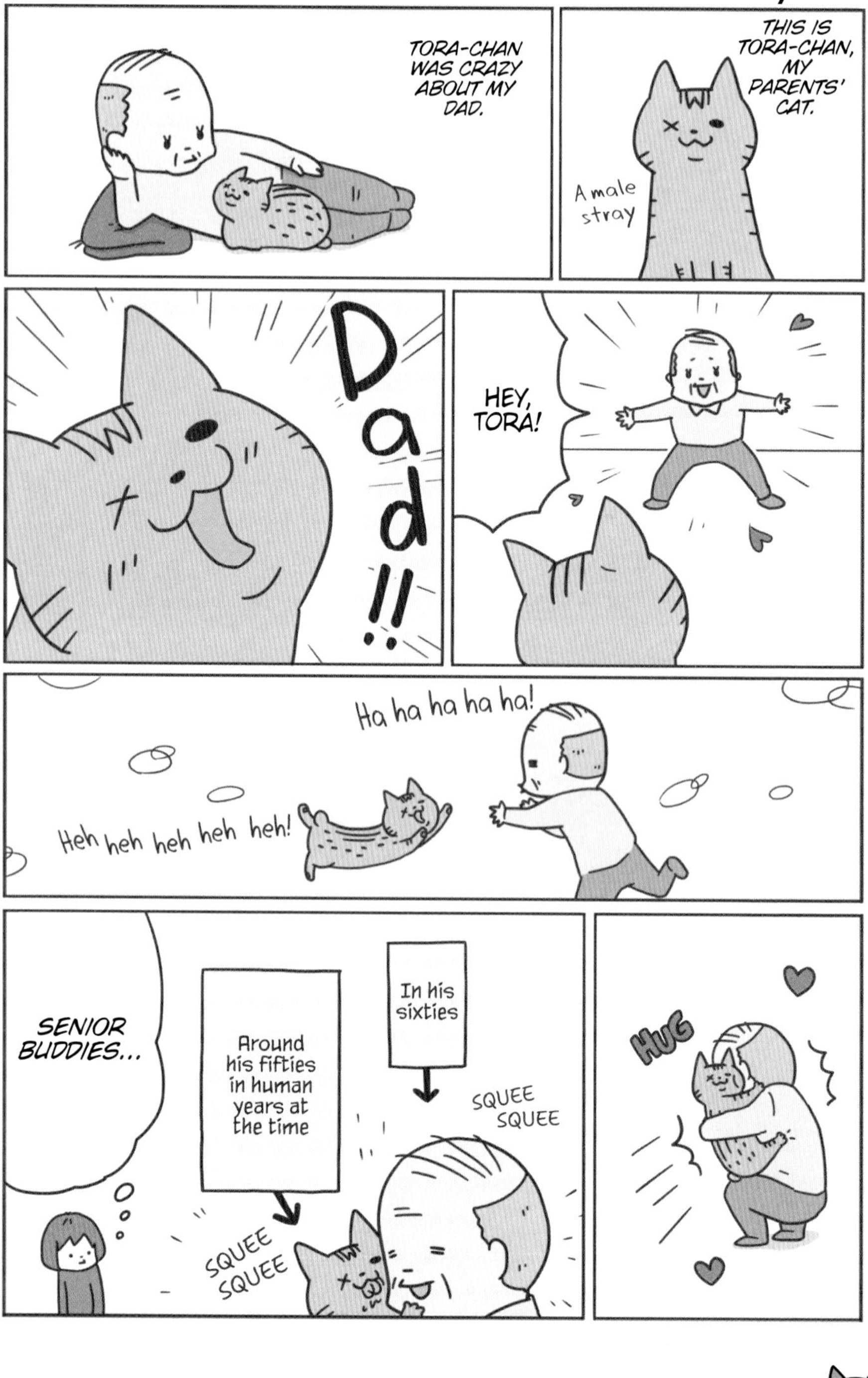
THIS IS TORA-CHAN, MY PARENTS' CAT.
A male stray
TORA-CHAN WAS CRAZY ABOUT MY DAD.
HEY, TORA!
Dad!!
Ha ha ha ha ha!
Heh heh heh heh heh!
HUG
In his sixties
SQUEE SQUEE
Around his fifties in human years at the time
SQUEE SQUEE
SENIOR BUDDIES...

Time, Place, and My Cat

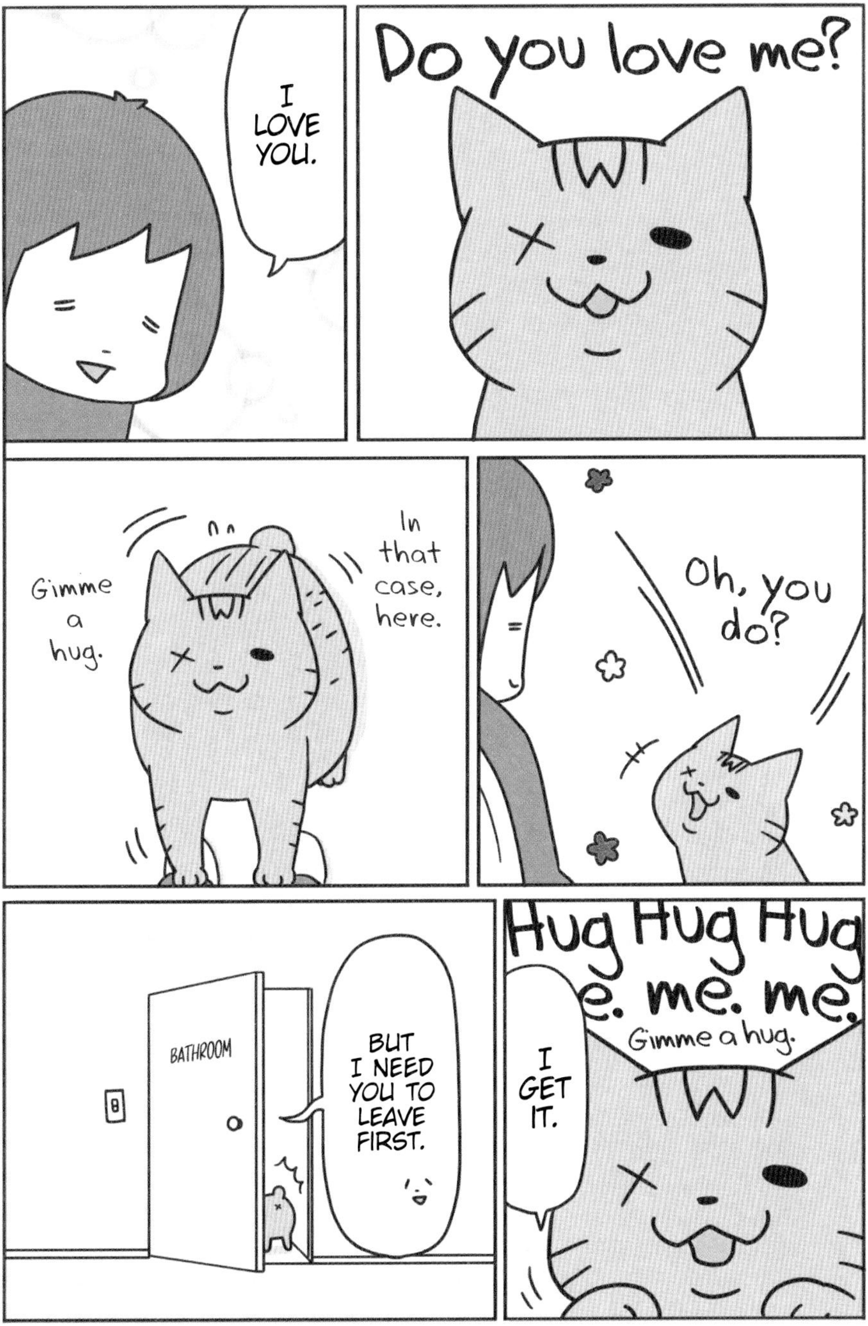
Do you love me?
I LOVE YOU.
Oh, you do?
In that case, here.
Gimme a hug.
Hug Hug Hug
e. me. me.
Gimme a hug.
I GET IT.
BUT I NEED YOU TO LEAVE FIRST.
BATHROOM

Dawn
AT DAWN AT MY PAR-ENTS' HOUSE...
SNORT
SNORT
WHAT'S THIS SOUND?
SNORT
SNORT
Snorting
Oh, you're awake!
Purring
PRRR
PRRR
PRRR
PRRR
Good morning! Good morning!
Uh, good morning... Pee-ew!
EXCITED
Here, smell my tooshie!
WHY DOES THIS HAVE TO HAPPEN TO ME?

These were the stories of my parents' cats!
See ya!!

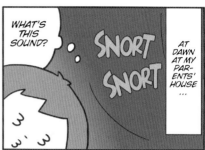

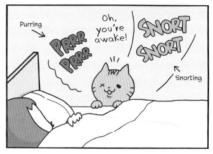

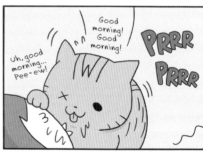

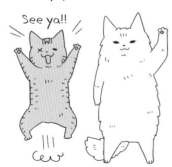

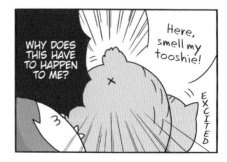

Chapter 7

Meeting My Cats

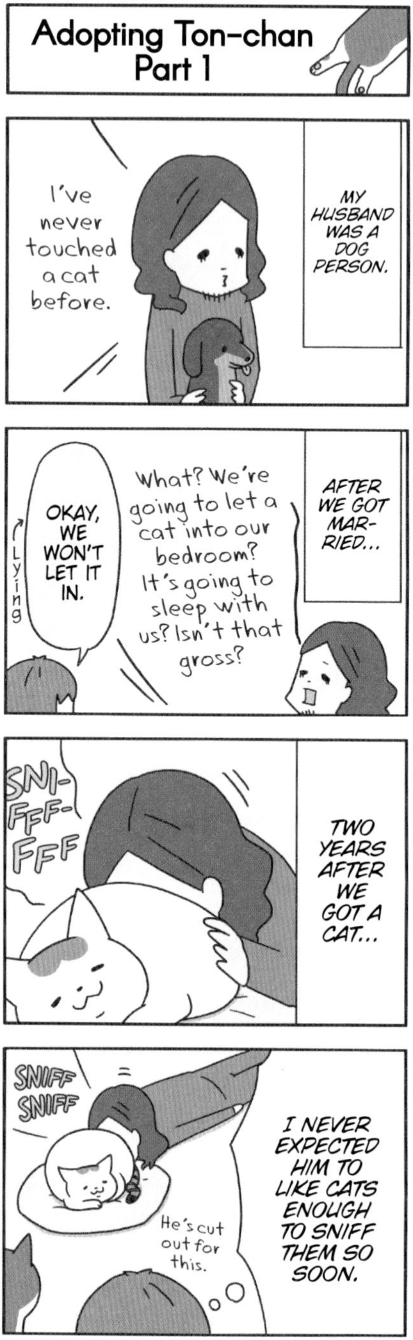
Adopting Ton-chan Part 1
MY HUSBAND WAS A DOG PERSON.
I've never touched a cat before.
AFTER WE GOT MAR-RIED...
What? We're going to let a cat into our bedroom? It's going to sleep with us? Isn't that gross?
OKAY, WE WON'T LET IT IN.
Lying
TWO YEARS AFTER WE GOT A CAT...
SNI-FFF-FFF
I NEVER EXPECTED HIM TO LIKE CATS ENOUGH TO SNIFF THEM SO SOON.
SNIFF SNIFF
He's cut out for this.

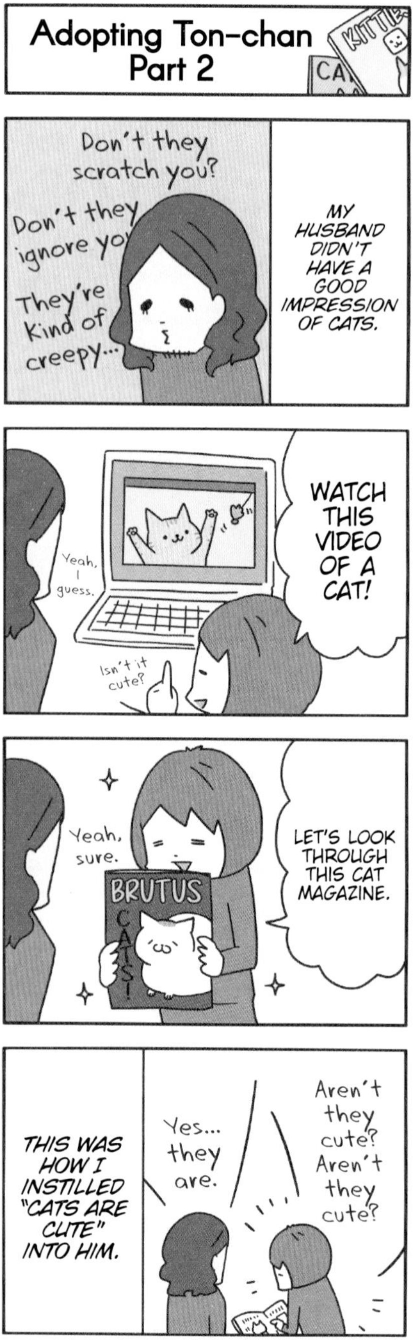
Adopting Ton-chan Part 2
MY HUSBAND DIDN'T HAVE A GOOD IMPRESSION OF CATS.
Don't they scratch you?
Don't they ignore yo
They're kind of creepy...
WATCH THIS VIDEO OF A CAT!
Yeah, I guess.
Isn't it cute?
LET'S LOOK THROUGH THIS CAT MAGAZINE.
Yeah, sure.
BRUTUS
CATS!
Aren't they cute? Aren't they cute?
Yes... they are.
THIS WAS HOW I INSTILLED "CATS ARE CUTE" INTO HIM.

Adopting Ton-chan Part 3

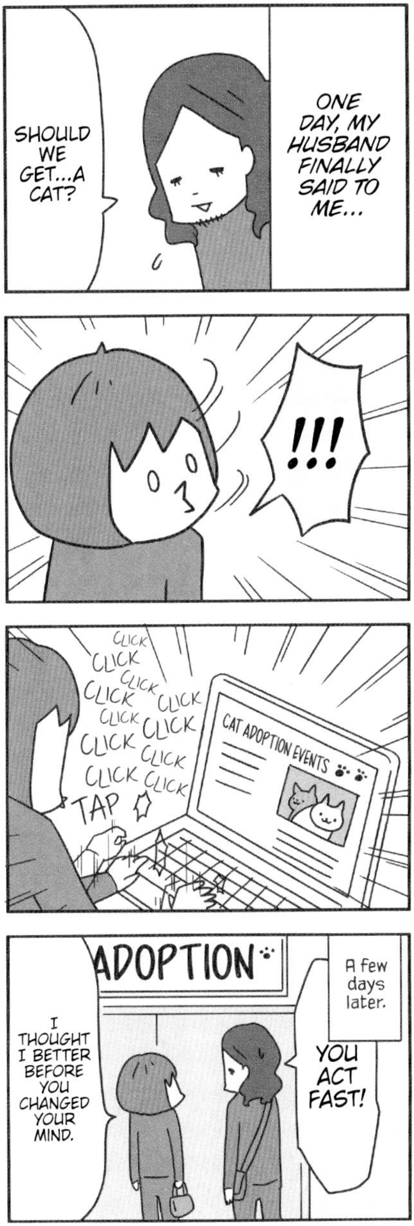
ONE DAY, MY HUSBAND FINALLY SAID TO ME...
SHOULD WE GET...A CAT?
!!!
CLICK CLICK CLICK CLICK CLICK CLICK CLICK CLICK CLICK CLICK CLICK
CAT ADOPTION EVENTS
TAP
ADOPTION
A few days later.
YOU ACT FAST!
I THOUGHT I BETTER BEFORE YOU CHANGED YOUR MIND.

Adopting Ton-chan Part 4

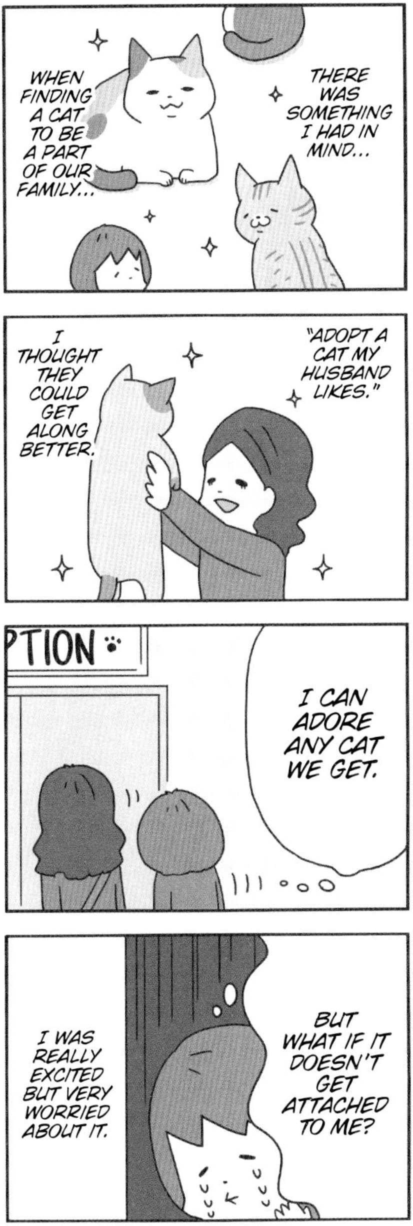
THERE WAS SOMETHING I HAD IN MIND...
WHEN FINDING A CAT TO BE A PART OF OUR FAMILY...
"ADOPT A CAT MY HUSBAND LIKES."
I THOUGHT THEY COULD GET ALONG BETTER.
PTION
I CAN ADORE ANY CAT WE GET.
BUT WHAT IF IT DOESN'T GET ATTACHED TO ME?
I WAS REALLY EXCITED BUT VERY WORRIED ABOUT IT.

Adopting Ton-chan Part 5

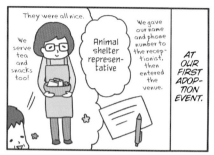

AT OUR FIRST ADOPTION EVENT.
We gave our name and phone number to the receptionist, then entered the venue.
Animal shelter representative
They were all nice.
We serve tea and snacks too!
THERE WERE ABOUT THIRTY CRATES IN THE RENTED SPACE.
Snacks
I KNOW IT'S OBVIOUS, BUT...
GLANCE
GLANCE
Who are you?
THIS IS NERVE-RACKING FOR ALL OF US.

We went there in the afternoon. More than half of the cats were already adopted.

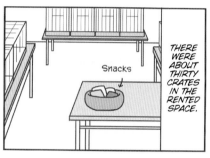

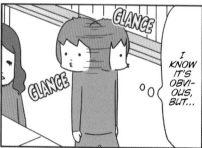

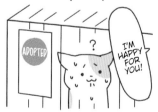

I'M HAPPY FOR YOU!
ADOPTED

You might have a better chance at finding a cat earlier in the day!

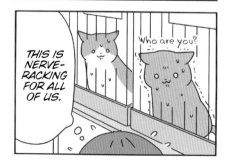

Adopting Ton-chan Part 6

At a venue

CATS

WE DIDN'T FIND A CAT AT THE FIRST ADOPTION EVENT. WE WENT TO ANOTHER ONE FOR A DIFFERENT SHELTER THE FOLLOWING WEEK.

THIS IS SO NERVE-RACK-ING.

They're all so cute.

THIS KITTEN SLEEPING WITH ITS BELLY OUT WOULD LATER BECOME OUR TON-CHAN.

Double take

This relaxed older cat was the most popular one that day.

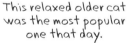

FUKUSUKE (TEMPORARY) 5 YEAR OLD, MALE 7KG

How cute!!

So ador-able!!

ZZZ

ZZZ

Aww!!

Adopting Ton-chan Part 7

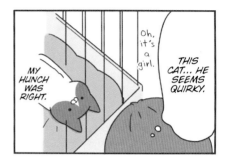

THIS CAT... HE SEEMS QUIRKY.
Oh, it's a girl.
MY HUNCH WAS RIGHT.
She's adorable!!
Yay! She likes you!
YAY!
WE INSTANTLY FELL IN LOVE WITH TON-CHAN AND STARTED THE ADOPTION PROCESS.
WE SUBMITTED THE APPLICATION WITH OUR IDENTIFICATION.
DRIVER'S LICENSE
APPLICATION
TAMAGOYAMA HUSBAND
TAMAKO
THEY SEEMED TO CONDUCT THOROUGH BACKGROUND CHECKS TO AVOID PET ADOPTION SCAMS AND ANIMAL ABUSE.
OUR APPLICATION GOT ACCEPTED, AND WE WERE SCHEDULED TO BRING TON-CHAN HOME A WEEK LATER.
We were so excited that we stared at the photo we took of her every day.

It didn't take us long to make the decision after we met her.

This was the photo of her that we stared at throughout the week.

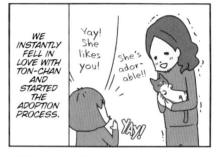

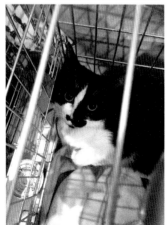

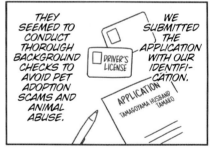

Adopting Ton-chan Part 8

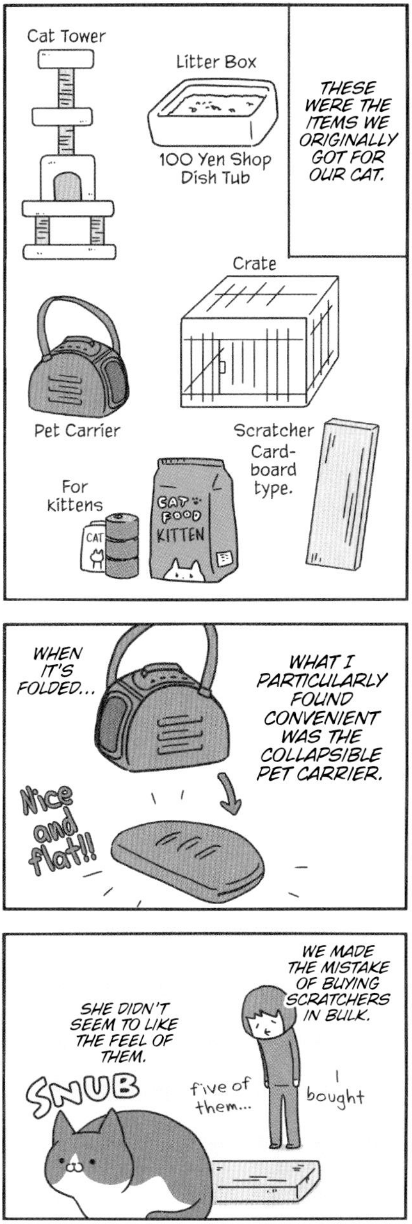
THESE WERE THE ITEMS WE ORIGINALLY GOT FOR OUR CAT.
Cat Tower
Litter Box
100 Yen Shop Dish Tub
Crate
Pet Carrier
Scratcher
Card-board type.
For kittens
CAT
CAT FOOD KITTEN
WHAT I PARTICULARLY FOUND CONVENIENT WAS THE COLLAPSIBLE PET CARRIER.
WHEN IT'S FOLDED...
Nice and flat!!
WE MADE THE MISTAKE OF BUYING SCRATCHERS IN BULK.
I bought
five of them...
SHE DIDN'T SEEM TO LIKE THE FEEL OF THEM.
SNUB

Adopting Ton-chan Part 9

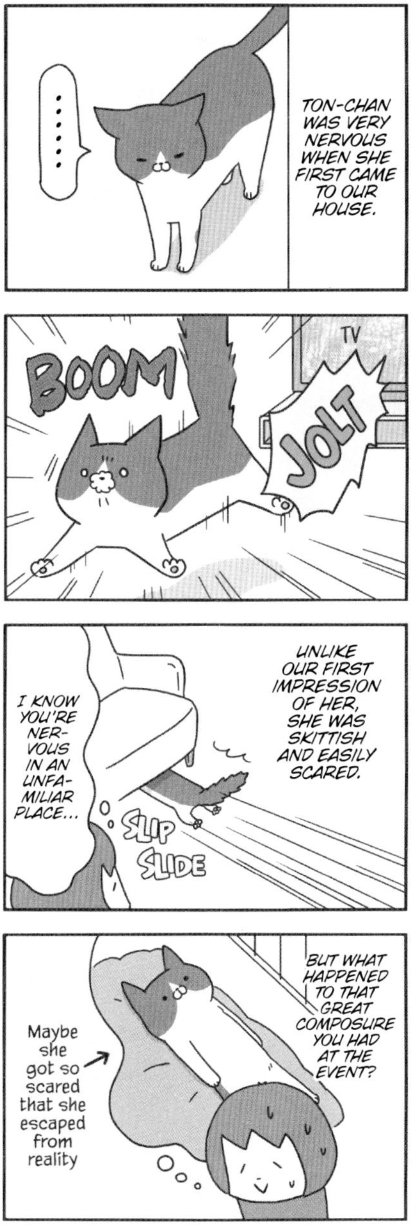
TON-CHAN WAS VERY NERVOUS WHEN SHE FIRST CAME TO OUR HOUSE.
......
TV
JOLT
BOOM
UNLIKE OUR FIRST IMPRESSION OF HER, SHE WAS SKITTISH AND EASILY SCARED.
I KNOW YOU'RE NERVOUS IN AN UNFAMILIAR PLACE...
SLIP SLIDE
BUT WHAT HAPPENED TO THAT GREAT COMPOSURE YOU HAD AT THE EVENT?
Maybe she got so scared that she escaped from reality

Adopting Ton-chan Part 10

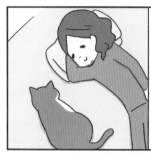

MY HUSBAND ADJUSTED TO LIVING WITH TON-CHAN SOONER THAN I EXPECTED.
TON-CHAN LOOKS HAPPY WHEN YOU PET HER.
Why is she showing me her butt?
SHE WANTS TO BE FRIENDS.
MY GULLIBLE HUSBAND, WHO WAS INCLINED TO BELIEVE THAT, SUCCESSFULLY BECAME THE CAT PERSON HE IS NOW.
Really?
Is this true?

I WOULD COMPLIMENT HIM TO GET HIM FIRED UP.
I think she likes you more than me. You're so lucky! Yay!!
YOU THINK SO? ...

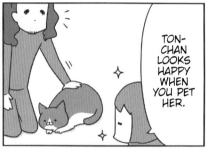

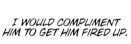

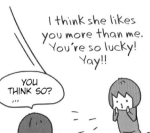

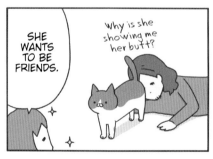

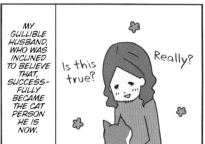

Meeting at the Adoption Event

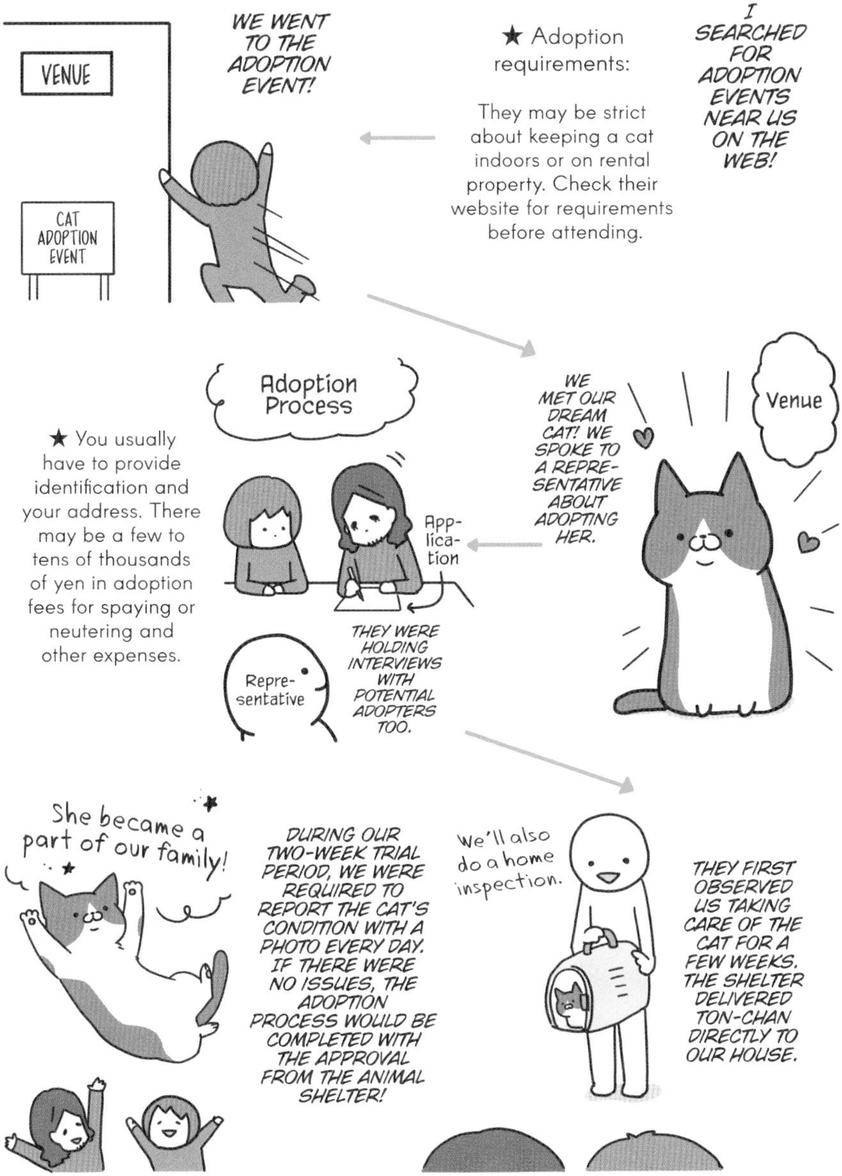
I SEARCHED FOR ADOPTION EVENTS NEAR US ON THE WEB!
★ Adoption requirements:
They may be strict about keeping a cat indoors or on rental property. Check their website for requirements before attending.
WE WENT TO THE ADOPTION EVENT!
VENUE
CAT ADOPTION EVENT
Venue
WE MET OUR DREAM CAT! WE SPOKE TO A REPRESENTATIVE ABOUT ADOPTING HER.
Application
Adoption Process
★ You usually have to provide identification and your address. There may be a few to tens of thousands of yen in adoption fees for spaying or neutering and other expenses.
THEY WERE HOLDING INTERVIEWS WITH POTENTIAL ADOPTERS TOO.
Representative
THEY FIRST OBSERVED US TAKING CARE OF THE CAT FOR A FEW WEEKS. THE SHELTER DELIVERED TON-CHAN DIRECTLY TO OUR HOUSE.
We'll also do a home inspection.
DURING OUR TWO-WEEK TRIAL PERIOD, WE WERE REQUIRED TO REPORT THE CAT'S CONDITION WITH A PHOTO EVERY DAY. IF THERE WERE NO ISSUES, THE ADOPTION PROCESS WOULD BE COMPLETED WITH THE APPROVAL FROM THE ANIMAL SHELTER!
She became a part of our family!

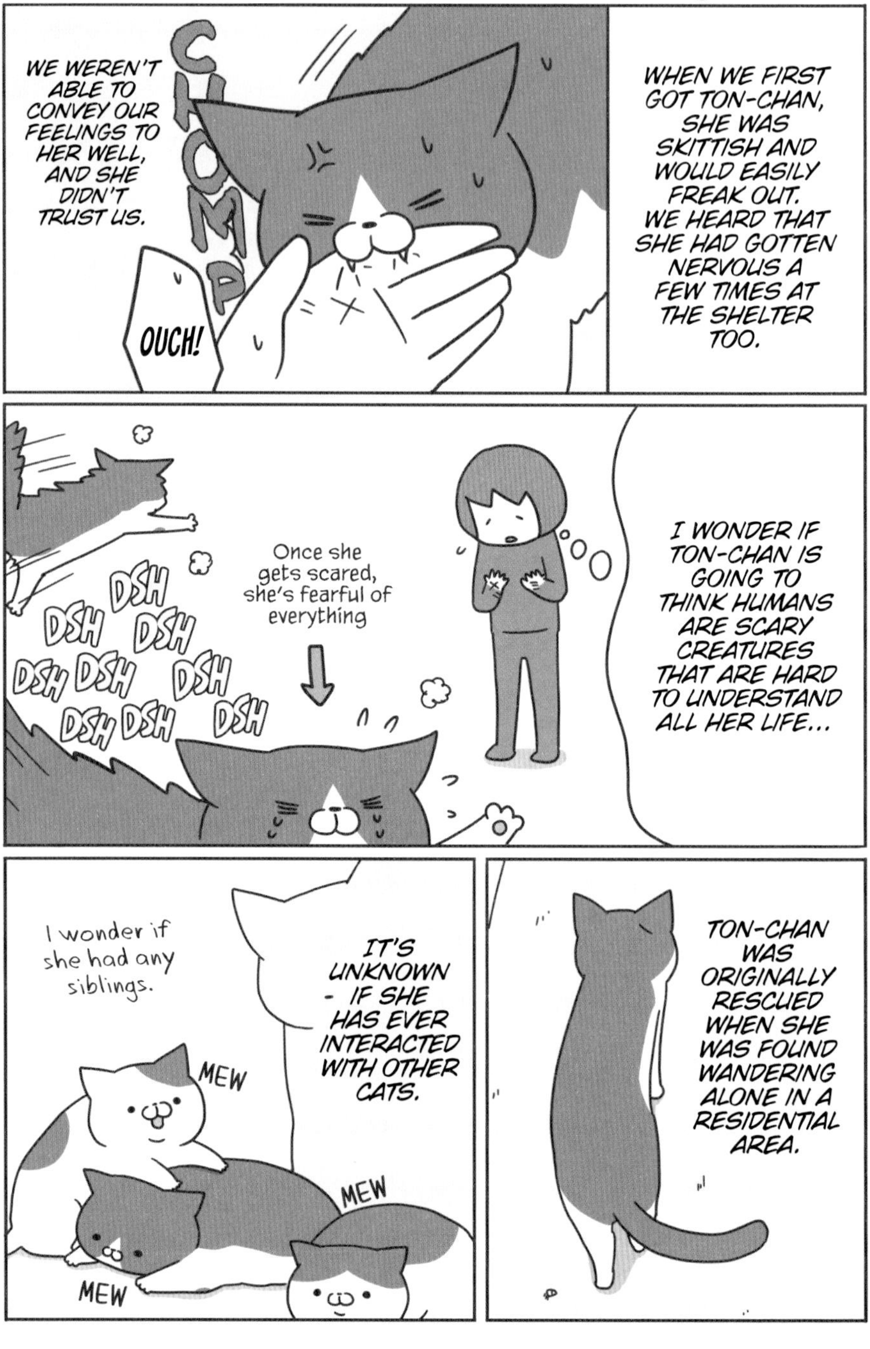
WHEN WE FIRST GOT TON-CHAN, SHE WAS SKITTISH AND WOULD EASILY FREAK OUT. WE HEARD THAT SHE HAD GOTTEN NERVOUS A FEW TIMES AT THE SHELTER TOO.
CHOMP
WE WEREN'T ABLE TO CONVEY OUR FEELINGS TO HER WELL, AND SHE DIDN'T TRUST US.
OUCH!
I WONDER IF TON-CHAN IS GOING TO THINK HUMANS ARE SCARY CREATURES THAT ARE HARD TO UNDERSTAND ALL HER LIFE...
Once she gets scared, she's fearful of everything
DSH DSH DSH DSH DSH DSH DSH DSH DSH
TON-CHAN WAS ORIGINALLY RESCUED WHEN SHE WAS FOUND WANDERING ALONE IN A RESIDENTIAL AREA.
IT'S UNKNOWN IF SHE HAS EVER INTERACTED WITH OTHER CATS.
I wonder if she had any siblings.
MEW
MEW
MEW

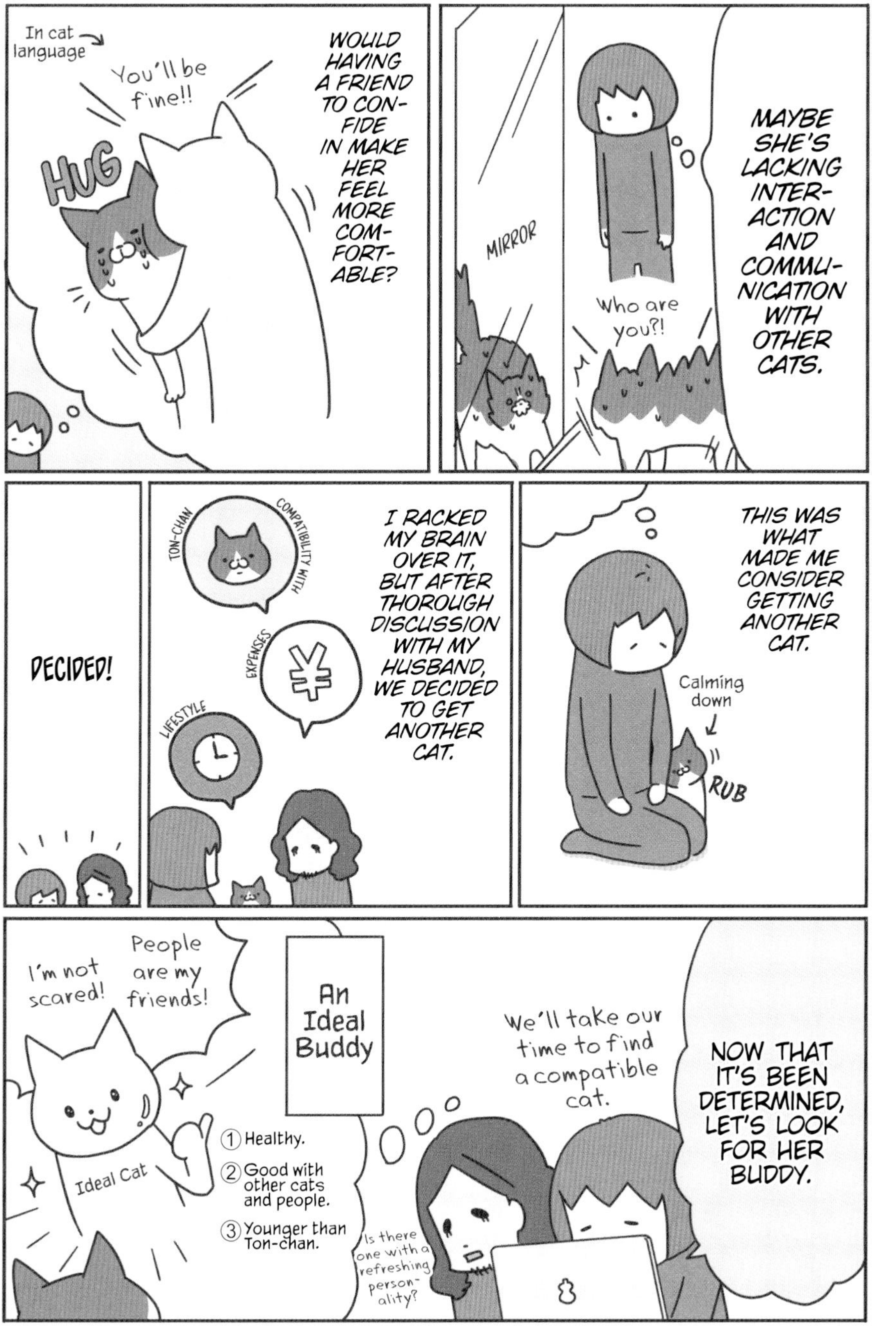

MAYBE SHE'S LACKING INTERACTION AND COMMUNICATION WITH OTHER CATS.
MIRROR
Who are you?!
WOULD HAVING A FRIEND TO CONFIDE IN MAKE HER FEEL MORE COMFORTABLE?
In cat language
You'll be fine!!
HUG
THIS WAS WHAT MADE ME CONSIDER GETTING ANOTHER CAT.
Calming down
RUB
I RACKED MY BRAIN OVER IT, BUT AFTER THOROUGH DISCUSSION WITH MY HUSBAND, WE DECIDED TO GET ANOTHER CAT.
COMPATIBILITY WITH TON-CHAN
EXPENSES
LIFESTYLE
DECIDED!
NOW THAT IT'S BEEN DETERMINED, LET'S LOOK FOR HER BUDDY.
We'll take our time to find a compatible cat.
Is there one with a refreshing personality?
An Ideal Buddy
① Healthy.
② Good with other cats and people.
③ Younger than Ton-chan.
Ideal Cat
People are my friends!
I'm not scared!

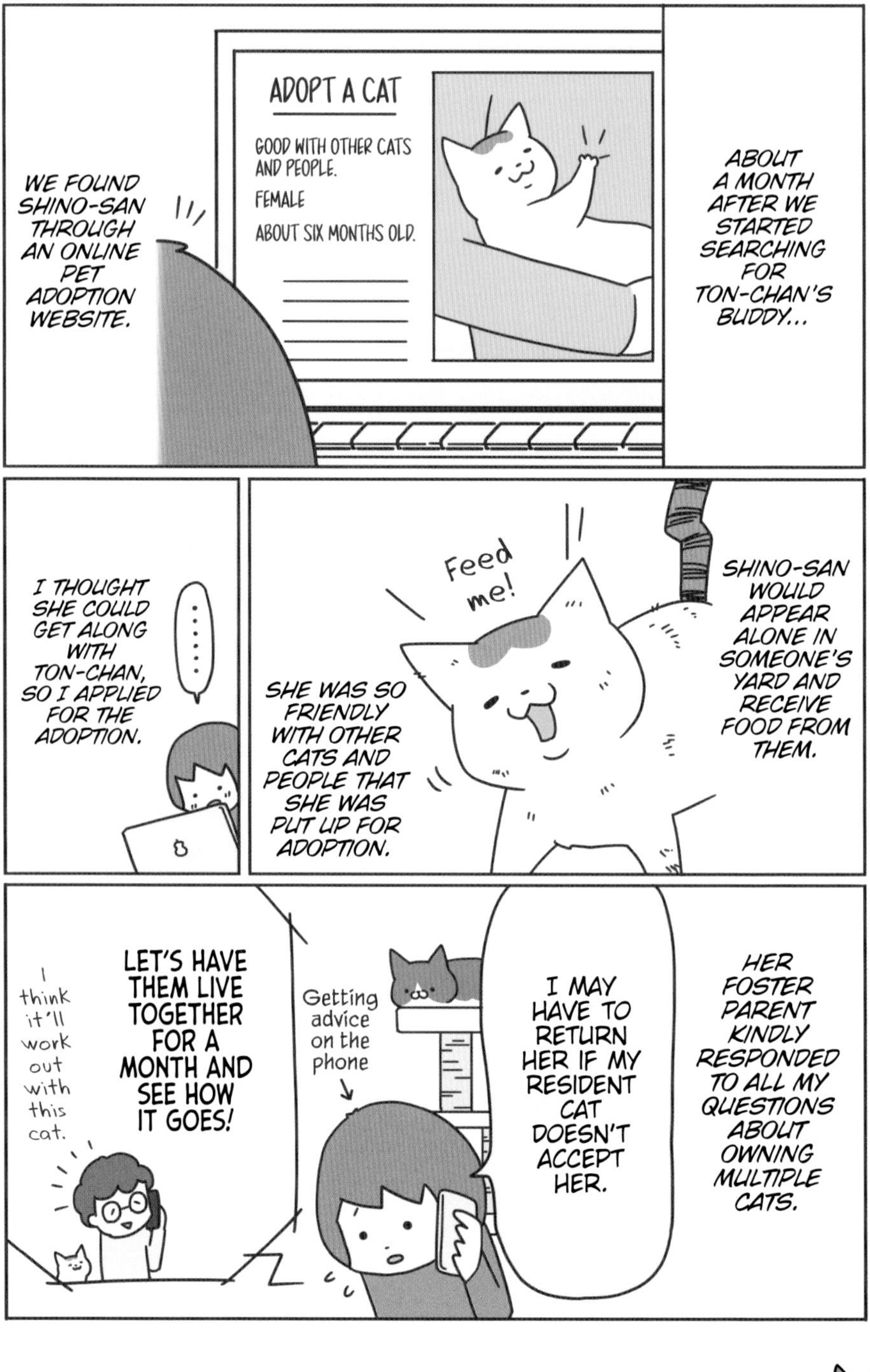
ABOUT A MONTH AFTER WE STARTED SEARCHING FOR TON-CHAN'S BUDDY...
ADOPT A CAT
GOOD WITH OTHER CATS AND PEOPLE.
FEMALE
ABOUT SIX MONTHS OLD.
WE FOUND SHINO-SAN THROUGH AN ONLINE PET ADOPTION WEBSITE.
SHINO-SAN WOULD APPEAR ALONE IN SOMEONE'S YARD AND RECEIVE FOOD FROM THEM.
Feed me!
SHE WAS SO FRIENDLY WITH OTHER CATS AND PEOPLE THAT SHE WAS PUT UP FOR ADOPTION.
......
I THOUGHT SHE COULD GET ALONG WITH TON-CHAN, SO I APPLIED FOR THE ADOPTION.
HER FOSTER PARENT KINDLY RESPONDED TO ALL MY QUESTIONS ABOUT OWNING MULTIPLE CATS.
I MAY HAVE TO RETURN HER IF MY RESIDENT CAT DOESN'T ACCEPT HER.
Getting advice on the phone
LET'S HAVE THEM LIVE TOGETHER FOR A MONTH AND SEE HOW IT GOES!
I think it'll work out with this cat.

Meeting through an Online Adoption Ad

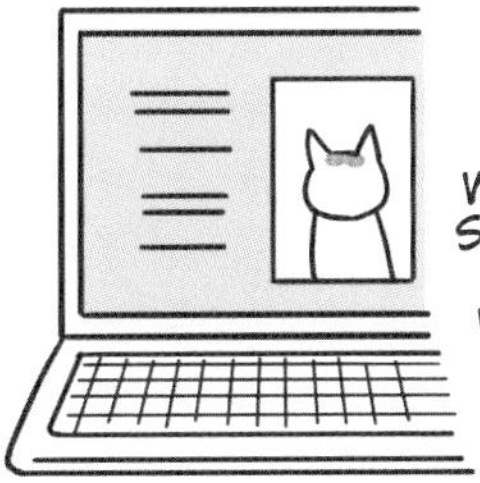

① WE FOUND SHINO-SAN ON A WEBSITE.

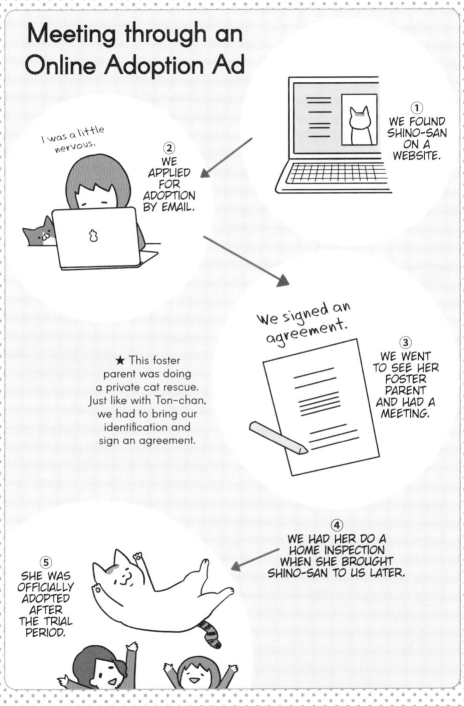

I was a little nervous.

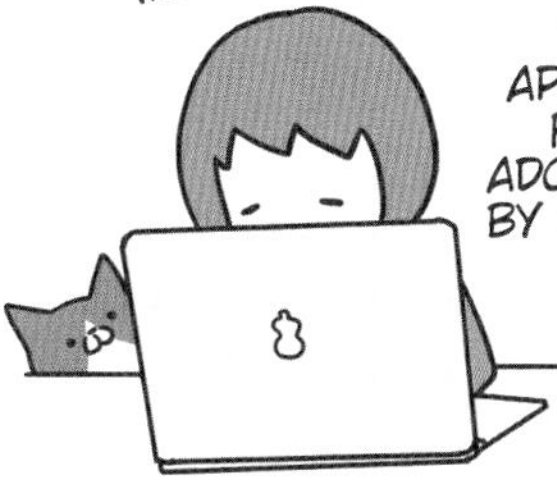

② WE APPLIED FOR ADOPTION BY EMAIL.

We signed an agreement.

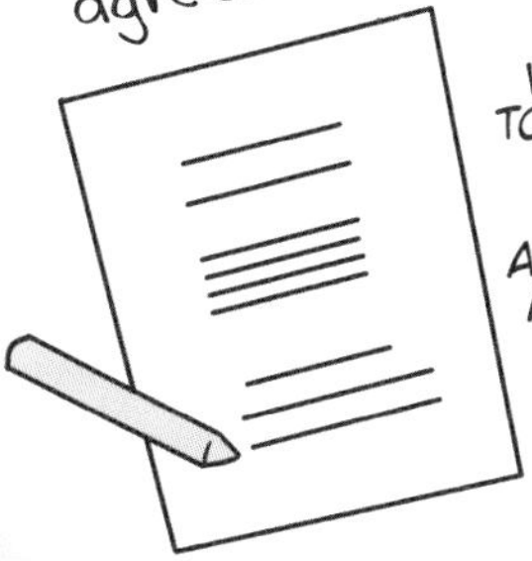

③ WE WENT TO SEE HER FOSTER PARENT AND HAD A MEETING.

★ This foster parent was doing a private cat rescue. Just like with Ton-chan, we had to bring our identification and sign an agreement.

④ WE HAD HER DO A HOME INSPECTION WHEN SHE BROUGHT SHINO-SAN TO US LATER.

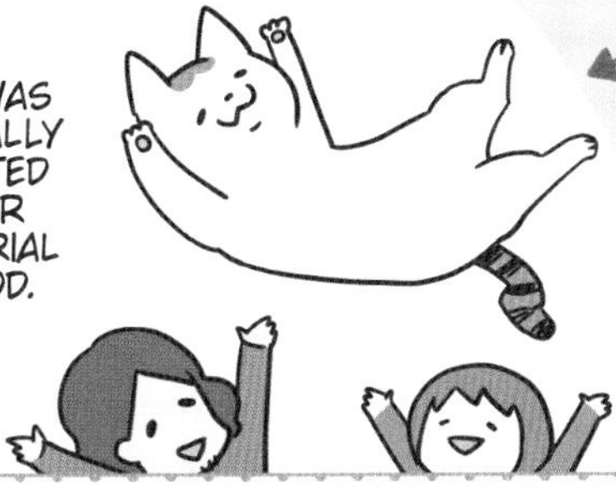

⑤ SHE WAS OFFICIALLY ADOPTED AFTER THE TRIAL PERIOD.

Meeting Shino-san Part 1

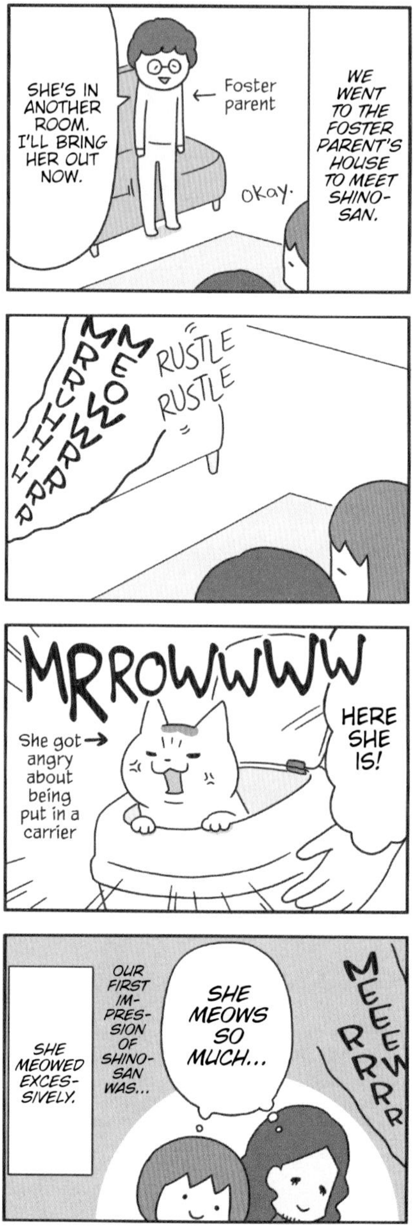
WE WENT TO THE FOSTER PARENT'S HOUSE TO MEET SHINO-SAN.
Foster parent
SHE'S IN ANOTHER ROOM. I'LL BRING HER OUT NOW.
okay.
RUSTLE RUSTLE
MMEOWW
MRRWRRR
HERE SHE IS!
MRROWWWW
She got angry about being put in a carrier
MEEEW
RRRR
SHE MEOWS SO MUCH...
OUR FIRST IM-PRES-SION OF SHINO-SAN WAS...
SHE MEOWED EXCES-SIVELY.

Meeting Shino-san Part 2

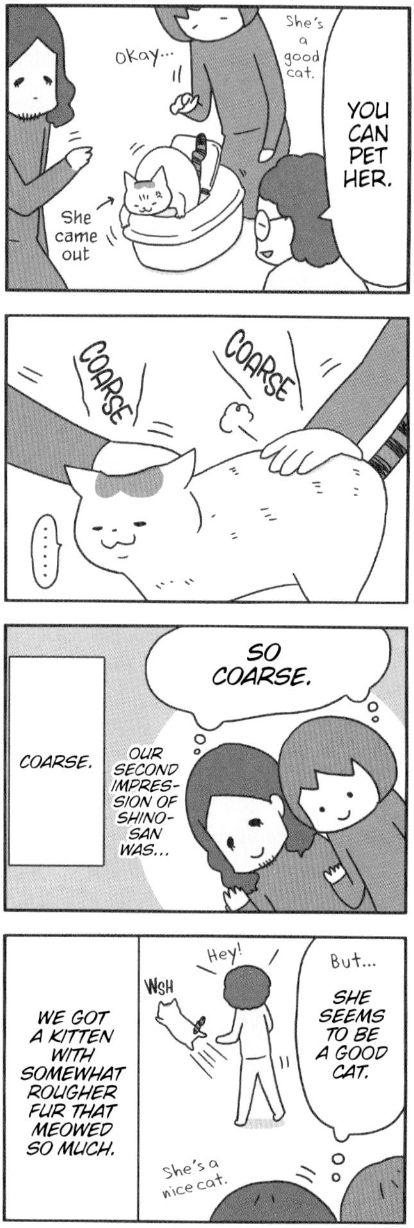
YOU CAN PET HER.
She's a good cat.
okay...
She came out
COARSE
COARSE
....
SO COARSE.
OUR SECOND IMPRES-SION OF SHINO-SAN WAS...
COARSE.
But...
SHE SEEMS TO BE A GOOD CAT.
Hey!
WSH
She's a nice cat.
WE GOT A KITTEN WITH SOMEWHAT ROUGHER FUR THAT MEOWED SO MUCH.

Living With Shino-san Part 1

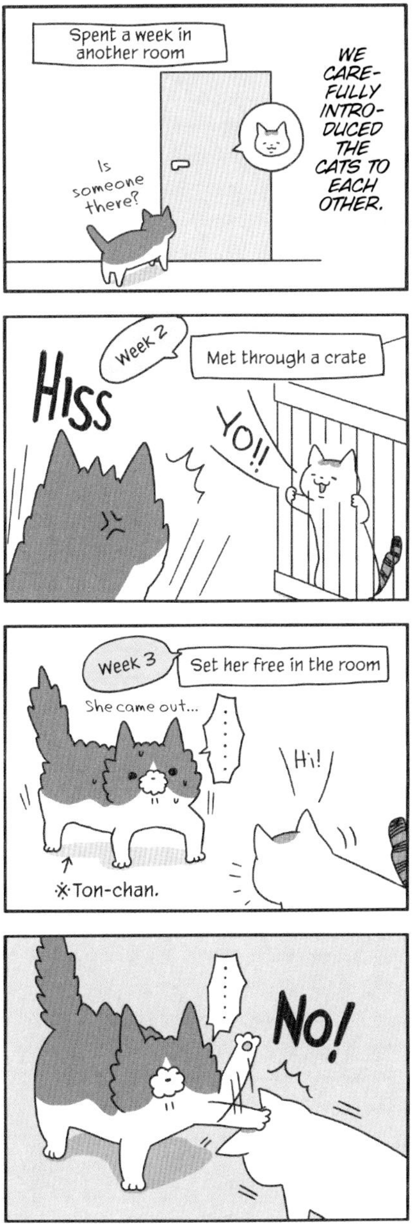
WE CAREFULLY INTRODUCED THE CATS TO EACH OTHER.
Spent a week in another room
Is someone there?
Met through a crate
Week 2
HISS
YO!!
Set her free in the room
Week 3
Hi!
She came out...
※Ton-chan.
NO!

They didn't try to hurt each other, but we were nervous as we watched them.

Living With Shino-san Part 2

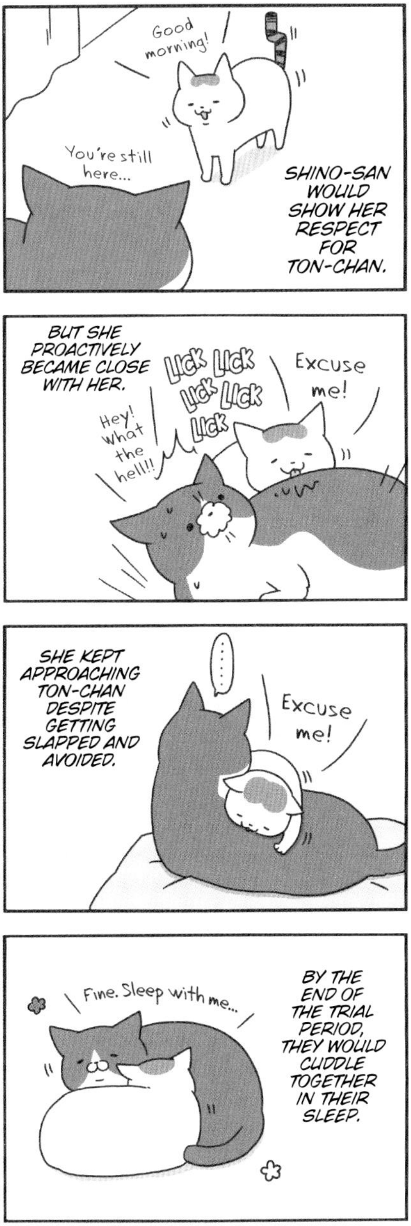
Good morning!
SHINO-SAN WOULD SHOW HER RESPECT FOR TON-CHAN.
You're still here...
Excuse me!
LICK LICK LICK LICK LICK
BUT SHE PROACTIVELY BECAME CLOSE WITH HER.
Hey! what the hell!!
Excuse me!
SHE KEPT APPROACHING TON-CHAN DESPITE GETTING SLAPPED AND AVOIDED.
BY THE END OF THE TRIAL PERIOD, THEY WOULD CUDDLE TOGETHER IN THEIR SLEEP.
Fine. Sleep with me...

Ton-chan's Development Part 1

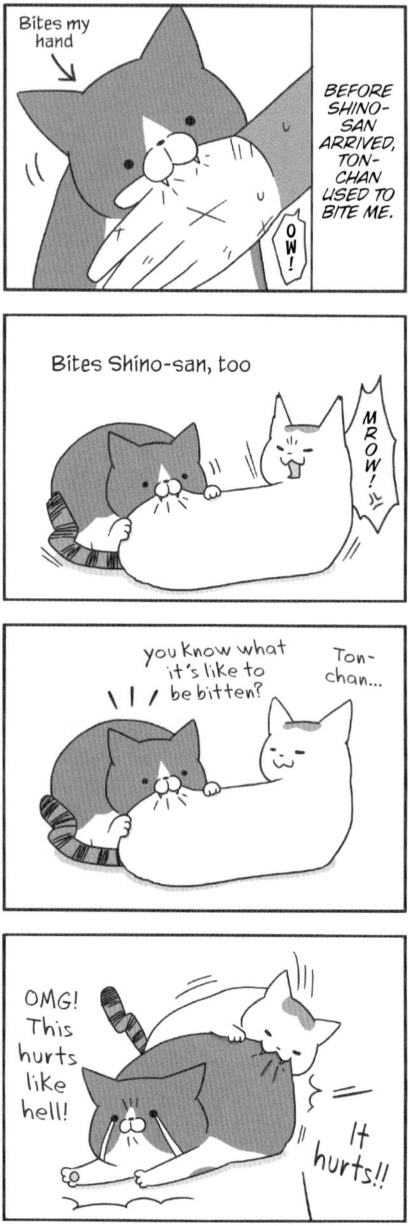

BEFORE SHINO-SAN ARRIVED, TON-CHAN USED TO BITE ME.
Bites my hand
OW!
Bites Shino-san, too
MROW!
Ton-chan...
you know what it's like to be bitten?
OMG! This hurts like hell!
It hurts!!

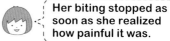

Her biting stopped as soon as she realized how painful it was.

Ton-chan's Development Part 2

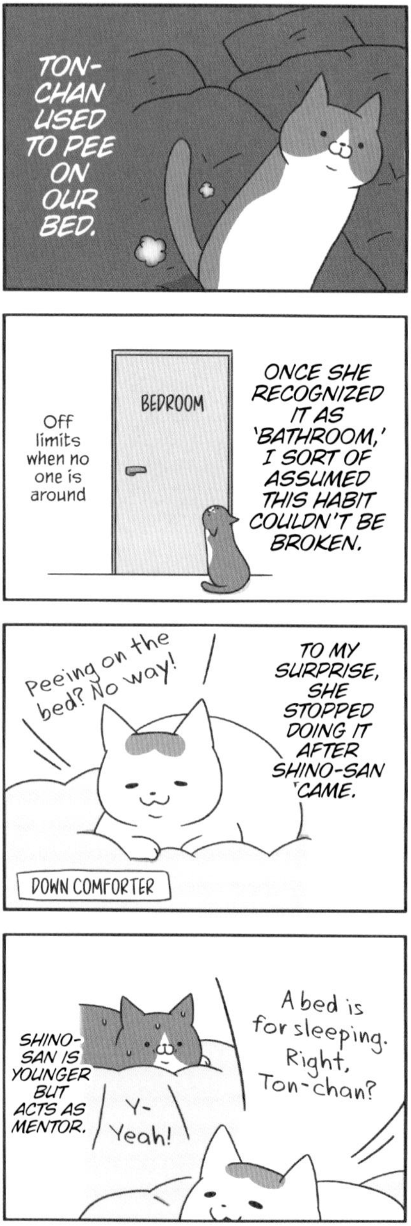

TON-CHAN USED TO PEE ON OUR BED.
ONCE SHE RECOGNIZED IT AS 'BATHROOM,' I SORT OF ASSUMED THIS HABIT COULDN'T BE BROKEN.
BEDROOM
Off limits when no one is around
TO MY SURPRISE, SHE STOPPED DOING IT AFTER SHINO-SAN CAME.
Peeing on the bed? No way!
DOWN COMFORTER
A bed is for sleeping. Right, Ton-chan?
SHINO-SAN IS YOUNGER BUT ACTS AS MENTOR.
Y-Yeah!

My Cats Today

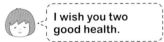

ZONED OUT
...
EVER SINCE SHINO-SAN CAME TO LIVE WITH US, TON-CHAN BECAME EXTREMELY CALM AND STOPPED PANICKING.
THE TON-CHAN I SEE NOW MUST BE HER TRUE SELF.
RUB
RUB
RUB
RUB
RUB
Let's sleep together.
No thanks!
SHINO-SAN IS CRAZY FOR TON-CHAN AS USUAL.
Oh, come on!
Urghh!
I FEEL LIKE SHE TREATS HER MORE POORLY THAN EVER BEFORE.

Thank you Shino-san for not giving up on loving the grumpy Ton-chan.

I wish you two good health.

Ton-chan's Full Name

WHEN WE WERE CONTEMPLATING TON-CHAN'S NAME...
This facial marking
THAT LOOKS POINTY.
TON-GARI-CHAN.
TON-CHAN'S FULL NAME IS TONGARI-CHAN.*
IT'S TON-CHAN FOR SHORT.
......
Ton-chaaan!
THIS STRANGE CAT WITH A WEIRD NAME HAS GROWN UP WITHOUT EVER GETTING A COLD.
ZZZ
ZZZ

*Tongari means "pointy."

THERE WERE TIMES WE WISHED WE HAD GIVEN HER A GIRLIER NAME...
NOM
NOM
NOM
NOM
BUT "TON-CHAN" SUITS HER THE BEST.

Shino-san's Full Name

WHEN WE WERE PONDERING OVER SHINO-SAN'S NAME...
LET'S SAY WHATEVER COMES TO OUR MINDS.
HOW ABOUT "CENTER" FOR CENTER PART--
REJECTED!
"HANNYAN" FOR MAKING THE DEMON FACE WHEN SHE MEOWS--
REJECTED!
MROW
AFTER A PROLONGED DEBATE, WE NAMED HER SHINONOME, FOR HER SUNNY DISPOSITION AND THE SKY AT DAWN REPRESENTED BY THE CLOUD-LIKE MARKING ON HER HEAD.
Her full name is
Shinonome
Shino-san for short.

WE OFTEN GET COMPLIMENTED THAT "SHINO-SAN" FITS HER PROFILE.
We use the honorific -san for her even though she's younger.
I'M GLAD WE DIDN'T END UP PICKING CENTER OR HANNYAN.

Ton-chan as a Kitten

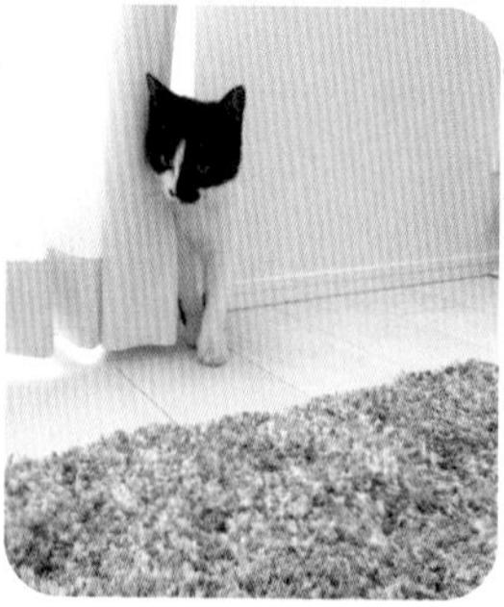

The day Ton-chan came to our house, she was hiding behind the curtain.

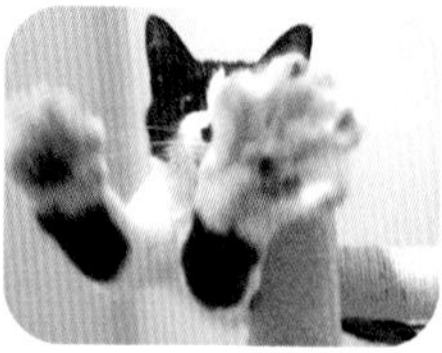

A bonus peek at her paw pad.

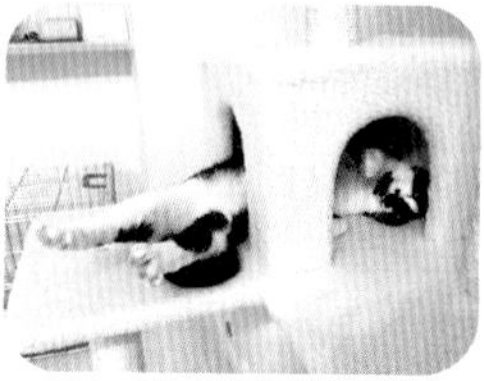

Now she fills up this box section whenever she sleeps in it.

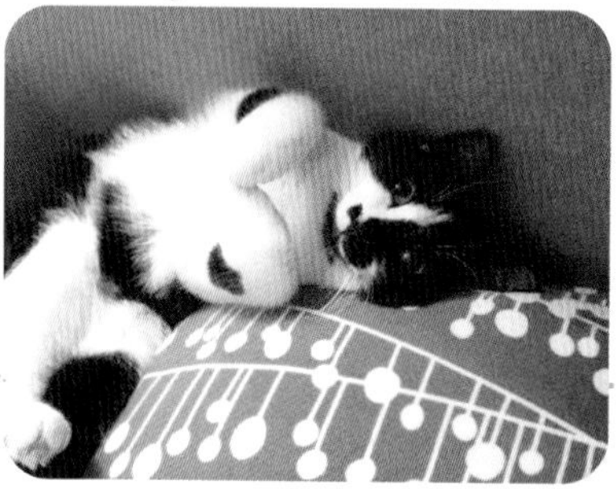

She was sucking up to me here. Her cuteness makes my heart throb.

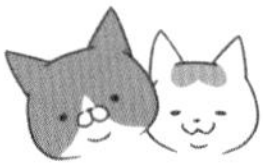

Memories of Ton and Shino

Shino-san as a Kitten

She was serious at playing and very speedy.

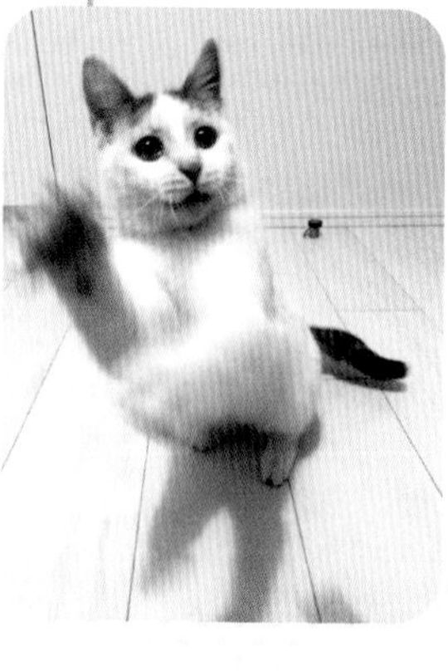

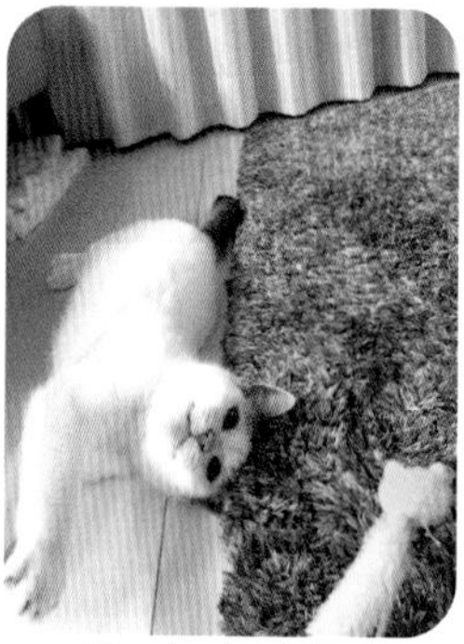

She looked like a kitten when she hunted prey.

She calms down when my husband holds her.

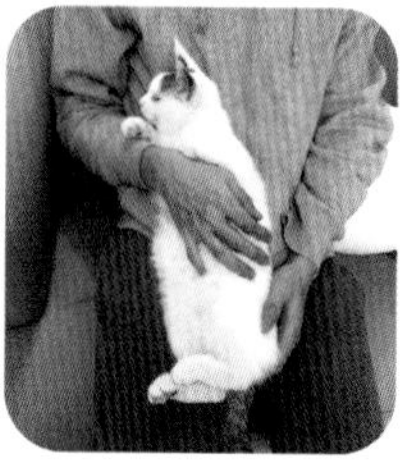

She acted wilder back then.

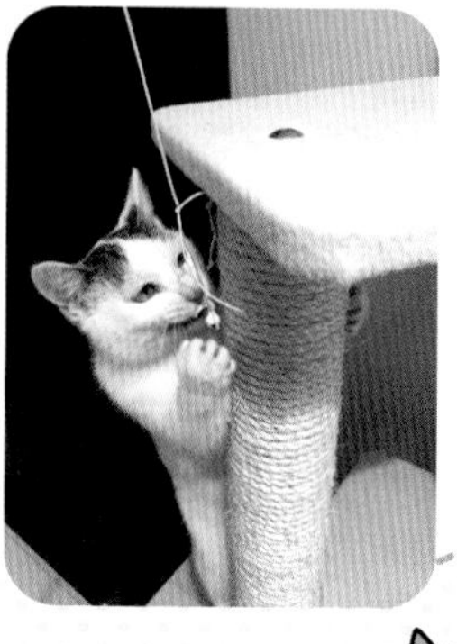

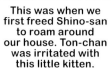

When Shino-san First Arrived

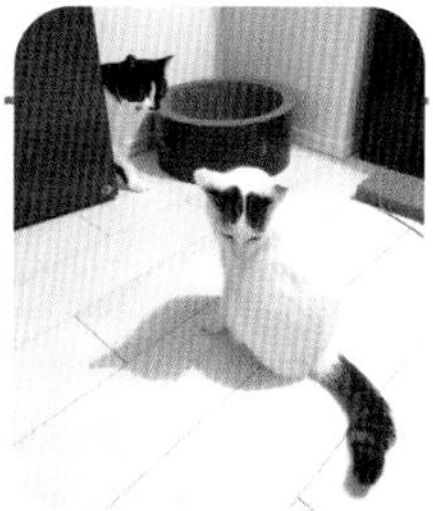

This was when we first freed Shino-san to roam around our house. Ton-chan was irritated with this little kitten.

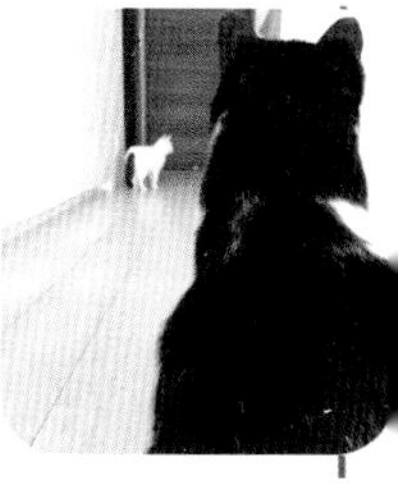

They weren't that close yet, but Ton-chan determined Shino-san was harmless.

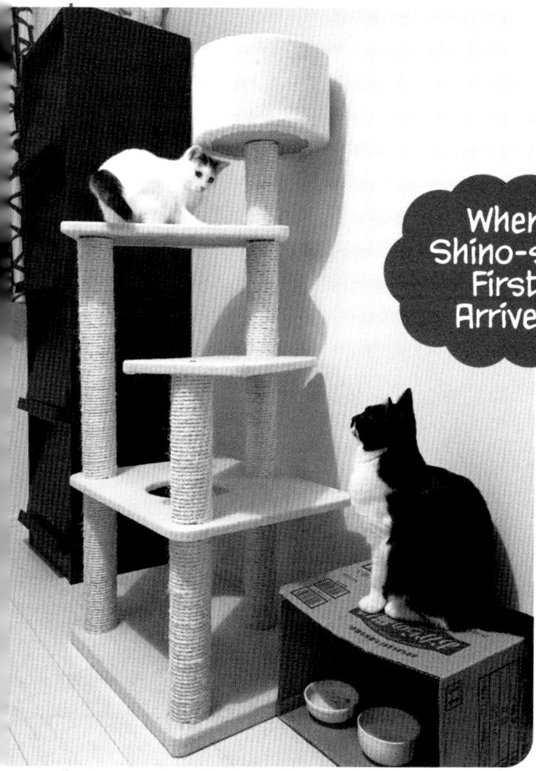

Ton-chan was watching Shino-san. She was anxious.

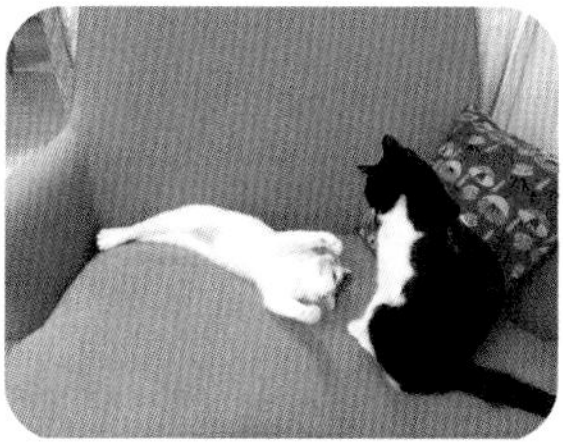

Shino-san isn't scared of other cats. Ton-chan gets annoyed but doesn't push her away anymore.

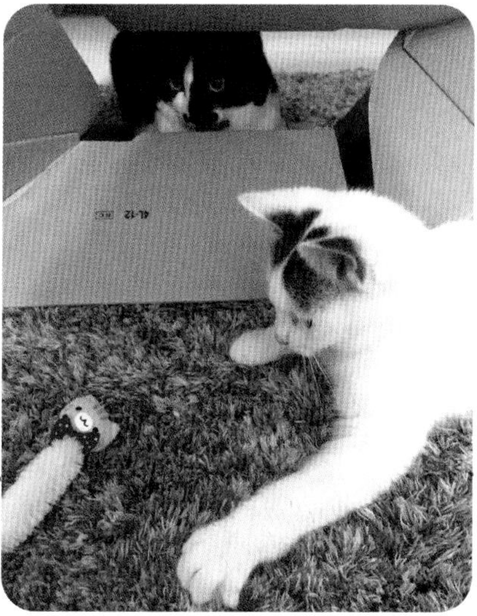

Shino-san was playing with Ton-chan to get closer with her. Ton-chan nervously approached the toy.

My Cats Today

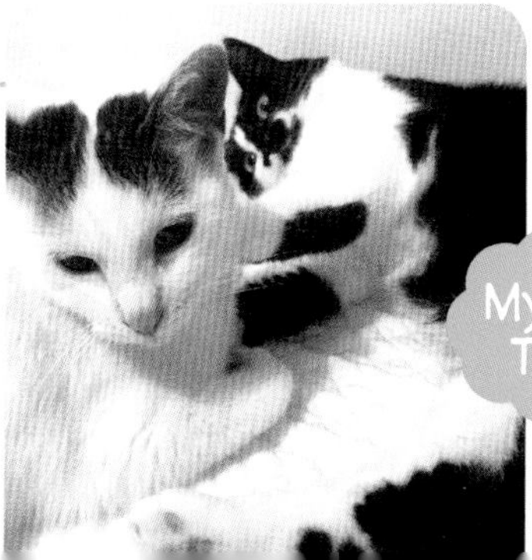

Occasional Play
<Shiro-san Version>

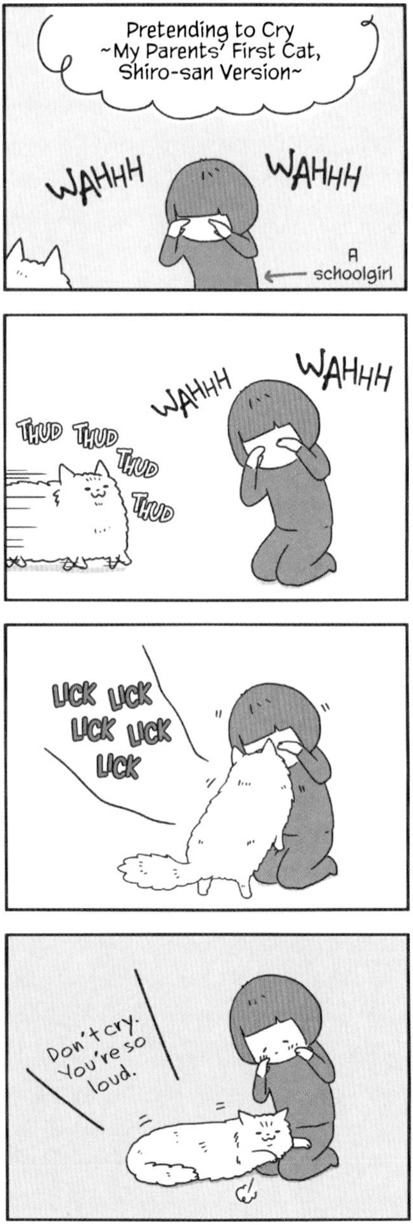
Pretending to Cry
~My Parents' First Cat, Shiro-san Version~
WAHHH
WAHHH
A schoolgirl
WAHHH
WAHHH
THUD THUD
THUD
THUD
LICK LICK
LICK LICK
LICK
Don't cry. You're so loud.

Occasional Play
<Tora-chan Version>

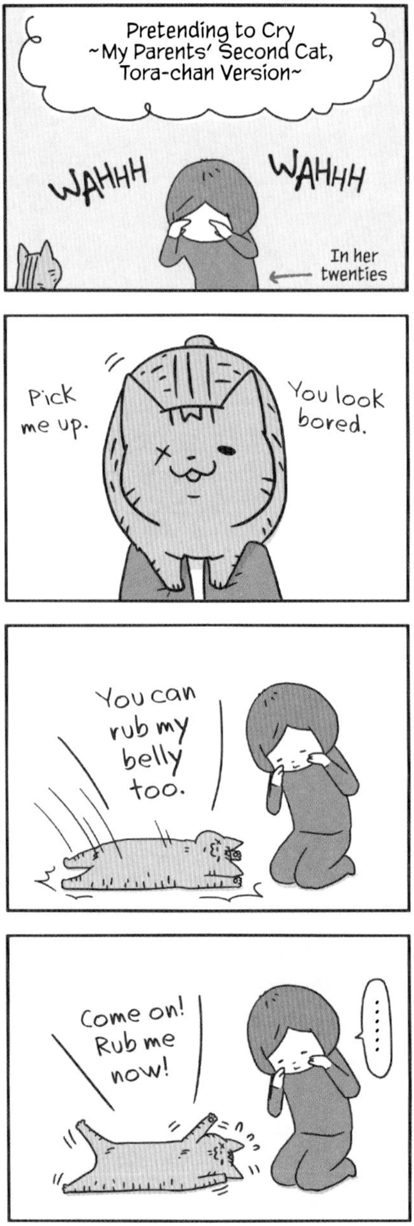
Pretending to Cry
~My Parents' Second Cat, Tora-chan Version~
WAHHH
WAHHH
In her twenties
You look bored.
Pick me up.
You can rub my belly too.
......
Come on! Rub me now!

Occasional Play
<Ton & Shino Version>

Pretending to Cry ~Ton-chan & Shino-san Version~
WAHHH
WAHHH
What the heck? Creepy!
WHISPER
WHISPER
Let's get out of here.
WHISPER
WHISPER

Their reactions are completely different, but they're all cute. Cats are great.

Kindness Ranking

1
2
3

 **afterword**

Thank you for reading this book all the way to the end.

I've always loved cats and manga since I was little, so I'm thrilled to have my cat manga published.

The difficulty in verbally showcasing the funny and cute things my cats do is what ultimately made me consider creating a manga about cats. Just as the title suggests, most of my manga covers the strange things my cats do, but I receive many comments from the readers through social media and my blog that they're common or that their cats act in similar ways.

Maybe these peculiar behaviors of my cats are universal in other countries.

I think my cats will continue to do odd things, which I want to portray in my manga.

I would like to give my deepest thanks to my editor, Shirakawa-san, who gave me many opportunities and advice; my designer, Chiba-san, who crafted such a cute binding; my desktop publishing manager, Ogawa-san; Yamamoto-san, who helped me create the manga; my husband, who is always supporting me; and most importantly, everyone who adores and cheers for Ton-chan and Shino-san.

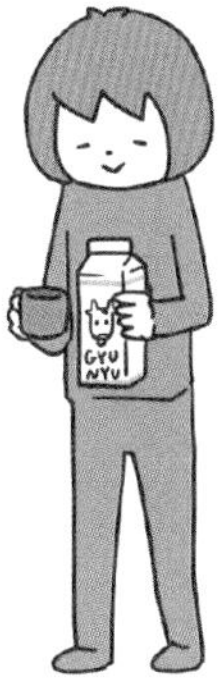
GYU NYU

Tamako Tamagoyama
February 2016

 SPECIAL THANKS

Pinch-Hitter
Airi Yamamoto

 STAFF

Book Design
Itsuko Chiba
(An-Butter Office)

Desktop Publisher
Takuya Ogawa
(Kokageya)

Proofreader
Etsuko Saiki

Sales
Mizuho Kobayashi

Chief Editor
Noriko Matsuda

Editor
Keigo Shiragawa

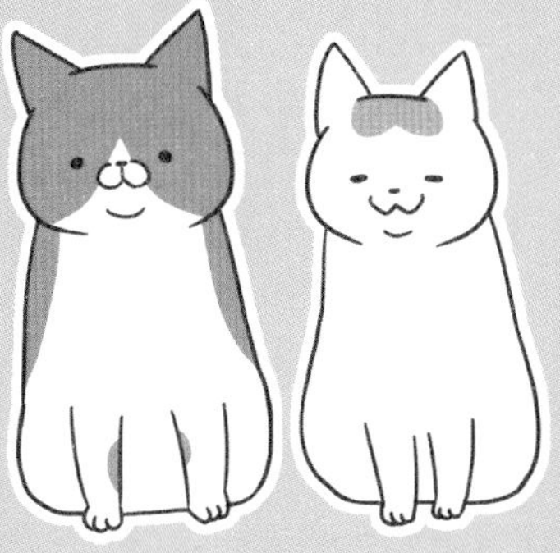

Ton & Shino

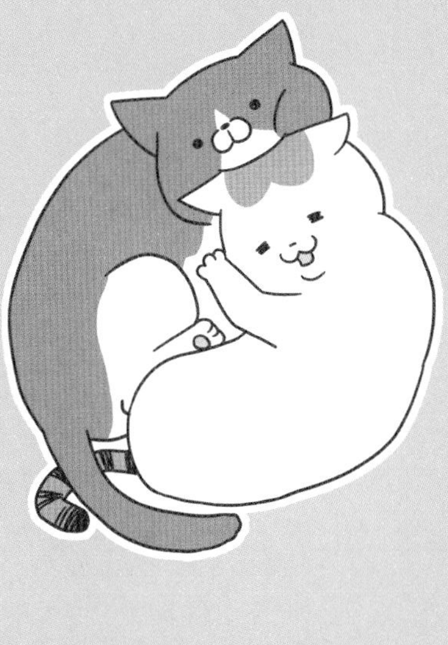

SEVEN SEAS ENTERTAINMENT PRESENTS

My Cat is Such a Weirdo

story and art by TAMAKO TAMAGOYAMA

VOLUME 1

TRANSLATION
Elina Ishikawa

LETTERING
Kaitlyn Wiley

COVER DESIGN
H. Qi

PROOFREADER
Danielle King

COPY EDITOR
Leighanna DeRouen

EDITOR
Linda Lombardi

PRODUCTION DESIGNER
Christina McKenzie

PRODUCTION MANAGER
John Ramirez

PREPRESS TECHNICIAN
Melanie Ujimori
Jules Valera

MANAGING EDITOR
J.P. Sullivan

EDITOR-IN-CHIEF
Julie Davis

ASSOCIATE PUBLISHER
Adam Arnold

PUBLISHER
Jason DeAngelis

UCHI NO NEKO GA MATA HEN NA KOTO SHITERU.
©Tamako Tamagoyama 2016
First published in Japan in 2016 by KADOKAWA CORPORATION, Tokyo. English translation rights arranged with KADOKAWA CORPORATION, Tokyo through le Bureau des Copyrights Français.

Seven Seas press and purchase enquiries can be sent to Marketing Manager Lianne Sentar at press@gomanga.com. Information regarding the distribution and purchase of digital editions is available from Digital Manager CK Russell at digital@gomanga.com.

Seven Seas and the Seven Seas logo are trademarks of Seven Seas Entertainment. All rights reserved.

ISBN: 979-8-88843-208-2
Printed in Canada
First Printing: October 2023
10 9 8 7 6 5 4 3 2 1

READING DIRECTIONS

This book reads from *right to left*, Japanese style. If this is your first time reading manga, you start reading from the top right panel on each page and take it from there. If you get lost, just follow the numbered diagram here. It may seem backwards at first, but you'll get the hang of it! Have fun!!

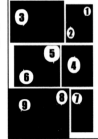

Follow us online: www.SevenSeasEntertainment.com